BEST PRACTICE

BEST PRACTICE
NEW STANDARDS FOR TEACHING AND LEARNING IN AMERICA'S SCHOOLS

STEVEN ZEMELMAN
HARVEY DANIELS
ARTHUR HYDE

HEINEMANN
Portsmouth NH

Heinemann
A division of Reed Elsevier Inc.
361 Hanover Street   Portsmouth, NH 03801–3912
Offices and agents throughout the world

Chapter 2: Excerpts from *New Policy Guidelines for Reading: Connecting Research
and Practice* by Jerome C. Harste. Copyright © 1989. Reprinted by permission of
the National Council of Teachers of English.

Chapter 6: Excerpts from *Lessons frm History: Essential Understandings and
Historical Perspectives Students Should Acquire,* edited by Charlotte Crabtree, et al.
Copyright © 1992. Published by the National Center for History in the Schools,
UCLA. Reprinted by permission of Charlotte A. Crabtree and the publisher.

Chapter 9: Excerpts from *A Community of Writers: Teaching Writing in the Junior
and Senior High School* by Steven Zemelman and Harvey Daniels. Copyright ©
1988. Published by Heinemann, a division of Reed Publishing (USA) Inc.
Reprinted by permission of the authors and the publisher.

Every effort has been made to contact the copyright holders and students for
permission to reprint borrowed material. We regret any oversights that may have
occurred and would be happy to rectify them in future printing of this work.

Library of Congress-in-Publication Data
Zemelman, Steven.
     Best practice : new standards for teaching and learning in
America's schools / Steven Zemelman, Harvey Daniels, Arthur Hyde.
          p.   cm.
     Includes bibliographical references and index.
     ISBN 0-435-08788-6
     1.   Teaching—Case studies.   2.   Direct instruction—Illinois—Case
studies.   3.   Active learning—Illinois—Case studies.
     4.   Educational change—United States.   I.   Daniels, Harvey. 1947–
     II.   Hyde, Arthur A.   III.   Title.
LB1025.3.Z46   1993
371.1'02—dc20   92–47034
                                                                                  CIP

Cover design by Mary Cronin
Printed in the United States of America
94   95   96   97   9   8   7   6   5   4

Contents

Preface and Acknowledgments

This book is not just about the schools and teachers in our own neighborhood, but it did start there. It all began around three years ago, amid the furious, exciting movement for school decentralization and reform here in Chicago. Since the three of us had been active for years in school change projects in the city, it was natural for us to pitch in. One problem in Chicago's reform process was immediately apparent: no one was paying attention to actual, day-to-day teaching and learning. Most of the early energy of reform was devoted to issues of governance, power, turf, logistics, authority, and money. Anyone familiar with Chicago politics knows that these topics always generate enthusiastic attention around here. There was non-stop chatting, scratching, wrangling, and logrolling about the arrangements of education, but just as at the national level, hardly anyone was talking about what the kids and teachers did together.

The three of us, as veteran teachers, staff development leaders, and curriculum specialists in several different fields, were worried about this direction. It seemed that reform might never get through the classroom door. So, as a way of helping to turn the dialogue from governance to curriculum, we decided to create a publication that would aggresively raise the issues of teaching and learning—the ultimate challenges of reform. We got a generous grant from the Joyce Foundation to create an instruction-centered newspaper that would be sent to all teachers, administrators, parent leaders, politicians, community groups, and foundation executives in the city—the whole constellation of people concerned with school renewal in Chicago.

Our inaugural issue was simple. All we did was draw together the current, national consensus recommendations about "best educational practice" in each of the traditional school curriculum areas: reading, writing, math, science, and social studies. We used mainstream sources only, nothing overly partisan or controversial, relying mainly on the key professional societies and research centers. We surrounded these recommendations with stories from Chicago teachers who were bringing them to life, practicing state-of-the-art instruction in their own classrooms every day. We optimistically named our sixteen-page tabloid *Best Practice 1*, printed 55,000 copies, and dropped 570 carefully labelled bundles on the loading dock at the Board of Education.

Why did we adopt the term Best Practice, first for our newspaper and now for this book? We borrowed the expression, of course, from the professions of medicine and law, where "good practice" or "best practice" are everyday phrases used to describe solid, reputable, state-of-the-art work in a field. If a practitioner is following Best Practice standards, he or she is aware of current research and consistently offers clients the full benefits of the latest knowledge, technology, and procedures. If a doctor, for example, does not follow contemporary standards and a case turns out badly, peers may criticize his decisions and treatments by saying something like, "that was simply not best practice."

In education, we mostly haven't had such an everyday standard: on the contrary, many veteran teachers will proudly *deny* the significance of current research or new standards of instruction. "I just give 'em the basics," such teachers say, "It's worked just fine for thirty years, and I don't hold with any of this new mumbo-jumbo." One wonders how long such self-satisfied teachers would continue to go to a doctor who says: "I practice medicine exactly the same way today that I did thirty years ago— I haven't changed a thing. I don't hold with all that newfangled stuff."

Perhaps one could argue that education as a field does not enjoy the clear-cut evolution of medicine, law, or architecture. But still, if educators are people who take ideas seriously, who believe in inquiry, and who subscribe to the possibility of human progress, then our professional language must label and respect practice which is at the leading edge of the field. That's why we have imported (and capitalized) the term Best Practice—as a shorthand emblem of serious, thoughtful, informed, responsible, state-of-the-art teaching.

Well, our *Best Practice* newspaper started quite a conversation around Chicago, and around the country (we now have subscribers from twenty states), and that story continues to be told in *Best Practice 2, 3* and beyond. What we discovered in assembling that first issue was an unrecognized consensus in American education, a surprisingly high level of agreement among seemingly disparate content fields, about how kids learn best. What is recommended across all subjects can only be called a neo-progressive transformation: virtually all the authoritative voices in each field are calling for schools that are student-centered, active, experiential, democratic, collaborative, and yet rigorous and challenging. As unashamed graduates of 1960s and 1970s school reforms, this renewed consensus sounded familiar and welcome to us.

So this book is, in a sense, the full-length version *Best Practice 1*, elaborated with stories from real schools in and beyond Chicago, and with more detailed treatment of the theoretical, historical, and political aspects of school reform in America. That means we have several goals:

- To concisely explain the current consensus on what constitutes Best Educational Practice in each of five key school curriculum areas, providing documentation from recent national reports, research summaries, and professional association position papers. We also want to trace the often ancient historical roots of these "new" ideas.

- To move beyond the subject-bound view of these principles and show the deep underlying commonalities in all these sets of best practices. We will also show how these connections and commonalities have their own surprisingly long history.

- To offer concrete examples of key classroom activities and practices which enact the new paradigm, especially by describing specific learning events in real classrooms.

- To suggest ways that teachers, administrators, and parents can work together to enact and extend the new curriculum.

We hope that this book will be a significant contribution to the growing literature on school renewal. We think it fills a gap for people who have read such disparate works as Jonathan Kozol's *Savage Inequalities*, Tracy Kidder's *Among Schoolchildren*, E.D. Hirsch's *Cultural Literacy*, John Goodlad's *A Place Called School*, Alan Bloom's *The Closing of the American Mind*, or Ernest Boyer's *High School*. We hope this book will be both complementary and challenging to this emerging canon of school reform. Among the distinctive features we hope you are about to enjoy, this book:

Is positive. This is not another critique of schools, but rather a hopeful map of specific, constructive strategies for change. We know that schools can and do change; the three authors have spent most of the last twenty years working on curriculum reform and instructional innovation projects.

Focuses on the classroom. In our view, too many other school reform books and reports perseverate on the governance, finance, and logistics of schools while overlooking the content and methods of learning. We focus here on how and what kids are taught.

Is authoritative. As much as we'd like to claim credit, these aren't our own ideas. The book draws its recommended practices from the existing knowledge base in major national reports from the key research centers and professional societies in each of five main teaching fields: reading, writing, mathematics, science, and social studies.

Is concrete. Everything in the book is illustrated with stories from real classrooms where teachers are putting Best Practice into effect every day, from kindergarten through high school.

Is practical. All the ideas we report on, while they do represent true progressive reform, are workable within the current educational system. Change needn't wait for large-scale structural reorganization or huge infusions of money, neither of which seems particularly likely.

While we do believe that this book deals mostly in facts, it also has a strong, unabashed, and partisan vision: we believe (and we hope we are about to prove) that progressive educational principles can and should govern classroom practice in American schools. While others belittle the past cycles of progressive reform during the 1930s and 1960s as meaningless fads, this book shows how the current wave of reform connects and culminates those past eras, and offers hope of creating the strongest and most enduring school renewal in this century.

Like all writers, we have may people to thank—though some of them might wish we hadn't remembered. First, we owe a special debt to our cherished colleague Marilyn Bizar, who has been our partner in leading the Best Practice network over these past four years. Her deep knowledge of literacy education, of cross-cultural curriculum, of school change processes—not to mention her dynamism and humor—have knitted our disparate group snugly together in a thousand critical ways.

Above all, this book reflects the brave, intelligent, and loving practice of the elementary and secondary teachers we work with, many of whom appear personally in these pages. Over the last fifteen years, we've had the privilege of gathering a family of brilliant, committed teacher-leaders in our Best Practice Network and in the Illinois Writing Project. These people not only bring the best of Best Practice to their own children every day, but also somehow find the energy and time to go out, after school and on weekends, conducting extended workshops for their city and suburban colleagues. It's when we're working closely with these dedicated professionals that we feel most confident—sometimes downright euphoric—about the prospects for reform in America's schools. We've seen schools change in deep and enduring ways when outstanding teachers like these are empowered to lead.

We also have some other, smaller networks of people who support us —our families. Steve wants to thank his wife Susan for pursuing her own teaching in the corporate world with demanding standards for herself, making her a valuable and sympathetic model to follow and share with. And he has especially admired his sons, Mark and Daniel, for their unremitting struggles to find meaning and joy and achievement as they've negotiated the school world. Their arts, their critiques, their searches have constantly reminded their parents about all that children can do, and about the freedoms and supports they need as they grow up.

Like the families of most writers, Harvey's has excelled at tolerating his absence, leaving him down in the basement hunched over the keyboard. Aside from thinking up ways to distract the children, Elaine contributed significantly to the content of the book: her expertise as a teacher educator, her years of experience as a public school teacher, and her special knowledge on issues of ability grouping and assessment all are strongly reflected here. Nick and Marny's learning processes, as well as their rich experience at Baker Demonstration School, continue to provide the first and strongest source for Harvey's thinking about education.

Art is blessed with a family who provides a continual testing ground for teaching ideas. Pam has wonderful insight into how to stimulate thoughtful connections among ideas in her third graders. With a clear sense of what builds real understanding, she keeps the university professors honest. For many years, Alicia, David, and Adam have offered an ongoing ethnography of schooling, teaching, and learning. Their running commentaries on human emotions, the forces of nature, and the absurdities of contemporary society have been the source of inspiration and delight.

1

Renewing Our Schools
An Emerging Consensus

This is an agitating, painful, and exciting time for America's schools. Since the mid-1980s, we have been enjoying and enduring the most intense period of educational reform in this century. Everyone has gotten into the act: politicians, parents, teachers, taxpayers, teacher educators, social critics, journalists, and researchers—all are passionately involved in school renewal. Education-oriented cover stories, blue-ribbon commissions, government reports, exposés, recommendations, talk shows, documentaries, conferences, jokes, gossip, and legislation abound. Indeed, we are writing this book during the reign of our nation's latest "Education President," in a state with a self-declared "Education Governor," and in a city that has begun the most radical school decentralization experiment in American history. For the moment, at least, education is the issue of the day.

This universal worry about the health of the public schools was deliciously portrayed in a recent *New Yorker* cartoon. A horrifying, ten-story-tall reptile, presumably from outer space, rampages through a downtown square as crowds of citizens run for their lives in every direction. One man at the head of the fleeing crowd turns to a fellow runner and comments: "Just when citywide reading scores were edging up!"

While all the heartfelt public concern about education is certainly useful, very little of this sudden interest has been admiring, pleasant, or even civil. Our national reappraisal of education began with widespread anger and worry about low test scores and the perceived slippage in American workers' global competitiveness. Indeed, the education crisis of the 1990s may have been fueled as much by the Hondas cruising America's highways as by the downhill ride of SAT scores. Much of the contemporary school reform movement's energy has been spent on blaming and finger-pointing: responsibility for our nation's educational disappointments has been enthusiastically and variously apportioned among television, video games, single parent families, ill-trained teachers, urban gangs, bad textbooks, sexual permissiveness, drugs, schools of education, and dozens of other causes.

Undeniably, the current debate about schools has included plenty of nonconstructive turmoil and rancor. Still, on balance, those of us who work in schools must welcome the scrutiny and even the fractiousness. After all, it is a rare and overdue moment when education leaps to the top of the national agenda—and it is during unstable periods like this one that true change often begins. So no matter what misgivings we might have about the current era of school reform, one thing is sure: today, millions of Americans are thinking hard and talking urgently about their schools. And that is welcome.

What About Learning and Teaching?

But one topic is peculiarly missing from this loud, ongoing conversation: **what** shall we teach and **how**? At first it seems unlikely that amid all this furor, the substance of education could somehow be overlooked, but the record of the reform era so far sadly bears this out. Most official discourse has concerned the structural and organizational features of schooling, not its ingredients. From the trend-setting book *A Nation at Risk* onward, most major reports, commission papers, books, and state and local reform efforts have focused on the logistics of schooling rather than its content and process: the central concerns have been the length of the school day and year, the credentials and pay of teachers, the roles and duties of principals, the testing and measurement of school "products," the financing of schools and of school reform, forging connections to the worlds of work and higher education, and articulating educational policy with national defense. Indeed, the federal government's touted "America 2000" reform package challenges virtually nothing in the current content or process of schooling, and promises only one direct governmental action in the name of educational renewal: a set of national examinations at fourth, eighth and eleventh grades.

Writing in *Educational Leadership*, our colleague James Beane recently addressed the peculiar imbalance in contemporary school reform debates. "It seems that no matter how radical restructuring talk may otherwise be, it almost never touches upon the curriculum itself. Much of what passes for restructuring is, in a sense, new bottles for old wine that has not gotten better with age. How is it that we can claim to speak of school reform without addressing the centerpiece of schools, the curriculum?" (1991). With the exception of a few school leaders like Beane, and the somewhat notorious E. D. Hirsch with his theory of "cultural literacy," surprisingly few reformers have paid serious attention to the **content** of schooling. What should schools teach? What should be the curriculum? What subject matter should children encounter and when? If our schools have indeed failed as utterly as so many blue-ribbon commissions claim, then immediate changes in the curriculum would seem advisable.

Similarly, the methods of teaching have been thoroughly ignored in the current debate. Except for John Goodlad, in his book *A Place Called School* (1984), few prominent reformers have focused systematically on teaching *processes*, the nature of the interactions between kids and teachers in school. Again, if our educational system has truly collapsed, then the careful critique and renewal of instructional methods would seem an urgent priority. We should be figuring out how to rearrange the basic ingredients of school—time and space and books and ideas and people—to maximize student learning. Instead, the topic of teaching methods is not just ignored; it is often explicitly ridiculed by mainstream school reformers as a time-wasting distraction best left to the pea-brained teacher educators in their despised colleges of education.

This neglect of what and how we teach has predictable results: nothing changes. After nearly ten years of zealous "reform," students are still sitting in pretty much the same classrooms with the same teachers, divided into the same instructional groups, doing the same activities, working through the same textbooks and worksheets, and getting pretty much the same scores on the many new standardized tests which are the only tangible legacy of a decade's exhortation. In a backhanded and ironic way, the mainstream school reform movement has actually ended up *endorsing* old modes of schooling. The experts have never really questioned the basic day-to-day process and content of American education; instead they blindly assume that if the same activities are conducted within an enhanced framework—with more time, more money, more teachers, more tests—then student achievement and outcomes will improve. In this version of reform, you simply do the same things harder, longer, and stronger. Now, this can be a perfectly fine approach to change if what you are already doing works well and merely requires intensification. Unfortunately, we are coming to understand that the basic things we do in American schools—what we teach and how—*don't* work: we don't empower kids, we don't nurture literacy, don't produce efficient workers, don't raise responsible citizens, we don't create a functional democracy. If we really want to change student achievement in American schools, we must act directly upon teaching and learning. More of the same is not the answer.

Real Reform

While legislatures, blue-ribbon panels, and media sages have tinkered with the logistics of education, another, quieter school reform movement has been growing. Our national curriculum research centers, a dozen subject-matter professional associations, many capable individual researchers, and thousands of on-the-line classroom teachers have been struggling to determine "what works" in the different school subjects, and to clearly define "best educational practice" in each teaching field. These groups and individuals share a curriculum-driven view of education: they assume that if American schools are to be genuinely reformed, we must begin with a solid definition of the content of the curriculum and the classroom activities through which students may most effectively engage that content. Unlike the better publicized (and often more official) reformers, they do not see the failure of American schools as an administrative breakdown, but rather as a failure of what we teach and how.

The last seven or eight years of tumultuous national debate, though it certainly hasn't concentrated upon instruction and curriculum, has nevertheless indirectly prodded further research in these areas. All the people in this alternate, uncoordinated reform movement—teachers, instructional researchers, subject area leaders—have been rethinking the substance, the content, the processes, the methods, and the dynamics of schooling. As a result, in virtually every school subject, we now have recent summary reports, meta-analyses of instructional research, bulletins from pilot classrooms, and landmark sets of professional recommendations. Today, there is a strong consensus definition of Best Practice, of state-of-the-art teaching in every critical field.

One might expect that when experts and practitioners from such disparate fields as science, mathematics, reading, writing, and social science sit down to define their own field's Best Practice, the results would be some very different visions of the ideal classroom, contradictory ways of organizing subject matter, and divergent models of what good teachers do. But, in fact, such polarities do *not* characterize these reports. Whether the recommendations come from the National Council of Teachers of Mathematics, the Center for the Study of Reading, the National Writing Project, the National Council for the Social Studies, the American Association for the Advancement of Science, the National Council of Teachers of English, the National Association for the Education of Young Children, or the International Reading Association, the fundamental insights into teaching and learning are remarkably congruent. Indeed, on many key issues, the recommendations from these diverse organizations are unanimous. Below is a list of these common conclusions, features that begin to define a coherent paradigm of learning and teaching across the whole curriculum.

Common Recommendations of National Curriculum Reports

- LESS whole-class, teacher-directed instruction, e.g., lecturing
- LESS student passivity: sitting, listening, receiving, and absorbing information
- LESS prizing and rewarding of silence in the classroom

- LESS classroom time devoted to fill-in-the-blank worksheets, dittos, workbooks, and other "seatwork"
- LESS student time spent reading textbooks and basal readers
- LESS attempt by teachers to thinly "cover" large amounts of material in every subject area
- LESS rote memorization of facts and details
- LESS stress on the competition and grades in school
- LESS tracking or leveling students into "ability groups"
- LESS use of pull-out special programs
- LESS use of and reliance on standardized tests

- MORE experiential, inductive, hands-on learning
- MORE active learning in the classroom, with all the attendant noise and movement of students doing, talking, and collaborating
- MORE emphasis on higher-order thinking; learning a field's key concepts and principles
- MORE deep study of a smaller number of topics, so that students internalize the field's way of inquiry
- MORE time devoted to reading whole, original, real books and nonfiction materials
- MORE responsibility transferred to students for their work: goal-setting, record-keeping, monitoring, evaluation
- MORE choice for students; e.g., picking their own books, writing topics, team partners, research projects
- MORE enacting and modeling of the principles of democracy in school
- MORE attention to affective needs and the varying cognitive styles of individual students
- MORE cooperative, collaborative activity; developing the classroom as an interdependent community
- MORE heterogeneously grouped classrooms where individual needs are met through inherently individualized activities, not segregation of bodies
- MORE delivery of special help to students in regular classrooms
- MORE varied and cooperative roles for teachers, parents, and administrators
- MORE reliance upon teachers' descriptive evaluation of student growth, including qualitative/anecdotal observations
  (Anderson, *et al.*, 1985; Bybee, *et al.*, 1989 and 1991; Harste,

1989; Hillocks, 1986; National Council of Teachers of Mathematics, 1989; National Science Teachers Association, 1985; American Association for the Advancement of Science, 1989; National Commission on the Social Studies, 1988 and 1989)

The latent agreement on these principles is so strong in the different subject fields that it seems fair to call it an "unrecognized consensus." Though school people are often portrayed as lost and fragmented, the fact is that a remarkably consistent, harmonious vision of best educational practice already exists. But this emergent consensus hasn't yet been widely recognized across subject boundaries. The coherence of this vision, the remarkable overlap across fields may be quite striking, but so far most people in government, the media, and even the educational system itself haven't quite grasped its significance and its potential transforming power.

By 1994 or 1995, however, this new paradigm will be much more widely recognized: with funding from the U. S. Department of Education, national "standards documents" are currently being prepared by subject field leaders in reading, writing, science, and social studies. These reports, which are mandated to follow the pathfinding format of the National Council of Teachers of Mathematics standards, will closely parallel and refine the recommendations outlined in this book, and should strongly endorse the neo-progressive model of Best Practice schooling.

Admittedly, this emerging consensus is not perfectly symmetrical across the different school subjects; some fields are ahead of others. Reading and writing are indisputably the most advanced fields in defining and implementing Best Practice. The Writing Across the Curriculum and Whole Language movements, which have been solidly in place for ten to fifteen years, have been leading the way for practitioners and researchers alike. While mathematics does not yet enjoy a complementary "Whole Math" movement, math leaders have made a tremendous contribution with the series of National Council of Teachers of Mathematics standards documents published since 1988. These frameworks and guidelines have shown other fields how learning goals for children can be described in Best Practice terms—progressive, developmentally appropriate, research-based, and eminently teachable. Science educators, on the other hand, have a decades-old tradition of supporting progressive, hands-on, student-centered instruction, but little success with implementation in schools. This relative lack of impact undoubtedly reflects the low priority given to science at all levels of American education: science often gets pushed to the bottom of the curricular agenda, while worries about reading, writing, and math gobble up time, attention, funding, and the energy for staff development and curriculum reform.

Finally and disappointingly, the field of social studies lags behind. At first, this seems surprising, since subjects like history and geography appear to cry out for collaborative, experiential, student-centered, cognitive approaches—key structures in the emerging Best Practice paradigm. But, as we'll detail in Chapter 6, social studies education is dragged down by its political baggage. Because this is the one school subject with the explicit duty to inculcate patriotic values and transmit "necessary" cultural information, it becomes a battleground on which partisans take a very strong stand. In a sense, social studies teachers have been frightened away from progressive change because of the vociferous traditionalism of high-profile outsiders like E. D. Hirsch, William Bennett, and George Bush. As a result, social studies is the one major curriculum field that lacks strong, current, unambiguous documents which clearly endorse Best Practice principles. At best, social science education is in transition; its leaders and organizations have offered the Best Practice movement a wary, dance-away embrace—but with some definite bright spots we'll outline later on.

As the above more/less chart also suggests, there is more afoot here than the congruence of certain teaching recommendations from the traditionally separate fields of the American school curriculum. A more general, progressive educational paradigm is emerging across content boundaries and grade levels. This coherent philosophy and spirit is reaching across the curriculum and up through the grades. Whether it is called Whole Language, or integrated learning, or transdisciplinary studies, by some other name, or by no name at all, this movement is broad and deep and enduring. It is strongly backed by educational research, draws on sound learning theory, and has, under other names, been tested and refined over many years.

What is the nature of this new/old curriculum? What assumptions and theories about learning inform this approach? What is the underlying educational philosophy of this re-emergent paradigm? If we study the more/less chart a little more systematically, we can identify thirteen interlocking principles, assumptions, or theories that characterize this model of education.

CHILD-CENTERED. The best starting point for schooling is kids' real interests; all across the curriculum, investigating students' own questions should always take precedence over studying arbitrarily and distantly selected "content."

EXPERIENTIAL. Active, hands-on, concrete experience is the most powerful and natural form of learning. Students should be immersed in the most direct possible experience of the content of every subject.

REFLECTIVE. Balancing the immersion in direct experience must be opportunities for learners to look back, to reflect, to debrief, to abstract from their experiences what they have felt and thought and learned.

AUTHENTIC. Real, rich, complex ideas and materials are at the heart of the curriculum. Lessons or textbooks which water down, control, or over-simplify content ultimately disempower students.

HOLISTIC. Children learn best when they encounter whole, real ideas, events, and materials in purposeful contexts, and not by studying sub-parts isolated from actual use.

SOCIAL. Learning is always socially constructed and often interactional; teachers need to create classroom interactions which "scaffold" learning.

COLLABORATIVE. Cooperative learning activities tap the social power of learning better than competitive and individualistic approaches.

DEMOCRATIC. The classroom is a model community; students learn what they live as citizens of the school.

COGNITIVE. The most powerful learning for children comes from developing true understanding of concepts and higher order thinking associated with various fields of inquiry and self-monitoring of their thinking.

DEVELOPMENTAL. Children grow through a series of definable but not rigid stages, and schooling should fit its activities to the developmental level of students.

CONSTRUCTIVIST. Children do not just receive content; in a very real sense, they recreate and re-invent every cognitive system they encounter, including language, literacy, and mathematics.

PSYCHOLINGUISTIC. The process of young children's natural oral language acquisition provides our best model of complex human learning and, once learned, language itself becomes the primary tool for more learning, whatever the subject matter.

CHALLENGING. Students learn best when faced with genuine challenges, choices and responsibility in their own learning.

The rest of this book, as it discusses each subject in the school curriculum, will spell out what these key principles really mean in practice. However, to explain why these ideas are so important, we'll elaborate on them a bit now.

Schooling should be CHILD-CENTERED, taking its cues from students' interests, concerns, and questions. Making school child-centered involves building on the natural curiosity children bring to school, and asking kids what they want to learn. Teachers help students to list their own questions, puzzles, and goals, and then structure for them widening circles of experience and investigation of those topics. Teachers infuse into such kid-driven curriculum all the skills, knowledge, and concepts that society mandates, though always in original sequences and combinations. But child-centered schooling does not mean passive teachers who respond only to students' explicit cues. Teachers also draw on their deep understanding of children's developmentally characteristic needs and enthusiasms to design experiences that lead children into areas they might not choose, but that they do enjoy and that engage them. Teachers also bring their own interests and enthusiasms into the classroom to share, at an age-appropriate level, demonstrating how a learner gets involved with ideas. Thus, child-centered education begins by cordially inviting children's whole, real lives into the classroom; it solicits and listens to their questions; and it provides a balance between activities that follow children's lead and ones which lead the children.

As often as possible, school should stress learning that is EXPERIENTIAL. Children learn most powerfully from doing, not just hearing about, any subject. This simple psychological fact has different implications in different subjects. In writing and reading it means that students grow more by composing and reading whole, real texts, rather than just doing worksheets and exercises. With mathematics it means working with objects—sorting, counting, and building patterns of number and shape; and carrying out real-world projects that involve collecting data, estimating, calculating, drawing conclusions, and making decisions. In science it means conducting experiments and taking field trips to investigate natural settings, pollution problems, and labs at nearby factories, universities, or hospitals. For social studies, students can conduct opinion surveys, prepare group reports that teach the rest of the class, and role-play famous events, conflicts, and political debates. The key is to help students think more deeply, to discover the detailed implications of ideas through direct or simulated immersion in them.

Effective learning is balanced with opportunities for REFLECTION. Too often, school is a process of stimulus-response. The work cycle is: "Do it, turn it in, get your grade, forget it, and move on." But learning is greatly strengthened when children have time to look back on what they've learned, to digest and debrief, to recognize broader principles, to appreciate their accomplishments and understand how they overcame obstacles. Of course it is hard to think reflectively in the middle of doing an experiment or revising a draft, but afterwards students can review what happened and apply what they learned to future efforts. Do children need to be taught this reflective process? No—we can find evidence of it in their play and family interactions all the time. But kids need *time* set aside for reflection, and they need to become consciously aware of its power and their ability to use it. Adding reflective thinking to school learning is one of the simplest of all instructional innovations. Though there are other, more elegant approaches, many teachers have found that the simple addition of a student learning log for each subject, with time set aside each day for responding to well-structured teacher "prompts" builds reflection into the day, and moves students into a new level of thinking.

Learning activities need to be AUTHENTIC. There is a natural tendency in schools to offer children simplified materials and activities, so that they are not overwhelmed with complexity. But too often we underestimate children and oversimplify things, creating materials or situations that are so synthetic as to be unlifelike—and, ironically, educationally worthless. The most notorious examples of this, of course, are the linguistically deprived stories appearing in many basal reading texts. We now understand that children routinely handle phenomenal complexity in their own daily lives—indeed, kids' effortless learning of the thousands of abstract rules underlying spoken language is proof of their ability to sort out the complex tangle of data the real world inevitably presents. What does authenticity mean in the curriculum? In reading, it means that the rich, artful, and complex vocabulary of Grimm's fairy-tales is far more educational than watered-down, "cleaned up" versions in basal readers. In math, it means that children might investigate ways of dividing a pizza or a cake, rather than working the odd-numbered fractions problems at the end of the chapter. Authenticity also means that children are reading and writing and calculating and investigating for purposes that they have chosen, not just because the teacher gave an assignment or because a task appears in a textbook. Yes, teachers can and should sometimes give assignments that a whole class can work on, to share and compare the resulting ideas they've generated. But if teachers don't also take steps to turn schoolwork into something the children truly own, then the results will be mechanical, more an exercise in dutifully following directions than in real valuing of thought and knowledge.

Learning in all subjects needs to be HOLISTIC. In the traditional American curriculum, information and ideas are presented to children in small "building blocks." While the teacher may find these subparts meaningful and may know they add up to an eventual understanding of a subject, their purpose and significance aren't always apparent to the children. This part-to-whole approach undercuts motivation for learning, because children don't understand why they are doing the work. But it also deprives children of an essential condition for learning—encountering material in its full, lifelike context. When the "big picture" is put off until later, later often never comes. We know that children do in fact need to acquire skills and abilities that are parts of a larger whole—skills such as spelling and multiplying and evaluating good evidence for written arguments. But holistic learning means that children gain these abilities most effectively by going from whole-to-part, when kids read whole books, write whole stories, and carry out whole investigations of natural phenomena. Brief lessons on use of quotation marks are learned fastest and remembered longest when the class writes scripts for plays they've decided to put on. And meanwhile, the focus on a rich whole text or inquiry ensures that children are simultaneously making far more mental connections—albeit often unconscious ones—than the teacher ever has time to directly teach within the one or two or three "skills" that she or he covers.

Teachers should tap into the primal power of SOCIAL relations to promote learning. Much research has shown how social interactions in the family and community support early language learning. This occurs unconsciously and naturally in families and groups of children playing together. Such spontaneous social helping is often called "scaffolding" because, just as a temporary scaffold allows bricklayers to construct a wall which finally stands on its own, these interactions support young language-builders along the way, but ultimately leave the child independent. Children are far from passive in this scaffolding process. They learn not only by imitating grownup behavior, but by taking an active part, constructing and testing hypotheses, and initiating behavior themselves. Babies learn language swiftly and effectively without being directly "taught" because they are learning words that help them get their needs met in their families. Following this model, schools can reverse their old counterproductive patterns of isolation and silence, tapping the power of social interaction to promote learning.

Some of the most efficient social learning activities are COLLABO-RATIVE. When we think of the social side of learning, we most readily envision group discussions, kids listening to one another's work, carrying out projects and writing letters and stories *for* one another. Collaborative learning goes on to promote children's learning *with* one another. Even in the workplace, we're recognizing how much collaboration actually goes on in American life, and how valuable group problem-solving is, compared to perpetual competitiveness and isolation. Collaborative small-group activity has been shown to be an especially effective mode for school learning—and solid achievement gains have been documented across the curriculum by Johnson and Johnson (1985), Slavin (1984), and others. Collaborative work allows learners to receive much more extensive feedback from fellow students than they can ever get from a single teacher who must spread his or her time among all students. Of course, group work requires training students and carefully designing meaningful, authentic activities—otherwise the effort of the groups can be inefficient and shallow. But cooperation does work very well when teachers employ the student training techniques that have been refined in recent years. It's worth the effort, because habitual cooperation pays off both in time better used in the classroom, and later on, as a valuable skill in life.

Classrooms can become more effective and productive when procedures are DEMOCRATIC. It is a classic bit of American hypocrisy that we claim to be a democracy and yet send our children off to profoundly authoritarian schools. But even if we don't choose to democratize schools as a matter of principle, there are instructional reasons for doing so. Certain essential democratic processes make learning more efficient, more widely spread throughout the classroom, and more likely to have life-long effects. First and most important, children need to exercise *choice*— choice in books they read, topics they write about, and activities they focus on during some parts of the day. This means that teachers must help children learn how to make intelligent choices, not just arbitrary ones or choices of avoidance. When children learn to make good choices, they are not only more committed to the work they do; they acquire habits that make them lifelong readers, writers, and continuing learners of math, science, and social issues—and, not inconsequentially, active, critical, involved citizens.

But democracy is not just freedom to choose. In a genuinely democratic classroom, children learn to negotiate conflicts so that they can work together more effectively and respect and appreciate one anothers' differences. They learn that they are part of a larger community, that they can gain from it, and must also sometimes give to it. They hear about differences in one anothers' cultures, religions, regional backgrounds, and personal beliefs. Too often, this valuing of community within difference is missing in both rich and poor neighborhoods, and its absence undercuts education in countless ways, leaving us with discipline problems, vandalism, hostility toward school, and low self-esteem among students. Democracy in the classroom is not just a frill or an isolated social studies unit, but an educational necessity.

Powerful learning comes from COGNITIVE experiences. Many teachers have moved well beyond believing that memorized definitions constitute real understanding, and are reorganizing their classrooms to facilitate higher-order, conceptual learning. Concepts are the abstract ideas that give special meaning to human experiences. Full comprehension and appreciation for such concepts as *tangent, democracy, metaphor,* and *photosynthesis* come from complex, varied experiences that gradually build deep understanding that is increasingly abstract, general, and powerful.

At the same time, *how* children think is intimately related to *what* they think. Teachers must help students develop the specific types of thinking that our civilization values, such as analytical reasoning, interpretation, metaphorical thinking, creative design, categorization, hypothesizing, drawing inferences, synthesis, and so forth. Students need to experience these kinds of thinking for themselves with appropriate modeling and facilitation from their teachers and others. When they do, language, thinking, and conceptual understanding are intertwined as students *construct* ideas, systems, and processes for themselves.

Along with thinking and concepts is *metacognition*, the notion that children can become increasingly aware of their own thinking and concepts. When teachers end an activity with reflective debriefing and questions such as "What happened?" "What did you do?" and "How did you come to that conclusion?" students become conscious of their own cognitive processes and can better monitor their own work and thinking. This mental self-awareness helps students develop more effective cognitive strategies for accomplishing tasks, making decisions, and reviewing their own work.

Children's learning must be approached as DEVELOPMENTAL. This is one of the most carelessly used words in current educational parlance, enlisted in the support of all sorts of contradictory ideas. To us, developmental does not mean labelling or teaching students according to their purported level on a fixed hierarchy of cognitive stages. Nor does it mean lockstep instruction according to some textbook company's scope and sequence chart. Instead, developmental simply means stage-appropriate; developmentally oriented teachers approach classroom groups and individual students with a respect for their emerging capabilities. Developmentalists recognize that kids grow in common patterns, but at different rates which usually cannot be speeded up by adult pressure or input. Developmentally-oriented teachers know that variance in the school performance of different children often results from differences in their general growth. Such variations in the speed, but not the direction or the ultimate degree of development, should not be grounds for splitting up groups, but are diversities to be welcomed and melded into the richness of a group.

In developmental schooling, we help children by recognizing and encouraging beginning steps when they occur—whether on schedule or not. We study the research on how children actually advance in math or spelling, and build our programs around this knowledge, rather than marching through arbitrary word lists or problems each week. In complex areas like writing, we chart children's progress in many ingredients of composing and understand how some abilities will appear to regress as children challenge themselves with other, more difficult rhetorical tasks. In math, along with review and exploration of this week's topic, we include challenging, enjoyable activities that go beyond the textbook unit, so that we find out what various kids are really ready for.

Children's learning always involves CONSTRUCTING ideas and systems. Studies of early language acquisition, of science learning in school, of reading processes, of mathematical cognition, and many other areas show that human beings never just take in and memorize material. Even when staring at clouds or smoke or trash in an empty lot, we are constantly trying to find and organize meaning in what we see. In a very real sense, people always *reinvent* whatever they encounter, by constantly making and revising mental models of the world. Inventing and constructing is exactly how we learn complex systems like mathematics, language, anthropology, or anything else. For example, when a two-year-old invents and uses words like "feets" or "goed," words that she has never heard from anyone, she is demonstrating constructivism. Children don't just imitate the language around them; they use it as a corpus of raw material from which to generate hypotheses, to reinvent the language itself. Along the way, they create original, temporary forms that serve until new hypotheses generate new structures. Kids don't merely learn to speak; every one of them, in a profound sense, rebuilds their native language.

Constructivist teachers trust that all children can reinvent math, reading, and writing no matter how "disadvantaged" their backgrounds, and they are eager to tap into the thinking abilities children bring to school. They know that the keys are experience, immersion, and engagement in a safe, interactive community. Kids need much time to practice reading, writing, mathing, experimenting. They need encouragement to reflect, to share their emerging ideas and hypotheses with others; they need to have their errors and temporary understandings respected; and they need plenty of time. Constructivist teachers cheerfully accept that their most helpful role isn't one of direct telling and teaching. Indeed, given the fundamentally internal nature of this deep learning, teachers can't help by presenting rules, skills, or facts. Instead, they create a rich environment in which children can gradually construct their own understandings. When teachers do create an appropriate, stimulating, healthy setting, children's urge to make sense of their world propels their own learning.

Influencing many of these principles is the PSYCHOLINGUISTIC base of children's learning. It's no accident that in discussing many of the above principles we've used the example of child language acquisition. Indeed, this magical and universal phenomenon has provided educators with one of our most important bodies of knowledge—and most generative of metaphors—about learning. Childhood language development is the most powerful, speedy, and complex learning any of us will ever do in our lives. We learn to speak without being directly "taught," and without conscious intention to learn. It happens in the social setting of families, and it becomes internalized through play and crib-talk. Once learned, oral language becomes the main tool for future learning, and provides the base for reading and writing. Outer speech gradually becomes storable as inner thought.

Teachers now recognize that the lessons of psycholinguistics aren't restricted to preschool children at home. The concept of scaffolding—the special kind of help provided by parents and siblings in a family—can be explicitly built into the structure of work in school. The ideas of hypothesis-testing and temporary linguistic forms help us to respect and learn from, rather then punish children's errors in school. The natural instincts of parents to engage, support, enjoy, and extend their children's utterances encourages us to rethink teacher feedback and evaluation practices. The fact that language is learned tacitly, during socializing and play, suggests that we make the classroom more playful and interactive.

Perhaps above all, the fact that we learn to talk by talking implies that children should simply be allowed to talk far more than they currently do in school. The school norm of silent classrooms must be abolished; ironically, when teachers enforce the standard of silence, they are in a very real sense making learning illegal.

Following all these principles means that school is CHALLENG-ING. While some people might think of experiential, collaborative, or self-chosen tasks as "easier" for students, teachers using state-of-the-art practices know that the opposite is true. Students are expected to take considerable responsibility, monitor their own learning, be sure they apply the abilities they've acquired, keep their own records, and elect new projects when they're finished with something, rather than just fill in an extra ditto sheet. As the students in a classroom gradually assume more responsibilities, the teacher attends to the needs of individual children, provides a safe space for experimenting with newer and more difficult tasks, and adds challenges as kids are developmentally ready for them. In classes where these approaches abound, kids love the challenge.

So What's New?

This set of ideas will be entirely familiar to anyone who worked in American schools during the late sixties and early seventies, someone raised on the ideas of Carl Rogers, John Holt, Herbert Kohl, A. S. Neill, Neil Postman, and Charles Weingartner. But then this list doesn't exactly hold any surprises for people who lived through the progressive era of the 1930s, or who have studied the work of John Dewey. Yes, today's "new" integrated and holistic educational paradigm can fairly be called a progressive resurgence. *Another* progressive resurgence.

But while it is harmonious with and descended from past progressive eras, this new movement is not identical to the open classrooms of the 1960s or the Deweyian schools of the 1930s. While still rooted in the characteristic view of children as fundamentally good, self-regulating, and trustworthy, today's movement is driven by more than an optimistic conception of children's nature. This time around, the philosophical orientation is better balanced with pedagogical pragmatism and insight about cognition. We are blending a positive view of children with our commitment to certain curriculum content and our improved understanding of how learning works. In the 1960s, many progressive innovations failed because they were backed with more passion than with practical, well-thought-out procedures for implementing them. Now, a generation later, we return to the same basic ideas, with the same fundamental understanding of kids' capabilities, but equipped with much better ideas about how adult helpers can make it work.

Yes, many of these ideas are old and familiar. And while this neo-progressive movement does indeed promise a revolution in education, it is the furthest thing from a fad. Though it has re-emerged now partly as a result of contemporary forces, it also represents a much older, ongoing, and long-coming shift in the educational philosophy of this nation. This closely related set of ideas has been struggling for acceptance in American culture for many generations, appearing and reappearing in forms which too many educators and citizens have mistaken for meaningless cyclical trends.

Now, near the turn of the century—indeed, the millennium—these ideas appear again, this time in a stronger, more coherent form. Perhaps the current cycle of progressive reform will have a more lasting influence on education in this culture than the innovations of the sixties and seventies, or even than the era of John Dewey. While the authors of this book have no doubt that this cyclical tendency will continue on into future generations, we also believe in progress. With each cycle, some things change that never change back, and some cycles leave a stronger heritage than others. We believe that today's is potentially the most important, powerful and enduring phase of progressive educational reform ever to occur in American schools.

How to Read This Book—and Why

Today we enjoy a rich base of research and exemplary practice that points the way to school renewal through curriculum reform. As teachers are showing in schools around the country, this progressive paradigm is not just a dream any more, but a real, practical, manageable, available choice. But this new/old model enacts learning and teaching in very different ways from those that most contemporary parents, principals, and teachers themselves experienced in school—and in some ways it directly contradicts teachers' professional training. So when teachers, schools, or districts want to move toward this new model, everyone involved in the change needs lots of information and reassurance. They need a chance to construct their own understanding of what the new curriculum means, what research and theory supports it, how it can be implemented, and why it holds so much promise for our children.

That's what this book is for: to help all the parties to school reform recognize, understand, appreciate, and start exploiting the remarkably coherent models for across-the-curriculum school reform that have already been built. Toward this end, we'll take several steps in the next few chapters. First, we want to provide a compact and accurate summary of current Best Practice research in each of five main school teaching fields, drawing upon the consensus documents from each subject area.

After each field's research base, we tell the story of one exemplary program, showing how some real teachers are implementing key content and processes in a variety of classrooms.

This pattern of organization, of course, restricts us for several chapters to the traditional subject-area boundaries. While we certainly don't wish to reify the compartmentalization of the curriculum, the fact remains that knowledge about schooling is currently generated and reported mostly within these customary divisions. The key research centers, professional societies, and even most individual researchers are identified with only one subject field each. Later in the book, we will talk about ways to move beyond the traditional school subject areas; after all, the new educational paradigm doesn't reach its full potential until Best Practice takes us beyond the old borders.

For all of us, the ultimate goal is more coherent, organic, and integrated schooling for American young people. But creating that kind of experience does not necessarily *begin* with rescheduling the school day, abolishing separate subjects, or instituting thematic interdisciplinary units. Vast changes and improvements in teaching can be made within the old subject boundaries. Indeed, we would warn that schools reorganizing their schedule and curriculum into interdisciplinary units without fully understanding the current research on reading, writing, mathematics, science, and social studies may merely devise an elaborate new delivery system for the same old superficial education. This problem leads us to the question of change, which is the final topic of the book. In later chapters we want to talk frankly and realistically—and we hope, practically—about the tough, but definitely not insurmountable problems of change in American schools.

There are different ways that different readers may approach this book, depending on their needs and interests. After all, according to the research on reading comprehension that we're about to summarize, meaning in any text is profoundly dependent upon the needs and knowledge of the reader. We'd be remiss if we didn't learn from our own inquiry, and we've designed the book to take this variability into account.

So if you are an experienced teacher trying to invigorate your science instruction, you may turn directly to the science chapter for guidelines and possibilities, browse several exemplary classroom segments to see how they actually work, study Chapter 7 for the classroom structures that enable new teaching strategies, and then consult Chapter 8, "Making the Transition," to consider what teacher-development activities to seek for your district. On the other hand, if you are a school administrator searching for policies to improve children's learning throughout your district, you might scan all the subject-area chapters, and then once you see the pattern they reveal, focus most strongly on Chapter 8 to think about the direction of staff development in the district. And if you are a school board member trying to imagine how changes in the curriculum might affect your own and your neighbors' children, you may appreciate most the classroom stories that illustrate how new-and-yet-old ideas are already making many schools the exciting and enriching places they ought to be.

Whatever your purpose as a reader, we urge that you view the recommendations and classroom examples in this book as elements of a process and not as examples of perfection. School districts or individual teachers rarely advance in one single, straight-line jump. None of the teachers whose classrooms we describe here considers him- or herself finished or a paragon; all of these professionals recognize that they are somewhere in the middle of a long, complex journey. Indeed, it is a defining characteristic of good teachers that they are learners themselves, constantly observing to see what enriches children's experience—and what makes teaching more invigorating and rewarding for them. Thoughtful readers will find many ways to improve upon and extend the activities described here. In fact, as we've talked with these teachers about their efforts, we've usually ended up brainstorming additional options and variations that bring even more principles of Best Practice into play. We certainly invite our readers to join in this process of extending and fine-tuning.

And we need to add a warning. It is tempting, as one reads any book about school reform, to be excessively impressed by innovative, highly-wrought, teacher-designed activities, implicitly assuming that increased student learning comes mainly from increased teacher doing. But it's not that simple. There needs to be a balance in the classroom, a balance between teacher-organized activity and children's own initiative and self-directed work. It is during kids' self-sponsored activities that much of the most powerful learning occurs, and the effects of good teaching get a chance to bloom. During the buzz and talk that goes on while small groups work, during the jotting and quiet considering of journal time, during the children's play with math manipulatives or puzzles, while kids sketch out a cluster of ideas on a piece of butcher paper—so much is happening that is valuable, even when there's a bit of digressing and fooling around, that an observer gets dizzy watching it.

A Story

When ten-year-old Kate, who has really struggled with reading and writing, finally composes her very first coherent story, it isn't part of an assigned, teacher-planned activity. Kate is a black fifth-grader at Washington Irving School, from a poor neighborhood on the west side of Chicago. She's belligerent much of the time, a non-participant in most lessons, and her teacher agonizes over Kate's seemingly bleak future. For several weeks the class has been working on inferential reasoning, imagining "the story behind" various objects and events, through reading books, brainstorming, and taking a walk in the neighborhood—all activities structured by the teacher. Now the class is generating a list of questions to ask a fascinating visitor who is coming after lunch—an investigator from the city morgue, which is located nearby and thus part of the neighborhood study.

Just now, the teacher discovers that Kate has been doodling in her journal, next to a drawing she's made of a trash-littered lot the class encountered on their neighborhood walk. The one ability Kate recognizes in herself is that she can draw quite well. Next to the drawing, Kate has begun writing a story titled "The Funky Boot," based on a mysterious object she noticed in the vacant lot. She asks in a whisper if she can work on her story right now, using the computer at the back of the room. Kate works there until lunch time, pauses impatiently for only part of the morgue investigator's talk, returns to the computer, and later asks to skip gym so she can continue writing—the longest continuous attention that she's ever given to any school task except drawing. The piece is barely coherent, but it is Kate's first attempt at authorship. While the classroom climate and activities have made this breakthrough possible, the timing and commitment come from Kate.

As much as we value well-structured teaching and creative classroom activities, in this book we hope to show why schools must also make time for kids—creating not just elegant teacher-orchestrated events but also simple, regular, predictable space for all of our Kates to achieve their own wonderful discoveries.

Works Cited

Anderson, Richard C., Elfrieda H. Hiebert, Judith A. Scott, and Ian A.G. Wilkinson. 1985. *Becoming a Nation of Readers: The Report of the Commission on Reading*. Washington, D.C.: National Institute of Education.

Beane, James. 1991. Middle School: The Natural Home of Integrated Curriculum. *Educational Leadership*. October.

Bybee, Roger, *et al.* 1989. *Science and Technology Education for the Elementary Years: Frameworks for Curriculum and Instruction*. Andover, MA: National Center for Improving Science Education.

———. 1991. *Science and Technology Education for the Middle Years: Frameworks for Curriculum and Instruction*. Andover, MA: National Center for Improving Science Education.

Goodlad, John. 1984. *A Place Called School*. New York: McGraw Hill.

Harste, Jerome C. 1989. *New Policy Guidelines for Reading: Connecting Research and Practice*. Urbana, IL: National Council of Teachers of English.

Hillocks, George. 1986. *Research on Written Composition*. Urbana, IL: National Council of Teachers of English.

Johnson, David W., Roger T. Johnson, Edythe Holubec, and Patricia Roy. 1984. *Circles of Learning: Cooperation in the Classroom*. Alexandria, VA: Association for Supervision and Curriculum Development.

National Council of Teachers of Mathematics. 1989. *Curriculum and Evaluation Standards for School Mathematics*. Reston, VA: Commission on Standards for School Mathematics.

A Nation at Risk: The Imperative for Educational Reform. 1985. Washington, D.C.: National Commission on Excellence in Education.

Position Statements on Preschool and Elementary Level Science Education and Science Education for Middle and Junior High Students. 1985. Washington, D.C.: National Science Teachers Association.

Science for All Americans: A Project 2061 Report on Literacy Goals in Science, Mathematics, and Technology. 1989. Washington, D.C.: American Association for the Advancement of Science.

Slavin, Robert, Sharon Schlomo, Karen Spencer, Clark Webb, and Robert Schmuck. 1985. *Learning to Cooperate, Cooperating to Learn*. New York: Plenum Press.

Social Studies for Early Childhood and Elementary School Children Preparing for the 21st Century: A Report from the NCSS Task Force on Early Childhood/Elementary Social Studies. 1989. *Social Education* (January).

Statements on Preschool and Elementary Level Science Education and Science Education for Middle and Junior High Students. 1985. Washington, D.C.: National Science Teachers Association.

The Tool Kit. 1988. Washington, D.C.: National Council for the Social Studies.

2

Best Practice in Reading

How Reading Was

Ask any group of middle-aged Americans to think back upon learning to read, and rich, diverse memories flood in immediately. Some people will start retelling stories about Dick and Jane and Spot and Puff, while others joke nervously about which reading level they were assigned to at the age of six. Most can recall lugging a thick basal text to their reading group each day, where the main activity was round robin oral reading—children took turns reading aloud while the teacher listened for mistakes. Many of us remember feeling dread as we waited for our turn; others recollect the embarrassment of making mistakes and being corrected in front of the whole group. Many of today's adults recall being separated from their friends by reading-group levels: some of us were shamed by being assigned to the low group, while others were pleased (and maybe just a bit pressured) to find ourselves among the "top" readers. Many of us can even recall the sometimes transparent nicknames given to the three levels of reading groups: maybe no teacher *really* called our groups "Bluebirds," "Chickadees," and "Buzzards," but even as first-graders, we could always crack whatever code camouflaged the winners and losers groups.

Most of us children of the 1950s and 1960s will also remember plenty of phonics, an important and time-consuming subject with its own curriculum, chunk of the school day, and slot on the report card. In Harvey Daniels' elementary school in suburban Minneapolis, for example, phonics was taught right after lunch every day, using special books and worksheets, and never coordinated in any way with reading, which was done in the morning. He remembers the kids' groans when the teacher commanded them to take out their phonics materials: it always signalled a long bout of silent seatwork, in which kids circled countless "same" or "different" sounding words.

21

What books did kids read in those days? In many classrooms, the basal textbook was the only source of stories, while the "Weekly Reader" and the science and social studies textbooks filled in the nonfiction side. Few classic tales or stories were contained in the basals, since these texts were expressly designed to provide carefully (and synthetically) controlled vocabulary and complexity. Children's books were read at home, if at all.

Was this kind of reading instruction effective? Test scores, many of which measured the presumed "subskills" of reading, when looked at over the long term, were remarkably stable (see Roger Farr's work on the historically flat pattern of U.S. reading achievement). Most children learned how to decode simple print. But we did not create a nation of mature, effective, voluntary, self-motivated, lifelong readers: on the contrary, most Americans gladly stopped reading the moment they escaped from school. And for those graduates forced to read on the job, their employers complained often and publicly about the inability of young employees to comprehend even the simplest texts which work put in front of them.

And yet some of us ex-students from this dull era, a sizeable fraction of us in fact, *did* somehow learn to read beyond the mere functional level, and we became fluent, skillful, lifelong readers. How did this happen? We share a vague sense that much of our learning, our positive connecting with literacy, happened outside of school—in families and communities where literacy was honored and practiced. When we think back on our warmest, most personally powerful formative experiences with reading and writing, those events are predominantly out-of-school. So does this mean that schools really can't teach reading? Or that the cultural situation of students constitutes an impenetrable ceiling over their reading achievement? Teachers and researchers today are finding encouraging answers to these tough questions.

Reading the New Way

Marianne Flanagan teaches fifth grade on the south side of Chicago, in a school and in a district where the basal reading program still holds sway over most teachers and administrators. And indeed, for part of each day, Marianne teaches reading the old way, leading her thirty-two Black and Hispanic students through stories in the basal text, sometimes even marching them through the exact questions prescribed by the thick, glossy teacher's manual. One thing Marianne won't capitulate to, though, is leveled groups; her whole class simply discusses the basal stories together.

At other times in the day, however, Marianne is experimenting with some very different reading activities. Today, for example, her kids' "Literature Circles" are meeting. You can hear the noise long before you reach the door to room 213: the buzz of Literature Circles echoes halfway down the stairwell. When you enter the room, you may not believe that *any* reliable communication could happen amid this din; indeed, that's exactly what a few of Marianne's colleagues, long bred to equate silence with effective teaching, seem to think as they walk past her doorway, shaking their heads. And yet as a visitor gets acclimated to the noise level, joins a few student groups, and tunes in to the ongoing conversations, the sophisticated quality of these literary discussions becomes apparent. Children are tucked up close to each other, talking with animation, seriousness, and sometimes passion about the novels they have chosen to read. Among the titles being discussed today are Katherine Patterson's *Bridge to Terabithia*, H. G. Wells's *War of the Worlds*, Beverly Cleary's *Dear Mr. Henshaw*, and Sid Fleischmann's *The Whipping Boy*. Using a set of rotating, formalized roles (Discussion Director, Literary Luminary, Vocabulary Enricher, Illustrator, and Connector) the children purposefully and independently discuss questions they have brought to the groups themselves. Even the all-boys group in the corner by the window is completely engrossed and on-task with *Lord of the Rings*. "Man, don't you understand that this book is supposed to be a fantasy?" Robert somewhat impatiently queries his circle-mate Tyrone. "It's not real, it's a fantasy!"

Marianne skirts around the edges, dipping briefly into the groups. Sometimes she gets drawn into the conversation if the book is one she has read herself; but she hasn't read all the books kids are discussing, and she doesn't worry about it. Her job is not to translate or interpret the books; it is to facilitate the work of the groups.

Marianne's Literature Circles turn traditional reading instruction upside down in almost every dimension. The children, not the teacher, pick the books. Everyone doesn't read the same book at the same time. In Marianne's room, with thirty-two kids, there are usually eight different four-member groups meeting at once, each reading a different book. The groups are temporary and are formed on the basis of student interest in a particular book. The readings are not short, linguistically controlled basal stories, but real, whole, unabridged books, drawn from the worlds of children's, young adult, and classic literature. Kids are pursuing their own discussion questions, not following the cues of the teacher or textbook study questions. The reading teacher's role has shifted from being a presenter/questioner at the center of attention to that of an unobtrusive, quiet facilitator. In this activity, the students are the ones making the assignments, raising the questions, doing the talking and working. Perhaps most distinctively, the kids love *this* reading class. They lobby Mrs. Flanagan for extra meeting time and complain noisily whenever the school events rearrange the schedule and shortchange their Literature Circles.

Marianne has worked hard over three years to get the kinks out of the Literature Circles: to refine the roles kids play in their groups, to help the children internalize the importance of coming prepared to circle meetings, and to build a growing classroom library of multiple copies. Nothing has been easy; she's had to solve plenty of problems along the way. During the same time, she's also been experimenting with other "Whole Language" activities: reading literature aloud more often, introducing regular journal writing, starting a writing workshop, publishing more student work, making more class time for literature discussion. Indeed, one of the things that makes Marianne such an effective reading teacher, especially in a setting where one could think of plenty of excuses, is that she loves to experiment. Marianne is willing to try any promising idea, and she doesn't worry about pre-planning an innovation to the last detail. She's secure in herself, and doesn't obsess about what might go wrong. She just tries things first and then fixes up the weak spots later. She doesn't expect perfection of herself or her kids. She knows that for kids and teachers alike, growth comes through risk-taking and mistake-making.

As she looks back on her efforts with literature circles, Marianne says that the work has been worth it: "My students are more eager and enthusiastic to meet in their discussion groups. They like the idea that they may choose the books and be in charge of their own discussions. I frequently hear conversations about what book the group plans to read next. The power of the literature groups has instilled in the students an incredible thirst for reading. Book club orders have increased. There are more trade books visible in my classroom than ever before. On library days children return eagerly displaying their selection for the week. The librarian has indicated that the children request works by many authors and various genres. Also, I have noticed more of my children using their time wisely by reading in between assignments."

Qualities of Best Practice in Teaching Reading

Reading invariably comes first on everyone's list of basic academic skills, and we certainly endorse that ranking. After all, much of the information that school (and life) has to offer is coded in print, and students' ability to unlock and use all this knowledge depends on fluent, skillful, critical, and independent reading.

This means that any credible model for the genuine refreshment of American schools had better start with a solid plan for teaching reading. Though the field of reading has certainly been subject to its own passionate internal controversies over the years, the basic consensus about state-of-the-art reading instruction is stronger and clearer than ever today. Reading is no longer much of a mystery: the experts now understand quite well how it works and agree, at least ninety-five percent, about how to teach it to the vast majority of children.

The following are the key qualities and characteristics of Best Practice in reading instruction, the approach validated by our best research—

the model that Marianne and thousands of other teachers are moving toward. Whether this approach goes under the name of "whole language," "strategic reading," or "process reading," it works. Two landmark documents have charted this course: *Becoming a Nation of Readers: The Report of the Commission on Reading*, published by the Center for the Study of Reading in 1986, and *New Policy Guidelines for Reading: Connecting Research and Practice*, published by the National Council of Teachers of English in 1989. Because the NCTE report is the more recent, and because it incorporates and goes beyond the findings of *Becoming a Nation of Readers*, we will draw mainly on the NCTE document here. Many of the statements that follow are close paraphrases or direct quotes from the NCTE report, with thanks to its author, Jerome Harste. (We should also note that as this book goes to press, the NCTE and the International Reading Association, the two largest professional societies concerned with literacy education, have appointed a joint task force to produce an even more comprehensive document on Best Practice in literacy education, a report that should be available in 1994.)

Reading means getting meaning from print. Reading is not phonics, vocabulary, syllabification, or other "skills," as useful as these activities may be. The essence of reading is a transaction between the words of an author and the mind of a reader, during which meaning is constructed. This means that the main goal of reading instruction must be comprehension: Above all, we want students to understand what is on a page.

Reading is a process. Reading is a meaning-making process: an active, constructive, creative, high-order thinking activity that involves distinctive cognitive strategies before, during, and after reading. Students need to learn how skillful, experienced readers actually manage these processes.

Hearing books read aloud is the beginning of learning to read for most children, and this practice should extend from the home into school, and up through the grades. Teachers should set aside time each day for reading aloud, selecting good literature of high interest to the children.

Beginning reading instruction should provide children with many opportunities to interact with print: listening to stories, participating in shared book experiences, making language-experience stories and books, composing stories through play, enacting dialogue through drama, and reading and writing predictable books. From the first day of school, books and paper and pens should be in the hands of children. If children do not have extensive book experiences prior to coming to school, teachers must begin by providing the reading experiences they have missed. Children should never be treated as though they have not had meaningful encounters with print; in fact, even those from the most deprived families have experienced much more interaction with written symbols than most teachers acknowledge. Instead, teachers should build from and extend what children already know about language, whether that knowledge begins with fairy tales in parents' laps or from the rich (but educationally underestimated) print appearing on television screens.

Reading is the best practice for learning to read. Independent reading, both in school or out of school, is strongly associated with gains in reading achievement. Effective teachers of reading provide time for silent reading every day, encourage reading for varying purposes, and develop creative ways for students to respond to literature.

An effective reading program exposes students to a wide and rich array of print and goes beyond the use of the basal. Access to interesting and informative books is one of the keys to a successful reading program. An effective reading program goes well beyond the basal reader to include a variety of materials both narrative and expository, provides experiences with children's literature, and encourages students' self-selection of books. The classroom is stocked with a rich array of print of all kinds, including poetry, newspapers, and trade books as well as content-area books and magazines. Fiction and nonfiction materials should be selected on the basis of quality and student interest and should represent a wide range of difficulty, both so that kids can experience successful independent reading regardless of their level and also so they can challenge themselves by moving up in difficulty. Content-area teachers should use multiple textbooks and trade books, and set up environments in which students work on self-selected topics within the required units of study. Children in all classrooms should have free and unlimited access to print materials.

Choice is an integral part of literate behavior. Children should be permitted to choose reading materials, activities, and ways of demonstrating their understanding of the texts they have read. Reading skills and strategies should be presented as options rather than as rules to be universally applied under all reading conditions. Teachers should issue invitations to read and write rather than make reading and writing assignments. Teacher-directed instruction in which all children in a classroom or reading group are required to make the same response may indicate that this guideline is not being met.

Yes, but . . . How can the teacher manage when kids are all selecting and reading different books? Won't many kids waste time, or choose unchallenging books?

Providing choice doesn't mean having a "lax" classroom in which little work is done or expectations are low; it simply recognizes the limits of whole-class or group instruction. The teacher can entice kids to try good literature through brief "book talks." She can use quick one-on-one conferences to help them make good choices. Short conferences later on help the teacher to learn how the child is progressing, in work habits, engagement, and understanding. When a student is found not to be reading or improving, the teacher's response is to observe, identify the problem or blockage, and design an activity or find a piece of reading that will address the student's need. All along the way, just as with whole-class instruction, the teacher must make behavior norms clear.

Teachers who use strategies like Marianne Flanagan's Literature Circles, described above, find that the children inspire one another to read and think more. They become involved in heated discussions and debates. One group overhears the excitement in another group and decides to read their book next. Kids share their ideas with one another and with the teacher in frequent journal entries. Motivation to work hard is probably the most powerful when it comes from your peers.

Teachers should model reading. Teachers should read widely right along with their students, explaining their own meaning-making and book-choosing, telling how they select books, authors, or genres. It is vital that children get to observe a "joyfully literate adult" using print in a variety of ways every day. This modeling not only encourages children but it demonstrates for them the complex mental processes involved in skillful reading, especially when the teacher "thinks aloud" about her own meaning-making processes. Children need to see this kind of literate adult behavior over and over to internalize it. Teachers who are good models help to ensure that schools don't just graduate students who can read, but people who *do* read.

Effective teachers of reading help children actively use reading and writing as tools for learning. Research shows that children tend to use learning strategies in the manner in which the strategies have been taught. Teachers can demonstrate the usefulness of literacy by offering opportunities for children to engage in meaningful reading and writing during content-area instruction. Brainstorming questions before a subject is explored, pursuing library research projects, integrating reading and writing in content-area learning logs, and classroom activities that engage students in reading and writing in the ways they are used outside of school—all of these strategies meet this guideline.

Children learn reading best in a low-risk environment in which they are permitted and encouraged to test hypotheses of interest to them. Experiences should be planned that allow children to take risks, make inferences, check their conclusions against the evidence at hand, and be wrong. Reading teachers should help children understand that predicting what will happen next in stories, jumping to conclusions, and confirming or disconfirming their hypotheses are effective and powerful reading strategies rather than errors. For the most part, teachers should avoid questions that suggest right answers and instead ask questions that encourage a diversity of well-supported responses. Penalties for being wrong, as well as an overemphasis on correctness, grades, and being right—by either students or teachers—are indications that this guideline is not being met.

While teachers are becoming sensitized to their own overdomination of reading instruction, and now are rightly concerned with structuring more student-directed reading activities such as SSR and reading workshop, they still need and want to do some direct teaching. When they take the floor for a structured reading lesson, **teachers should provide pre-reading, during-reading and after-reading activities**. Before reading, teachers help students to activate prior knowledge, to set purposes for reading, and to make predictions. During reading, teachers help students to monitor their comprehension and construct meaning. After reading, teachers help students to savor, share and reconstruct meaning, and to build connections to further reading and writing.

The goal of teaching word analysis is meaning. The ambiguous research findings on phonics have engendered fierce professional and public partisanship for nearly forty years. Both sides insist that the case is closed—in their favor. The fact is that most kids—eighty to ninety percent—will learn all the sound-symbol strategies they'll ever need from naturalistic, fluent, ample real reading and (especially) from practicing invented or developmental spelling in their own writing. A fraction of children, which disproportionately includes poor, minority kids, don't acquire their sound-symbol ideas in this embedded, automatic way, but can learn and use these strategies when they are taught directly. Therefore, effective teachers have a broad-based approach to teaching word analysis that includes wide contextual reading experiences, focused word study, and student writing. They spend their instructional time judiciously; they carefully balance direct phonics instruction with more holistic, integrated reading and writing activities, and are alert to the potential boredom of decontextualized drills. In any case, such brief, well-designed lessons in phonics should normally be concluded by the end of second grade.

> **Yes, but . . . phonics worked just fine for me. I can even remember how much fun it was when I realized I could figure out what a word was.**
>
> Learning is complex, and people—adults as well as children—aren't always aware of all the processes going on simultaneously. You, as a

first grader, were very likely discovering things about context clues, picture clues, ingredients of a story, shapes of whole sentences, recognizable words, sounds of letters, gradually and in an unpredictable order. Kids in middle-class families are usually exposed to all this automatically, both at home and at school. And, as a fund of fascinating research has revealed, they come to school having absorbed much of it *before* officially "learning to read." Best Practice teachers have learned to identify and build on this prior knowledge, rather than start arbitrarily from scratch on just one piece of the puzzle. Then the kids who didn't get started at home for one reason or another must be given help with all the elements.

Teachers should provide daily opportunities for children to share and discuss what they have been reading and writing. As part of this sharing time, the teacher should help children to value the reading strategies they already have, and also continually introduce, and invite children to try, new ones. Author sharing times, peer tutoring activities, and collaborative research projects can help students reach this goal. Observing this work will provide teachers with much information for gauging students' progress. In an effective reading program, students **spend less time completing workbooks and skill sheets**. There is little evidence that time spent in these activities is related to reading achievement and they often consume precious chunks of classroom time. Effective teachers critically evaluate skill activities before giving them to students and replace them, where appropriate, with whole, original activities. Once students have internalized the behavioral norms of reading and writing workshops, these structures provide far more valuable and individualized "seatwork" than any prepackaged ditto sheet.

Writing experiences are provided at all grade levels. As well as being valuable in its own right, writing powerfully promotes ability in reading. Effective teachers provide a balance of different kinds of writing activities, including both individual, self-sponsored writings like those in journals or writing workshops, as well as teacher-guided writing activities that help students try new genres, topics, and forms for writing.

Reading assessment should match classroom practice. Many of the current standardized reading achievement and basal series tests focus on atomized subskills of reading, and do not stress what we really value in reading, which is comprehension. The best possible assessment would occur when teachers observe and interact with students as they read authentic texts for genuine purposes, and then keep anecdotal records of students' developing skills, problems, changes, and goals in reading.

Yes, but . . . When does the teacher find the *time* to do all this?

Many of the more traditional approaches to reading eat up loads of class time without moving kids ahead very efficiently. During traditional round-robin reading, when kids take turns reading aloud, only one child is actually reading at any given time, while the others often barely pay attention. When kids are completing boring worksheets, the teacher often needs to focus on maintaining discipline. When every activity focuses on teacher direction and information-giving, the teacher cannot give children much individual attention—or much sense of their own motivation for reading.

But when every child is reading a book of her own choice, the teacher can easily stop by the desks of three or four or five kids who need some special attention, or who are scheduled for a conference. It's not difficult to jot down a couple of phrases on the outcome during or after each conference. When children are discussing books in small groups, the teacher can circulate, observe the comments of individuals and take note of children's level of understanding. Indeed, as teachers grow into the habit of "kid-watching," they begin to notice all sorts of behaviors that indicate the level of individual children's literacy. This kind of observation is clearly a major part of the teaching described by Lynn Cherkasky-Davis at the end of this chapter.

Teachers are professional decision makers who decide how and what to teach. They plan lessons using a variety of materials. They organize flexible groups for varied instructional purposes. They model appropriate reading behaviors by demonstrating effective strategies, encourage students to discuss and interact, read aloud to students at all grade levels, and build classroom norms that facilitate fluent reading.

Effective administrators and school board members recognize teachers as learners and support their professional right to try to improve the status of literacy instruction. They do so by actively encouraging teachers to test their best hypotheses about what works for kids. Teachers should be provided with inservice training and time off to attend professional meetings. Professional self-development can be fostered through the creation and encouragement of teacher support groups. As we'll discuss more fully in Chapter 8, teachers need time to gradually try out and fine-tune each element of a new approach in reading—or any other subject. And they need to be allowed to make thoughtful choices for themselves about where to start and how to adapt practices to their own styles, settings, and students.

Schools that are effective in teaching reading have an ethos that supports reading. These schools are characterized by vigorous leadership and high expectations for student learning. These schools maintain well-stocked and managed libraries with librarians who encourage wide reading and help match books to children.

We think that the foregoing list of ideas and practices is amazingly simple. These recommendations certainly don't require any complex, futuristic innovations; instead, they invite a thoughtful return to certain fundamental instructional strategies that amply predate the basal era: reading good literature aloud, having kids read lots of whole, real books, providing much writing practice, encouraging the patient and varied discussion of the ideas in books, and making the teacher a model of literacy.

How Parents Can Help

The crucial role of home experience in the development of effective readers is well-documented and has been widely publicized in the professional and popular press. By and large, when children grow up in print-rich homes, where parents model reading and writing, where literacy is a tool of day-to-day family life, where stories and words are treasured, where reading aloud is a bedtime ritual, good readers usually emerge. But the research doesn't only single out perfect, academic middle class homes: many effective young readers also watch a lot of TV, and even poor families who don't own many books can create rich print experience with newspapers and library books.

Teachers still worry about the children who come from homes where none of these foundational experiences are known about or practiced. Some parents are so stressed, distracted, or exhausted by their own lives that there's no energy left for reading at home; obviously this set of problems especially afflicts poor, single-parent families, and it is their kids who disproportionately fail at reading. What can or should the school do to support at-home literacy?

Without becoming intrusive missionaries, teachers can begin to help parents teach, showing them how simple and natural literacy-building experiences can be integrated into the family routine. In Lynn Cherkasky-Davis' kindergarten class on the south side of Chicago, each week begins with all the children reporting about the stories their parents read to them most recently. In many inner-city schools like this, teachers assume that parents cannot or will not read to their children regularly. Lynn simply requires that some adult—a grandparent or sibling or neighbor if parents aren't available—does the job. The project begins at the start of the year, when Lynn meets parents for the first time and tells them about the importance of reading to their children. She's sensitive to the parents' own limitations as readers, and makes it clear that strict "school" reading isn't the goal. "Just look at the book together, read it, enjoy it, talk about it," she says. She's pretty direct, though. She tells the parents that their kids must come prepared each week having been read to. In the face of Lynn's energetic commitment to the bedtime stories, saying "no" just isn't a viable option. Once each week, when Lynn's five-year-olds go home to the housing projects where most of them live, each child has identified a book to read that evening with someone. Those who don't have books at home leave the classroom carrying a plastic-handled bag with a book inside, withdrawn overnight from Lynn's large classroom library. These books are always treated with care and respect, and returned on time.

In Milwaukee, Jim Vopat runs a Parent's Literacy Project where inner-city parents meet one night a week to build confidence in their own reading and writing, as well as their ability to help their children. In a safe, trusting atmosphere of fellow parents, they hear stories read aloud, they write or draw in response to these stories, they keep journals, they interview each other, they learn how to use their public library, and they learn exactly what's happening in their children's schoolrooms from their kids' teachers. During each weekly meeting, parents try one new literacy experience within the deepening familiarity of the workshop; then, every week, they return to their own families to try out a variation of this experience with their own children: reading aloud, talking, making lists, interviewing, keeping journals. Everything the parents do in the workshop underscores and supports what teachers are doing with their children every day.

But what about those kids whose parents and families, for whatever reason, presently fail to nurture literacy? What do we do for these children? If we are convinced of the power of parent-child reading (and we certainly are), and if this experience has been missed, then it must be substituted, provided in some analogous form, by the people at school. Every child needs to go through the "lap stage" of reading development, ideally at the age of two, three, and four with his or her own parent. But if this doesn't happen, then the school must help the child recapitulate this critical experience with someone else, later on. Echoing the intimate, one-to-one reading relationship is exactly what special tutoring programs like Reading Recovery are all about. School must be ready, not to *be* the parent, but to fill in analogous adult-child literacy experiences if they are missed at home. If some children aren't connecting with reading because they were never drawn into it through intimate personal modeling the way most kids are, then they must be offered some lap learning, too. Ditto sheets and phonics drills can never fill this elemental gap.

How Principals Can Support Best Practice in Reading

In Chicago, our group of about one hundred teacher-leaders from the Illinois Writing Project and the Chicago Project on Learning and Teaching have been giving reading workshops for teachers for several years. Recently, these teacher-consultants created a list of advice for aspiring Whole Language principals:

1. Be a reader and a writer. Visit classrooms and read aloud or discuss books with children. Write and share your writing in the school community.

2. Be an audience for students. Read kids' work on the walls and in classrooms. Let the authors know you've read and appreciate their words. Have a principal's mailbox, and enter into active correspondence with kids.

3. Make sure classrooms have all the supplies and materials needed to create a true workshop atmosphere: above all this means *books*. Help teachers tap the right budget lines to buy books, encourage parents to raise money for more books, run bake sales if necessary to get more and more books into classrooms. For their writing workshops, teachers and kids need plenty of paper, pens, folders, notepads, scissors, blank books, post-it notes, computers, typewriters, etc. You can purchase a hot-glue book-binding machine for less than three hundred dollars—a superb way to honor the importance of kid-made books.

4. Celebrate literacy in your school. Incorporate reading and writing into special school events and programs. Create space and occasions for displaying and sharing written work noncompetitively. Everyone needs an audience, not a contest with few winners and many losers. Contests that stress only quantity of reading or writing degrade literacy and invite cheating.

5. Help teachers communicate with parents: *proactively*, to let them know how reading and writing are being taught; and *reactively*, to help uninformed or skeptical parents understand and support the program.

6. Use your role as instructional leader, supervisor, and evaluator. Let teachers know it's good to use language arts/reading time to read aloud, do storytelling, conduct a daily reading or writing workshop, share dialogue journals, or to adopt other promising practices. In your classroom visitations, evaluate congruently: if teachers are using a process approach, you'll see non-presentational, highly individualized, student-centered workshop activities in which the teacher mostly takes a facilitator/coach role.

7. Work at the district level to align the curriculum guide and the standardized testing program with the holistic approach: e.g., help the school get off atomized subskills, and onto real reading

and writing. It may be necessary to work for the *dis*adoption of basals, skill-and-drill workbooks, certain standardized tests, or other materials that undermine the new curriculum. Talk to fellow administrators, and help them to understand and buy into the new paradigm.

8. Bring in teacher-consultants, the local writing project, or other genuinely facilitative people to help your teachers explore the philosophy and classroom practices of Whole Language. After the workshop phase, provide the necessary followup and support to help teachers "install" new practices in their classrooms.

9. Nurture continuing growth and emerging peer leadership among your staff by sending volunteer teachers to workshops, courses, summer institutes or teachers-training-teachers events. Support your outstanding and committed teachers by giving them a chance to lead, to share with colleagues.

10. Even though you don't have time: Read the research, scan the journals, and pass along ideas and articles to your teachers. Order books that teachers request for their own growth—from Heinemann, Richard Owen, NCTE, IRA, Boynton/Cook, and others.

11. Help teachers get TIME to talk about teaching together, exchange ideas, work on joint projects, think and grow as a faculty.

Connecting with Progressive Principles

It is important to recognize how the many recommendations in this chapter reflect our thirteen principles of Best Practice outlined in Chapter 1. While we leave it to the reader to recognize these connections in later chapters, we want to offer here at least one "guided tour"—showing that, in the field of reading, those thirteen principles are not just pro forma abstractions, but powerful guides to both general policy-making and practical teaching. Later, in Chapter 7, we'll return to the principles to reflect on ways they are commonly applied in all of the major school subjects.

Perhaps the most fundamental theoretical construct in Best Practice reading instruction is its **psycholinguistic** orientation, which simply says: children learn to read the way they learn to talk, and school ought to operate accordingly. When young children are learning to speak, adults do not try to teach them the subskills of talking or put them through speaking drills. Mostly, what they do is surround kids with real, natural language, talking to them and around them all day long. Young children listen and vocalize, playing and pretending with sounds and words, creating successively better approximations of talking. Parents treat all of the child's utterances, no matter how fragmentary or idiosyncratic, as meaningful. If a nine-month-old infant murmurs "ta," nearby parents are likely to rush to the cribside exclaiming: "She said Daddy!" Parents intuitively offer heaps of immediate feedback and indiscriminate encouragement for any communicative effort. By the time children are five, they have mastered more than ninety percent of the structures of adult language, not through direct teaching or correction, but through immersion and experimentation.

In the same way, children learn to read **experientially**, by being immersed in real texts and real literacy events from an early age. No one needs to break written language down into segments or sequences for kids: they learn best **holistically**, when they are exposed to complete, real texts that exist in their world, including books, menus, signs, packages, and so forth. They learn to read by playing at reading, by making closer and closer approximations of reading behavior. A familiar example of this is when young children memorize a book that has been read to them repeatedly, until they can recite it while the pages turn. Parents sometimes worry that this is not "real reading" because the child has "only" memorized the words—but teachers recognize that this is the essence of becoming a reader.

Children who are learning to read are not just receiving and absorbing a system that exists outside of them, but rather are **constructing** that system anew, for themselves. In oral language, we recognize this phenomenon in kids' use of unheard forms like "goed" or "foots." The existence of these invented, but entirely logical, word forms shows that the kids are not merely absorbing an adult system, but creating new intermediate language systems, using rules which they originate. In literacy, we see this constructivism clearly in the phenomenon of invented spelling, where children who are first trying to spell the short vowel sounds will substitute from their existing inventory of long vowel sounds the one with the most similar manner of articulation in the mouth. And, of course, all this literacy learning is individually **developmental**—that is, it proceeds through a number of predictable and well-defined stages. But while the sequence is roughly the same for all kids, the age and rate of change will differ significantly from child to child.

Children learn to read best when the materials they read are **authentic and challenging**. Basal textbooks were originally supposed to offer near-perfect texts for beginning readers by limiting length and controlling vocabulary, but this intention backfires. Now we know that the controlled, synthetic stories custom-written for basals are often harder for kids to read than seemingly more complex and uncontrolled literature. This is because logic, or playfulness, or sheer interest are often sacrificed in the effort to control linguistic features, thus rendering the story unreadable. In other words: the fake easy stuff is harder to read than the real hard stuff. Of course there's nothing too new or shocking about this: it has always been somewhat peculiar for adults to "control reading vocabulary" for six-year-olds who know and routinely use words like

pterodactyl, tyrannosaurus, and Jurassic. We must not belittle the powers
of emerging readers any more than we patronize young speakers. If we
respect what kids can do with language, they'll not only tell us a lot, they'll
also choose whole, real books for themselves.

Wise reading teachers are **child-centered**, encouraging kids to follow
their interests and choose their own books regularly. One of the insights
from family literacy research is that in the ideal parent-child bedtime epi-
sode, the child, not the parent, picks the book and sets the pace for reading and talking. Learning to read, like learning anything else, is driven by
curiosity and interest on the part of the learner; if these elements are
missing, the motive for learning is absent. In school, when teachers always
and only pick the stories or books to be read, motivation is sacrificed for
most students most of the time.

Literacy is **socially** constructed and socially rooted. While there are
obviously some solitary moments in the reading and writing process when
the reader or writer bends over a page, still the beginning motive and
ending payoff for most literacy work is profoundly social. In the "real"
world, people read and write for social purposes, to get or give information from or to someone else, for some real reason. The traditional school
approach to literacy has cut kids off from this social connection and purpose for literacy, rendering too many reading activities into solitary,
alienating exercises. Instead, children grow better amid rich and regular
interaction, in classrooms where **collaboration** is the norm, where there
are many chances to read and write and talk with other readers. Of
course, classroom reading instruction itself is a complex social enterprise
with powerful relationships and meanings. For just one example, students
have traditionally been grouped in three levels for reading by some measure of "ability," past reading achievement, or intelligence. We now recognize that this practice is unnecessary and often destructive: the
research on such tracking shows that it invariably harms the achievement
and attitudes of the children assigned to the low group while proving little or no benefit for even the highest ranked group. Today we seek a more
heterogeneous classroom, not just for the **democratic** model it provides,
but for the genuine richness and stimulation that a diverse class of readers provides. Teachers are perfecting classroom structures and
strategies—like Marianne Flanagan's literature circles—that make tracking irrelevant and unnecessary. Such activities are inherently individualized; when kids group themselves, flexibly and temporarily, no one needs
to be classified and segregated. Everyone benefits and everyone can work
in the same room.

The progressive approach also stresses that reading is a **cognitive**
process. Not only do growing readers need to develop a repertoire of cognitive strategies for predicting, monitoring, and evaluating texts, they also
need to practice metacognition. Kids need to become **reflective,** actively

examining the meanings they construct from what they read, as well as noticing their own reading processes and strategies. This is one reason why journal-keeping and portfolios are both such important tools in Best Practice classrooms. Both of these structures invite students to regularly reflect—keeping track of what one reads and writes, jotting down responses and plans, reviewing one's own history and accomplishments as a reader, and pondering the nature of one's own thinking processes.

Exemplary Program
A Day in the Life of a Developmentally Appropriate Whole Language Kindergarten

Lynn Cherkasky-Davis
Foundations School, Chicago

We begin at the beginning, with a program that encompasses young children's entire day at school. The account is in the words of Lynn Cherkasky, of the Foundations School in Chicago, a school that sits in the middle of an extremely poor neighborhood. A visitor knows when he or she is approaching Lynn's room because the kids' work spills out the door and down the hallway. A metal cabinet full of narrow drawers with a child's name on each serves as the class mail system. A huge bulletin board is encrusted with materials—not the usual neat rows of kids' essays or drawings, because that couldn't possibly hold it all. Instead, there are ceiling-to-floor charts listing books the class has read in two categories, "real" and "make believe." A "brick wall" of reading is made up of colored squares with the title of a book someone has read on each, and an inscription above, stating, "This brick wall is under construction. Hopefully it will take a lifetime to complete. Welcome to our community of readers." One section holds letters from parents, the mayor, visiting teachers, letters from the kids to visitors, and "letters to an absent teacher." Several projects hang in thick clusters, each grouped together on a ring. One is a science project, "Fish or Not Fish," with a news article about whales and dolphins, and the kids' own research on sea animals. Another, on math, includes a read-aloud book, *Fruit Salad*, plus charts and graphs comparing the numbers of each kind of fruit the children brought in to *make* fruit salad. A book on a particular theme—*In My Bed*—is grouped with kids' versions of similar stories and maps of their bedrooms. But there's plenty more going on *in* the room, as Lynn will tell you.

The children enter the classroom for family style breakfast at 8:45. They "sign in" outside the door, thereby taking their own attendance. The first day of school the children may draw their "portrait" as signature, or may choose a color and shape to use as theirs until they are able to sign their names or parts thereof. From the first day, children use writing for authentic purposes, never for isolated tasks. We sign up for photographs, learning centers, literature preferences, activity helpers, field trip participation, etc.

Following breakfast the children blend into the rest of the classroom for family reading. Children may read alone, in pairs, or in small groups. Volunteer parents, a part-time teacher aide, and I read with the kids. We listen to them picture read, approximate read, or actually read— whatever stage they're at. Children may listen to literature tapes while following along in books, read from charts, content area books, Big Books, literature sets, song books, poetry, library books (with their mandatory library cards), magazines, literature from home, and/or materials written by other children (or themselves). Our reading period illustrates the cooperative and collaborative nature of the classroom. The students are comfortable risk-takers who, without hesitation or embarrassment, will simply tell you what they can't read or need help on. But they don't stop there, because they've learned how to gather context clues and continue on with their story. While the myriad of reading activities goes on, I am a participant as well as evaluator, making note of further instruction particular children need.

Calendar activity comes next, and we address many content areas: math, language arts, science, and social studies. We tally, seriate, categorize, classify, write, pattern, order, and rhyme, as well as develop number, pattern, place value and time sense. We classify the days as rainy, sunny, windy, etc., count them up, discuss the groupings, and so on. The children take the lunch tally and record the day's weather. They are empowered to do all "housekeeping business," following patterns set by children before them.

Several times throughout the day I read to the children. The books are alternately of my choosing (on a theme or particular subject matter) and the children's. Discussion follows. Another reading activity is author's circle. When a student has gone through all the writing process steps and a work is ready for publication, he or she comes to "author's circle." Today Shanika read a book she wrote. The class was interested in her title page and how she produced the book as well as the story and illustrations. Shanika explained her writing process clearly, and her sequencing of information. She called for questions and comments when she finished "reading" her story, and the children eagerly verbalized their thoughts and feelings.

The rest of our day is spent in a literate, "hands on," problem-solving environment. The children circulate to various learning centers—some of their own choosing, some as a result of teacher and child evaluation. Teacher planning underlies all the activities, but they are all child-centered, and the children construct their own knowledge. The classroom is set up to provide opportunities for children to explore, discover, experiment and create their own sense of their kindergarten world and tasks.

Let's tour the classroom to view some of these activities as they're organized in thematic centers. We have a home and family center where children role play, write shopping lists (while consulting peers and other class resources for color sequencing and correct spellings) and family stories. I am consulted as a last resource. Today I observed Daniel trying to figure out how to spell "hamburger." He asked a peer who replied, "I don't know. Research it in our 'Food text set.'" Not finding it there, Daniel flipped through previous lunch menus, looking for "H" and "A," two letters he was sure about. He found "Ha" and knew it was the word he was looking for. Daniel has been encouraged to be self-sufficient, self-directed, and resourceful. He could construct what was unfamiliar from the familiar.

Continuing our tour, we find the science center filled with things to manipulate and experiences to create and re-create. In the transportation center, children can build "cities" in conjunction with the construction site adjacent to it. They map their designs, post signs, and write speeding tickets. They may also explore various means of travel and building.

Around the corner from the manipulative shelves and math materials are art materials, musical instruments, and easels in the Fine Arts center. Back to back are the writing table and publishing and bookbinding cart. At the typewriter and resource desk (the only desk in the classroom), the kids experiment with reading and writing connections. Here they keep writing portfolios and "works in progress," and conduct conferences with peers. These are but a few of the learning centers the children can work at.

What ties all these centers together are books, books, books, and writing, writing, writing! Out in the hallway you will find the kids' mailboxes. Children write to each other, to me, parents, principal, volunteers, upper graders, and anyone else. Today two children wrote to a publisher, explaining that the tape for Goldilocks does not match the words in the book in two places. In the mailboxes one will find some of the "letters" and stories written in full sentences with just about perfect spelling. Others combine functional spelling, letter strings, recognizable words, and pictures. Some may be pictures only, but interestingly each is addressed, dated, and signed by its author in clear letters.

On the walls around the room, the writing that the children do fills so much space that we're continually in trouble with the fire marshall. One chart shows how each child is progressing with various tasks surrounding the bedtime story parents are expected to read to them each week. In another area, pocket folders hold projects kids have done as part of their "Book of the Month" club. Each kid has a folder with his or her name and picture, and a list of the books selected. Charts list things in various categories—"Films we have seen," titles of books about families, books about food, etc. Another display lists various items, one hundred of which children brought for counting—one hundred noodles, one hundred beans, etc. There are so many charts that some must be rolled up and pinned. This leaves room for others and allows us to unroll them when we need to take a look at them.

Looking around my class today I saw that Lakita and Jinae were busy in the writing center. Jinae had written a story, and Lakita was her peer reviewer (yes, even in kindergarten!). She posed such questions as, "Did you leave spaces between words? What kind of letter must your sentence begin with? Check your punctuation. You need to research the spelling of that word." (The children follow my style of integrating phonics instruction into reading and writing.) With that, Jinae got up from the writing table and went to the housekeeping/grocery area where she thumbed through menus, recipe cards, shopping lists, books, magazines, and the class lunch menu to figure out the spelling of the word in question. She committed the word to memory but knew that it needed an "s" at the end to make it a plural. This she double-checked with her peer reviewer. (The previous phonics lesson of "More Than One" had not been an isolated lesson but was a natural part of a story we wrote as a class. The plural "s" was introduced during the story where it was needed. Thereafter, it will be pointed out often in books we read. All letters and sounds are learned in this context of real literature.)

When Jinae's writing process was completed, another classmate was summoned to do final editing. This kindergarten child followed a checklist the class devised earlier in the year. "Do the illustrations match the print? Are the pages numbered and ordered? Is it ready to be bound?" At this point Jinae signed up for a writing conference with me during the next learning center time, to fine-tune her work and decide on the binding (as it is a multiple page story). She will then go to the publishing center and, with the help of a parent volunteer, bind her work. After completion, Jinae is ready for Author's Chair. Anyone who collaborated on the story will join in.

My eyes scanned the room. Donald was in the math center making three-part patterns and recording them. He was using Unifix cubes, chips, and colored toothpicks. Another student was checking him. Donald put his findings in his math journal and went on to seek out books in our class library that will reinforce his patterning (although books, like writing materials, abound at all learning centers). Donald has integrated math and reading. I noted this behavior in my anecdotal records. That, with his recordings, will go into his evaluation portfolio. Using this and my "kid watching" guide, we will evaluate his progress, needs, and desires.

Moving about this small room, which has no front or back but is fluid in its space, I discovered several children moving ahead with what had begun, earlier in the week, as a teacher-directed whole class activity on categorization. The kids often take off with such activities and go as far as they are presently able. Today Antoine, Octavius, and Carla had taken books out of the classroom library and were categorizing them by "books about school," "books about home," or "books about food." They went one step further and noted that some books fit into more than one category and some fit into neither. Carla wandered off to the Bean Bag to read one of the books about food she thought looked interesting. She then decided to make a "text set" with other books on cooking and placed them in the kitchen area. Meanwhile, the two boys continued to list the books in their appropriate categories. Octavius called Nicky over to read the list with him. Nicky then decided to categorize his own list. He chose another section of books and classified them according to "real" or "make-believe." He took a survey of classmates to discover and graph how many preferred fact over fiction and vice versa. When I left him, he was graphing his findings.

It was time to clean up for lunch. Later in the day we wrote in our journals, used a guided imagery activity during writers workshop, did shared reading, listened to each others' Bedtime Stories during Literature Circle, followed guided reading, sang, and worked on problem-solving during a whole group "hands on" math lesson. Following this, children broke into small groups (by interest, not ability) to delve further into the new math concept with parent volunteers. After they recorded their discoveries in their math journal, the children were free to return to the learning centers.

Patrice sat in the rocking chair by the post office drafting a letter to her pen pal. She needed to spell "spaghetti." She went to the recipe box and child-written menus in the kitchen/housekeeping area (a popular spot today). She asked her friends for help and seemed satisfied. Seeing that I was busy with another child, she consulted her classmates first. Although she knows she can come to me after she has exhausted all other resources, she did not this time. However, I looked at the letters to her pen pal and saw, "We eight bus spgte pasta." (We ate busghetti, spaghetti, pasta.)

When the second learning center time was over, we used what I had learned from the children during the day for our culminating lesson. We brainstormed a list of food categories: meats, liquids, junk, pasta. Of course, under the pasta category, we listed spaghetti. Several purposes and subject areas were served here: consensus building, reading, writing, speaking, listening, science, nutrition, and setting another research base. This chart will be kept at an appropriate spot in the classroom, available as a resource.

At 2:15 we completed our daily diary. Children got coats, and signed out. Patrice quickly went to the "out" mailbox, carefully opened the envelope to her pen pal, and did something to it. The bell rang and she didn't have time to re-glue or tape her envelope. I told her I'd do it. Patrice gave me a hug, filled out her exit slip and ran to meet her auntie.

The children are home. For the first time since 8:30, it is quiet. I read the student exit slips (I too am a learner!) and review and alter my plans for the rest of the week: 1) Upper Grade Reading Buddies will visit; 2) parent volunteers will transcribe the stories children dictated into the tape recorder; they will illustrate, order, and enumerate pages to ready them for "read-aloud" or publication; 3) children will direct and act out stories they have written for the preschoolers; 4) the class will design covers for books they bind and sell to authors from other classes; 5) favorite literature will be discussed, compared, and contrasted for books-of-the-month club; 6) we will do an author study of Stephen Kellogg; 7) scientific experiments, readings, and recordings regarding plants will take place; 8) we'll begin our study of Black authors and illustrators for age-appropriate literature; and 9) a new learning center will be introduced. My lesson plans are a hodgepodge.

There is never enough time. I read Patrice's exit slip. This is her "lesson plan." It says: "Today: I speled my letter write. Tomorrow: I want to write a store book." I read the letter she has written her pen pal before sealing it. It says, "We eight bus, spgte, pasta." as before, but she has crossed it out. (The children do not erase, knowing I like to see the steps in their writing process.) It now says: "We eight spaghetti." No reading series, ditto page, isolated skill drill would have accomplished this.

Creating a literate, problem-solving, risk-free, higher-level critical thinking, encouraging environment for all twenty-five Patrices, taking into account their individual needs, desires, and learning styles—this is the embodiment of Best Practice in any developmentally appropriate classroom, not just kindergarten but preschool through grade twelve. Best Practice is not vase-filling. Rather, it is fire-lighting.

Works Cited

Anderson, Richard C., Elfrieda H. Hiebert, Judith A. Scott, and Ian A.G. Wilkinson. 1985. *Becoming a Nation of Readers: The Report of the Commission on Reading.* Washington, D.C.: National Institute of Education.

Farr, Roger. 1979. *The Teaching and Learning of Basic Academic Skills in Schools.* New York: Harcourt Brace Jovanovich.

————. 1992. Putting it All Together: Solving the Reading Assessment Puzzle. *Reading Teacher* (September).

Harste, Jerome C. 1989. *New Policy Guidelines for Reading: Connecting Research and Practice*. Urbana, IL: National Council of Teachers of English.

Shannon, Patrick. 1990. *The Struggle to Continue: Progressive Reading Instruction in the United States*. Portsmouth, NH: Heinemann Educational Books.

Weaver, Constance. 1988. *Reading Process and Practice*. Portsmouth, NH: Heinemann Educational Books.

BEST PRACTICE IN TEACHING READING

Increase	Decrease
Reading aloud to students	Exclusive stress on whole class or reading-group activities
Time for independent reading	Teacher selection of all reading materials for individuals and groups
Children's choice of their own reading materials	Relying on selections in basal reader
Exposing children to a wide and rich range of literature	Teacher keeping her own reading tastes and habits private
Teacher modeling and discussing his/her own reading processes	Primary instructional emphasis on reading subskills such as phonics, word analysis, syllabication
Primary instructional emphasis on comprehension	
Teaching reading as a process:	Teaching reading as a single, one-step act
Use strategies that activate prior knowledge	
Help students make and test predictions	
Structure help during reading	
Provide after-reading applications	
Social, collaborative activities with much discussion and interaction	Solitary seatwork
Grouping by interests or book choices	Grouping by reading level
Silent reading followed by discussion	Round-robin oral reading
Teaching skills in the context of whole and meaningful of literature	Teaching isolated skills in phonics workbooks or drills
Writing before and after reading	Little or no chance to write
Encouraging invented spelling in children's early writings	Punishing pre-conventional spelling in students' early writings
Use of reading in content fields (e.g., historical novels in social studies)	Segregation of reading to reading time
Evaluation that focuses on holistic, higher-order thinking processes	Evaluation focused on individual, low-level subskills
Measuring success of reading program by students' reading habits, attitudes, and comprehension	Measuring the success of the reading program only by test scores

3

Best Practice in Writing

The Way It Used to Be

Steve Zemelman looks back on his own education in writing: "In third grade, we had to do a geography 'project,' and I chose Canada. I went home, pulled out the family copy of *World Book Encyclopedia*, recently bought by my father for just such moments, and marked the passages I planned to use. I can still picture the maps with those tiny corn plants and coal cars that showed the products of various regions. I meticulously traced a map of Canada, complete with corn plants and coal cars, and put my mother to work typing up the passages direct from the encyclopedia. 'Are you *sure* this is how you're supposed to do this?' she asked diplomatically. I told her it was just fine and went to work on the cover. I don't know what the teacher really thought, but I received the expected 'E' for excellent. We were shown no models of what a good report might look like, had no audience for our work, generated no particular questions that we wanted our "research" to answer, and received no help getting started. It's no surprise that we simply copied from encyclopedias.

"On another occasion, we were to write about a family event. I innocently described the exhilaration I felt when my father drove at high speeds on family road trips. This clearly violated the teacher's sense of propriety and she humiliated me before the entire class with a lecture about my shocking disrespect for the law.

"Oh, yes: there were also all the boring routines—endless worksheets, and sentences to be copied fifty times off the board, equating writing with punishment. The purpose of book reports was simply to prove that you read the book, so even if the reading was enjoyable (*Winnie the Pooh* and *Wind in the Willows* were my favorites), the reports were just a job to be dispensed with as quickly as possible. Otherwise, writing meant 'spelling quizzes.' I was good at those, which is no doubt one of the reasons I felt comfortable when I became an English major and then a teacher. And it meant 'handwriting.' As a lefty, I was regularly ridiculed, told that I held my pencil wrong, and that my script was hopeless. I really don't know why I didn't come to hate writing as most of the other kids did."

Writing the New Way

Pat Bearden teaches a second/third grade combination class in an urban school. The children range from some who are highly verbal and acclimated to school routines, to one or two who angrily resist and one child who appears to sleep much of the time. The neighborhood is made up of small single-family bungalows, but the residents are poor and working-class people. It is not unusual to be approached for a handout as you park your car outside the school, and children talk of the violence they see and fear around their homes. The building, however, is a newer cinder-block structure, with brightly painted hallways. Pat and several of her fellow teachers have participated in extended inservice programs on teaching writing.

Pat would have never allowed the sad waste of time that was the "Canada" project to get started in the first place. An observer can see that Pat resolutely wants to try new techniques for teaching writing, and most of them are aimed at giving *kids* ownership of their own work. As she introduces more writing activities, her classroom develops in unexpected directions, and the results surprise and please her. One major technique used by Pat and many other teachers involves using journal-writing in a workshop-style setting.

On a typical day as the kids come chattering back from gym, they can be seen getting to work on their journals. Children move around the room to find comfortable positions for working. Three boys join a visitor at the back table. Two girls scoot underneath another table to share their writing—they are supposed to read to a partner once they've finished a piece. Two others settle in a hidden corner, planning excitedly.

When it's time to share work aloud, everyone demands a turn. Danyelle offers to share hers, and Cherisse giggles nervously. "There are parts the boys aren't allowed to hear," Danyelle warns. She begins to read her piece, an explanation of how to play "Girl Talk," a game that adult non-television-fanatics may never have heard of. When she reaches a crucial spot, all the girls in the room jump up and point menacingly at the boys: "COVER YOUR EARS!" The boys instinctively obey, Danyelle plunges on, and the girls scream deliriously. Everyone is laughing, including Pat.

Later, on a more serious note, David reads a piece about why various kids in the room make him angry, ticking off a list of insults and conflicts that occurred out on the playground. The children listen solemnly and discuss the justice or injustice of each charge. David is writing *for* himself, *to* the class. Later, Cherisse is found upset, at the back of the room, and

David comes over to see what's wrong. She opens her journal to a page of captioned cartoon squares with a stick-animal in each. "These are my pets," she says. "They've all died." The teacher, briefly at a loss as to what to say next, quietly says, "It's hard being a child, isn't it?" David and Cherisse nod their heads gravely.

These children are discovering how writing connects with their own lives and extends in many directions. In the events described above, writing serves many purposes, including entertainment, explanation, persuasion, and personal expression. It is a valued channel for human pleasure, negotiation, feeling, rather than just a classroom exercise. The children are likely to remember this basic writing lesson long after they've forgotten the day-to-day events of this classroom.

What is the teacher's role in this writing workshop? Sometimes Ms. Bearden simply sits and writes along with the kids—after all, if writing is important, adults should be doing it, too. Often she can be seen circulating among the children, to monitor the stages of each one's effort and to see who needs immediate help. Then she spends a few minutes each with several children, her responses attuned to particular needs. If a child can't think of a topic, Pat asks questions about what is occurring in the child's life at present, places visited, stories read, events that evoked a feeling, etc. If a piece is supposedly "finished" but needs revising, she asks what part the child likes best and what aspect of writing he or she wants to improve. Pat can press the issue because each child has a folder where all writing is kept, along with a sheet that lists elements the child has mastered and several the child and teacher have agreed to work on next.

How does the teacher help children improve mechanics and spelling? She stresses that in the journals and first drafts, children should focus on ideas and hold off on corrections until later—this is their "sloppy copy." Since most beginning writers actually worry *too much* about correctness, she tells them to draw a "magic circle" around words they are unsure of, so they can comfortably put them off until later. Then every few weeks each child chooses a favorite piece from his or her folder to revise and polish for publication and a grade. Children work on revising in pairs, consult classroom editing "experts," and learn to look for correct examples in the surrounding environment of books and posters. Before an editing session, Ms. Bearden will choose one element that she considers most needed in the children's work and gives a focused "mini-lesson" on it.

Publication is a vital activity in this classroom. Every day, children take turns reading for a few minutes at the end of each writing session. The walls are covered with the kids' writing, including interviews of one another with mug-shot photographs attached, written responses from adult guests and famous people the class has written to, and a student-of-the-week bulletin board where each child gets a turn at displaying his or her best work, family photos, bios of favorite music stars, and other materials displaying their special interests.

Ms. Bearden uses evaluation carefully to promote learning, and does not let it overload her or discourage the children. She uses the "responsibility sheets" in the children's writing folders to keep track of the aspects of writing that children have learned (including both mechanics and processes). She holds evaluation conferences with children after they've finished and polished up their pieces, to discover what the children perceive they've improved and learned, and she closely "grades" only the polished pieces that are turned in once every two to four weeks. Even on those, she actually marks just samples of a few items, so that the writers can focus on patterns of errors and look for some themselves instead of having the teacher do all the work.

Qualities of Best Practice in Teaching Writing

The blossoming of research and pedagogical experiment on writing has, over the past dozen years, created a clear and consistent picture of an effective writing program. Following are some of the main characteristics and strategies employed in a classroom like Pat Bearden's. The ideas and practices come from a body of research generated in the past twenty years, a key summary of which is found in George Hillock's *Research on Written Composition*.

All children can and should write.

A pre-schooler recites a story from her "pretend" writing and then repeats it nearly word-for-word much later, as her parents chuckle over her "cute" imitation of adult behavior. But it's more than that. The constancy of meaning she associates with written symbols shows the child not only comprehends what literacy is, but is already practicing it.

Most children have been writing long before they reach kindergarten. Beginning writers can make meaningful marks on paper, starting with drawing and moving though their own imitation writing, to more conventional messages that can be understood by a widening range of audiences.

Children of all backgrounds bring with them to school extensive involvement in literacy, though the particular cultural patterns of language use can vary widely—not just in grammar or pronunciation, but in purposes and occasions for particular kinds of talk. Teachers can hope to succeed with children from many cultural backgrounds only if they seek to build on these strengths and then explicitly help children widen their repertoires. Therefore, it is vital that teachers listen to children and learn the particular language abilities and needs they bring to school, rather than assume the teachers' own language styles and customs are universal.

Writing should not be delayed while reading or grammar is developed first; rather, experimenting with the ingredients of written language is one of the prime ways of advancing reading achievement and mastering the conventions of language. Children of all grades need sufficient writing time to fully complete and reflect on communicative tasks, for writing is one of the most complex and important of academic abilities. However, it can readily be incorporated as one of the tools for learning other skills, rather than merely competing for time during the day.

Teachers must help students find real purposes to write.
Just before Halloween, Ms. McWilliams' class has talked over various versions of folk stories they've heard about a ghost named "Bloody Mary." Now they've decided to write up the many ghost stories they've collected from their families and friends, to produce a Halloween play. All protest vigorously when writing time is over for the day.

When the topic matters to them, children work hard to express themselves well, and are willing to invest time and effort in crafting and revising their work. The best language-learning occurs when students attempt actual communication and then see how real listeners/readers react. Arbitrarily assigned topics with no opportunity for choice fail to give students practice in this most crucial of steps in writing. Meaningful writing tasks bridge the cognitive demands of school and the issues of students' cultures and developing personalities. If the writer has no real commitment to the topic or the audience, he or she cannot effectively interpret feedback to learn about how words communicate between people.

Students need to take ownership and responsibility. Writing means making choices. The more choices teachers make, the fewer responsibilities are left for students. For a significant percentage of writing activities, students should choose their own topics. When revising, students must be helped to decide which pieces are worth continued work, to look critically at their work, and to set their own goals.

Yes, but . . . Does this mean that teachers don't teach? Many students don't know how to do these things!

In fact, there's as much or more teaching to do than before, but it's focused on higher level thinking abilities. Since students don't automatically know how to make their own choices or to critique their own work, good teaching means helping students learn these true authoring processes. Teaching techniques to promote real authorship and good decision-making include:

- modeling topic choosing and self-evaluation processes using the teacher's own writing
- brief one-to-one conferences between teacher and student (effective, however, only if the teacher asks real questions about the student's thinking process and ideas, rather than

just telling the student what to fix, or using "read-my-mind" queries)

- small group collaborative work and peer evaluation (requires training of students so that they work constructively and meaningfully together)

Effective writing programs involve the complete writing process. Many children, having never seen skillful writers at work, are unaware that writing is a staged, craft-like process which competent authors typically break up into manageable steps. Teachers must help children enact and internalize the stages of writing by using classroom activities appropriate to each stage. The stages many teachers focus on are:

- selecting or becoming involved in a topic
- pre-writing—includes considering an approach, gathering one's thoughts or information, freewriting ideas
- drafting—includes organizing material and getting words down
- revising—focused on further developing ideas and their clear expression, and the audience's need for understanding
- editing—focused on polishing meaning and proofreading for publication

Teachers can help children recognize that the process varies between individuals and between various writing tasks. Just as with other crafts, not all pieces are worth carrying through all stages, and children can learn from focusing on just one or two stages for a given piece of writing. If they save their revising and editing efforts for their best pieces, the work will be most meaningful and they are most likely to put real effort into it.

Teachers can help students get started. Support begins from the very start. Children can be helped to develop abundant ideas about their own topics—or when topics are teacher-assigned, to generate plenty of ideas and connections between the topic and students' own questions. Lists of these topics and questions can then be kept in students' folders or on wall charts so that students can get started on successive writing tasks on their own. Skillful teachers help student writers gather and organize material for writing through such pre-writing activities as:

- memory searches
- listing, charting, webbing, clustering raw ideas
- group brainstorming
- freewriting (a specific process for free probing of thoughts)
- large- and small-group discussion and partner interviews
- reading and research on questions students generate

Teachers help students draft and revise.

"Is this your first draft or did you revise it already?" Lakesha asks her partner as they sit down in a corner to read each other's work. For these children, revising writing is a regular activity, and they've learned to ask lots of questions to find out what stage the writing is at and what needs the writer perceives before they begin discussing a piece.

Successive stages in the writing process are often ignored in traditional approaches. Children need to realize that good writing usually does not come from doing it once quickly and forgetting about it. Teachers can model revision of their own work and can conduct group revising of anonymous samples from previous years, so that students see what the process is like. Children need instruction in how to revise their work. By using role-plays, modeling, and group problem-solving activities, teachers can illustrate a number of complex thinking processes:

- reviewing one's work and comparing what one has said to the intended meaning
- seeing the words from the point of view of a reader, who may have a different point of view, and may not know all that the writer does about the topic
- being aware of various styles and strategies for explanation that can be used to clarify ideas—usually learned through reading and seeing ways that other writers do it
- generating multiple options for expressing an idea, and choosing the one most appropriate for what the writer wishes to express

Revision is about thinking and communication, not just fixing up mechanical details. Simply telling the child how to fix a piece may achieve a better piece of writing, but it doesn't teach the child the thinking process involved in revising. Once the teacher has modeled revising processes, she can promote meaningful revising most by asking real questions about the topic and the process of thinking about it, questions that very often open up alternatives for the writing.

Grammar and mechanics are best learned in the context of actual writing. Grammar should be integrated into the later stages of the writing process and connected with writing in which students have built some investment. When work that writers care about is going public, they want it to look good and to succeed. In contrast, research has shown for decades that isolated skill-and-drill grammar lessons simply do not transfer to actual writing performance. Beginning writers in primary grades should be encouraged to use invented spelling, so they'll develop fluency and not waste half the writing period waiting for the correct spelling of a word.

Yes, but . . . Don't we owe it to children to help them succeed in our culture by teaching correctness?

As with other aspects of writing, a shift in philosophy does not mean that the teacher doesn't teach about this vital concern. Rather, the aim is to make the teaching efficient and effective, something that most teachers will agree traditional grammar teaching has not achieved. Brief focus lessons can be conducted during the editing phase, when correctness is more likely to matter to the writer (if, that is, the writing has a communicative purpose and destination), and doesn't interfere with motivation or the development of ideas. Specific grammar and mechanics lessons can then be efficiently centered on items appropriate to the kind of writing students are doing, or on needs the teacher has observed the students actually have.

Grammar elements actually need re-teaching less often than we think. When young children get a lot of practice reading and writing, their spelling gradually moves more and more toward conventional forms, even without direct spelling lessons. Teachers can use strategies that promote student responsibility. For example, students can keep lists in their writing folders of the elements of grammar and mechanics they've mastered, so that they can remind themselves to proofread, rather than wait for a teacher's complaints.

Students need real audiences, and a classroom context of shared learning.

A teacher and three junior high writers listen to a fourth read her narrative about the months she spent in bed recuperating from a broken back. She knows it lacks an ending and everyone makes lame suggestions. Finally, she talks more about the experience and declares, "I was never so happy as the day I came back to school." The whole group cheers with delight as they realize she's found her ending—not through directives or criticism, but through supportive talk and listening.

Publication of student writing is vital: making bound books, cataloging student works in the school library, setting up displays in classrooms, in school hallways, at the local library, in neighborhood stores, or even placing class anthologies in local doctors' and dentists' waiting rooms. The old idea that the teacher is the only legitimate audience robs students of the rich and diverse response from audiences that is needed to nurture a writer's skills and motivation.

But connecting student writers with a wider community means more than just sending letters and books to people. Within the classroom itself, building a supportive context for working collaboratively and sharing writing is perhaps the most important step a teacher can take to promote writing growth. In fact, if the students don't experience their classroom as a constructive place where it is safe to try new approaches and say what they really believe, then even the most sophisticated, up-to-date "writing process" techniques are likely to fall flat. However, when students hear and read one another's work in a positive setting, they are inspired to try new topics and learn new writing strategies. When they listen to each other's compositions, students discover, by examining their own reactions, what readers need to know in order to understand what writers intend.

Teachers build this kind of interactive learning context through lessons about listening and respecting other people's ideas, and through guided practice with working responsibly in small groups on collaborative projects as well as peer critiquing. Teachers must be sure to model respect and supportive questioning in their own conferences with children as well. Then in collaborative groups, children can readily learn to give responses that lead the writers to critique themselves, and figure out their own improvements. This approach yields much more learning than does direct advice about how to "fix" a piece, because the writer experiences the actual problem-solving. And writing comes to have greater value because it serves to promote learning and friendship by helping to build a classroom community. This community in turn becomes the most powerful motivator available for further efforts at carefully crafted communication.

Writing should extend throughout the curriculum. Students value writing and use it more when it becomes a part of many other learning activities. Writing is, in fact, one of the best tools for learning any material because it activates thinking. Brief, ungraded writing activities should be used regularly in all subject areas to activate prior knowledge, elicit questions that draw students into the subject, build comprehension, promote discussion, and review and reflect on ideas already covered.

Writing for the study of other subjects need not absorb large amounts of class time or create an impossible paper load. Instead, spontaneous, exploratory efforts can easily be used to make learning tasks more engaging and more efficient. Such activities include:

- First Thoughts—two- to three-minute freewrites at the start of a new topic or unit to help students realize what they already know about

- K-W-L Lists—charts of what students Know about a topic, what they Want to know (or questions they realize they have, to put it another way), and then later for reflection, what they've Learned

- Admit Slips and Exit Slips—a few sentences on a notecard handed in at the *start* of class, summarizing the previous day's

work or reading; or stating something learned (or not understood) to be handed in at the *end* of class

- Dialogue journals—in response to material read or discussed,
  students write and react to each other's ideas in pairs, or
  between student and teacher
- Stop-n-Write—brief pauses during teacher presentations or
  reading periods when students can jot down responses to the
  ideas, questions they have, and/or predictions about what is coming next

Teachers can collect these, but should read them quickly to learn which
concepts are understood and which need further explanation. Students
simply receive a "check" or a "minus" to monitor the work. (For more
about these writing-to-learn activities, see Chapter 7.)

Effective teachers use evaluation constructively and efficiently.
Good teachers know that masses of red marks on a page discourage children, and don't really provide effective help for learning how to revise or
to proofread. They also recognize the research indicating that writers
grow more by praise than criticism. Better strategies for evaluation
include:

- brief oral conferences at various stages of the work
- folder systems for evaluating cumulatively
- focusing on one or two kinds of errors at a time
- thorough grading only of selected, revised pieces
- student involvement in evaluation, including self-goal-setting
  and self-evaluation, particularly through conferences with the
  teacher to reflect on what has been learned and what improvements might come next

**Yes, but . . . Won't all this additional writing and revising and
conferencing take more time than a teacher can possibly
give?**

Students need to write a lot, so much that teachers couldn't possibly mark every error in every paper. However, research strongly
shows that the traditional intensive marking of student papers
doesn't promote improvement. Instead, a brief conference, or
marking a sample paragraph for just one type of problem results in
more real learning. The child can then take more responsibility for
making the improvements in the rest of the paper. Students can

periodically submit their best revised piece for in-depth evaluation. Thus, different types of evaluation—brief/informal, vs. extensive/ formal are employed to suit particular purposes. Good teachers aim for learning within the *child*, not just achieving a correct *manuscript*.

Along with more selective marking of papers, one can keep a sheet in each child's folder listing skills and processes the child has learned plus brief notes on broader aspects of growth. Such recordkeeping allows for flexibility and individualization, helps the child reflect on his or her progress, focuses on actual learning rather than just the written product, and yet maintains clear accountability for both students and teachers.

Growth in writing always means trying something new and making mistakes in the process. Students must feel trust in the teacher and the situation to take that risk, and evaluation practices should support this necessary condition for learning.

How Parents Can Help

Since the most efficient and powerful language-learning humans ever experience—learning to speak as babies—occurs at home and with complete naturalness, home should also be a place where writing is encouraged. Parents can best do this by reenacting the same sort of "scaffolding" they unconsciously used to promote their children's first language-learning. Detailed study of early language-learning shows that this parental support is characterized by *playfulness* and *closeness*, focus on *meaning* rather than language forms, *modeling* of adult language, regularity and *predictability* of language activities, growth of shared *terminology* for talking about language, and *role-reversal* in which children take the lead to ask questions and make decisions.

First and foremost, there should be *pleasure* and *closeness* associated with children's writing at home. Writing done at school or at home should be celebrated and enjoyed, just as families celebrate first words, clever remarks and other oral language achievements. Playful notes can be exchanged on the refrigerator, slipped under a closed bedroom door, or included in the child's lunchbox.

The focus should be on the *meaning* of children's writing. Parents can support good teachers' efforts to help children become invested in, and take responsibility for, the ideas that they have. It's best for parents not to respond first or primarily to a grade (whether good or bad) or red marks on a school paper, but to read what the child wrote and take an interest in it. Writing can be given meaning at home by using it for real purposes— chores completed, birthday present lists, grocery lists, vacation itineraries, labels in family photo albums, invitations, letters to grandparents (encourage them to write back, so children get a response), requests to companies for free information and brochures. Parents can *model* this practical literacy for their children. When a letter goes to grandma, two sheets can be written at the same time, one from the child and one from an adult in the house—and the two can each talk over what they're deciding to say. Reading stories aloud at bedtime also provides models: It's pleasurable and immerses children in the language of good writers, which can increase children's motivation for both reading and writing.

Parents can make literacy regular and *predictable* at home. A special corner with writing implements and a convenient flat surface, regular times for writing and/or reading, ritualized note-leaving, letter-writing, and word-game times, all help children to see literacy as a stable and dependable part of their lives that becomes a treasured memory of childhood as they grow older. Gifts on holidays and birthdays—such as a desk lamp, blank-page diary, dictionary, typewriter—can further reinforce the regularity of writing. This ritualizing of writing will naturally lead to special family *terminology* that allows parents and children to further personalize writing and to talk over the various activities associated with reading and writing: book, author, character, ending, illustration, chapter, etc.

At the same time, it's good for parents to let the child take the lead, and be open to *reversal* of parent-child roles. Children will want to make decisions about what to read and write about, how long to work on a project, whether to display or abandon it, etc., and will take more ownership of their writing when they have this control.

Parents should urge that writing be given a high priority throughout their child's school, and should look for and ask about the kinds of teaching practices described in this chapter. When possible, parents should visit their children's classes to help with publishing projects, to tell about the role of reading and writing in their work, or to serve as writing coaches and audiences. Good teachers will organize as much of this involvement as possible.

What Principals Can Do

Obviously, as an instructional leader, a principal will try to encourage state-of-the-art teaching of composition in his or her building. The principal can let teachers know it's valuable to use language arts/reading time to conduct a daily writing workshop, to have journal writing, or to adopt other promising practices. In classroom visitations, a principal should evaluate congruently: if teachers are using a process approach, one will see non-presentational, highly individualized, student-centered workshop activities in which the teacher mostly takes a facilitator/editor role.

For long-range development, principals must help teachers get time to talk about writing together, exchange ideas, work on joint projects, think and grow as a faculty. And in the short range, it's important to make sure classrooms have all the supplies and materials needed to create a true writing workshop atmosphere: plenty of paper, pens, folders, notepads, scissors, blank books, and even typewriters or computers.

Principals can also work at the district level to align the curriculum guide and any standardized testing program with the process approach; e.g., get away from grammar drills and on to work with whole texts. Similarly, principals can help teachers communicate with parents. It's best to do this proactively, to let them know how writing is valued and how it is being taught. Then, when necessary, principals can react to complaints or concerns, defending teachers from skeptical parents and communicating the goals of the program.

But along with this larger leadership role, the principal should also be a model, and an encourager and celebrator of literacy, as an adult and professional in the school. The principal can be a writer, writing and sharing writing in the school community. He or she can be an audience for students, read kids' work on the walls and in classrooms, and let the authors know their words have been appreciated. Every school can have a principal's mailbox, so that the leader of the school can enter into active correspondence with kids.

The principal can make certain that writing is incorporated into special school events and programs. Space and occasions can be created for displaying and sharing written work noncompetitively. The principal can help children and teachers find outlets for "publishing" writing beyond the school building, can help find community sponsors for writing projects, and can support kids' efforts to print a magazine, even buy postage stamps for letters and pen-pal projects. And even though there's never enough time, principals can read the research, scan the journals, pass along ideas and articles to teachers, and order books that teachers request for their own growth.

EXEMPLARY PROGRAM
Writing About Local Architecture

Phyllis Mabry, Chuck Force, Ginny Hays, Julia Heiden,
Marilyn Kostenski, and Fred Krueger
Eisenhower High School, Decatur, Illinois

What follows is a description of an unusual project—a high school writing program that involved all subject areas and that produced a publication of significance to an entire community. The typical givens in a high school—departments, forty-five minute periods, kids' complicated class schedules—forced the project to be run more as an extracurricular activity than as regular coursework, though teachers subverted this distinction whenever they could by giving credit to any participating students who were in their own classes.

Of course this is not the first time that creative and insightful teachers have developed an outstanding integrated curriculum unit, and some experimental schools have even succeeded in abolishing the bells and schedules that limit such projects. Only through such broader restructuring can we fully achieve an integrated, high-level, high-involvement learning process for students. But the Eisenhower effort is especially important because it illustrates how teachers in a typical, traditional American high school can begin to expand the possibilities. And even with a limited scope to the effort, students become deeply involved in writing and learning, discover connections among subjects, and widen their own perspectives and interests.

> I don't know at this point whether I should thank you for my mini-grant or have my head examined, as the other five teachers of the team suggested I do. With bits and pieces of the research, essays, poetry, interviews, problem-solving, and art and science experiments in different

stages of readiness, bringing this project to its completion is, to say the least, a monumental task. But it has been a labor of challenge, of exploring, and of love.

So Phyllis Mabry began her report on the year-long project she organized at Eisenhower High School to study about, and then publish a magazine on, four architecturally significant sites in Decatur, Illinois. The project involved six teachers, each in a different subject area:

Chuck Force—Math

Ginny Hays—Art

Julia Heiden—Chemistry

Marilyn Kostenski—History

Fred Krueger—Architectural Drafting

Phyllis Mabry—English

Thirty-two students signed up and formed four eight member teams, each to research one of the four sites and contribute to the magazine in one or more of the subject areas involved.

As Phyllis explained in her initial grant proposal to the National Writing Project, "Decatur's architecture ranges from Italianate and Second Empire to Frank Lloyd Wright and Art Deco"—a special heritage in the city that the teachers and students wanted to explore and to bring to the attention of local citizens. They therefore chose sites representing those four listed architectural styles:

- The Powers-Jarvis Mansion—Italianate landmark built in 1909
- The Wabash Train Depot—Neo-classical structure that was the hub for the Wabash line
- #2 Millikin Place—Decatur's Frank Lloyd Wright House
- The Staley Corp. Office Building—Art deco-style headquarters for the largest manufacturer of starch in the U.S.

The project began with tours of all the buildings. Decatur's Architectural and Historical Sites Commission, delighted with the project, contributed additional support to bring in a restoration expert as a one-week architect-in-residence. A newspaper reporter provided contacts with local history buffs. And as Phyllis put it, "The students have met and talked with the movers and shakers in their city, and the movers and shakers have met a group of enthusiastic, dedicated students."

Students then began working on historical essays, poems, personal and fictional pieces, floor plans, elevation drawings, stipple drawings, sketches, and photographic studies of important details. Science and math inquiries included chemical analyses of paint samples from the buildings (though Staley did not allow studies that might have revealed pollution residues from their starch manufacturing operations!), mathematical analysis of the absence of the Golden Mean in Frank Lloyd Wright's architecture, and topological study of room layouts in the various floor plans. One student even conducted a feature analysis of Frank Lloyd Wright windows in order to write a computer program that generated Wright-like graphics. Such efforts went far beyond what the teachers had conceived when they planned the project.

Because of the timing of the grant and the complexity of high school course scheduling, the students could not be placed in a single course or set of courses together. Instead, the teachers allowed those students who were in their regular classes to substitute project work for various other assignments. Project students who were in Ms. Kostenski's history classes simply wrote term papers on the history of one of the buildings, rather than on something else. Art, drafting, and math students were able to follow similar procedures. Such substitution was not possible in chemistry, however, given the curriculum and the need for special lab time and equipment. And for the teachers, much of the work had to take place outside regular class time. This was an obvious drawback, not only creating extra work for everyone, but disrupting schedules when field trips and special activities were planned and students were forced to miss other classes. The teachers have talked about ways to schedule students and work within at least some of the courses when they run similar projects again, by recruiting students the spring before an effort begins. On the other hand, the semi-extracurricular quality of the project made it especially attractive to the students, and several said that they really preferred to do the work on their own time, at their own pace.

One learns most about such a project by simply listening to the thoughts and reactions of teachers and kids. They tell not just of glitzy activities conducted or content taught, but they also reflect on the value of independent learning, on how their teaching and studying has been permanently altered, and on ways they would change or strengthen the project when it is run again. It's a story of education gradually and thoughtfully evolving toward something better.

Fred Krueger, the drafting teacher, was happy to have students who, instead of moaning and complaining about assignments, launched into them eagerly and welcomed challenges. The project was not a burden for him, because he simply allowed the project students who were part of one class to work on their floor plans and elevations in place of other assignments he would have given them.

Marilyn Kostenski, teaching history, enjoyed the project for herself. As a lover of local history and architecture, she relished the tours and opportunities to talk with interesting Decatur people. Many local folks regularly drive past the Powers-Jarvis home to stare, but she had the pleasure of wandering through all its nooks and crannies. She was inspired to put together a display of newspaper articles on Decatur history for all of her students to see, and plans to make her own set of slides for class activities on Decatur history.

Chuck Force gleefully pushed math activities beyond the rather mundane expectations the other teachers had for his students' contribution. Network theory, symmetry, use of the golden mean, and computer-aided graphic design simply hadn't occurred to the others before they came to him. He, too has been surprised. He's so excited about the motivating power of hands-on learning he's seen this year that he's planned his own student project for next year, using computer Logo programming to guide Lego robots. The kids will build the robots and create programs to put them to work, similar to cybernetic and robotic experiments going on at M.I.T.

Chuck and the chemistry teacher, Julia Heiden, both struggled with the issue of student initiative. Students' initiative, making their own decisions about how to study the buildings, was a key element in the program, but kids lacked knowledge of what sorts of questions could be asked in fields like math and chemistry, and were well-trained by schools to let teachers take the lead. Both these teachers found that they themselves had to do some groping and mulling to discover possible directions of inquiry, and so they made lists for the students of possibilities that were suggestive without being very specific. The science list looked like this:

Exterior	Interior
Structural support system	Ease of climbing steps
Waste-sewer system (then and now)	Heating–type, efficiency
Chimneys	Plumbing
Roofing	
Paint and exterior finishes and how they've weathered	Presence of Pb in water
	Presence of radon
pH of soil, drainage of soil	Illumination
Windbreaks, light exposure	Insulation
Effectiveness against wind and weather	Elevators
Nature of site before structure was erected	How windows go up and down
	Electrical system; did it ever have gas lights?
Effects of pollution	Efficiency of fireplaces
Construction materials	Asbestos present

The idea was to provide support but still leave the considering and tentative trying-out and decision-making to the kids. Both teachers said that when they participate in future interdisciplinary projects they'd work harder to move students into and through this writing-to-learn process.

Julia acknowledged that it took discipline not to intervene constantly to provide expertise and answers. The experiments and answers students came up with were not glamorous or earth-shattering, she says—just simple processes of using photospectrometry to determine lead content in paint samples. However, the students were engaged because the work was their own. And because they were allowed to use lab equipment at Staley Corp. and Milliken University, they rubbed shoulders with real chemists working on expensive equipment. And, she adds, those professionals in the Decatur community enjoyed contact with the students, a piece of good public relations for the school and for teenagers that is almost entirely missing in most cities. Ginny Hays, the art teacher, shared this same appreciation for the community relations the project fostered— "At first people worried about unruly kids invading their homes and offices. Now they're disappointed to realize the year is almost over."

Ginny wondered, with us, about how to extend such projects to a larger segment of the student body. The teachers had hand-picked and invited strong students to join in because they wanted to make sure the work would get done, and so they picked students who could handle the extra commitment involved. The students, too, had to make choices. Fifty were invited to participate and not all accepted. The teachers also took on a number of students who heard about the project and asked to be included. However, one bright and concerned Black student, Consuelo, remarked to a visitor, "The students who *really* need this extra motivation and excitement are the ones I tutor, the ones who don't realize the value of reading at all!" Ginny Hays agreed that this was an important insight.

"How would we do this, though, with our usual classes of thirty-five unmotivated kids?" she wondered. Preserving small teams of no more than eight students seemed vital to her. Also important was students' sense of choosing, making a commitment, and having the freedom *not* to join the effort if one wishes. Students would need to elect the project at course registration time, the spring before it began. Teachers would need to be skilled at organizing small group work in their classrooms. There would be hassles, she pointed out. It was easy for a couple of teachers to pack eight kids into their cars and zip off to one of the sites for a visit arranged at the last minute; but much more complicated to schedule a bus for thirty-five the necessary two weeks in advance and then cross your fingers that the bus actually shows up. And so the brainstorming went on.

Ask the students what they've learned, and the response is immediate and unanimous: "We always thought Decatur was a dull place and we didn't care about it. Now we're really proud to be here, and we want to make sure these buildings and others like them are preserved and restored. Decatur has a history and a special character. Everyone should know about it." Thus, the kids developed a powerful sense of purpose and audience for their writing. As one student, Kara, explained, "I used to look at the old buildings downtown and think, 'Ugh!' But now—this is history in plain sight!" What about the more traditional subjects of school? Stephanie observed, "I got to use the knowledge I've gained in past years." Employing her understanding of acids and bases, she analysed and wrote about the chemical content of the patina on a copper balustrade in the Powers-Jarvis Mansion.

The students expressed a desire to make the work more collaborative. While the teams of eight visited the sites together, most conducted their investigations and write-ups on their own. They had other thoughtful suggestions—"We did this as juniors and seniors, and that's too late. Younger students should have this kind of experience to make the rest of high school more meaningful." And they differed on the question of including lower-achieving students. While some felt this was essential, others had clearly accepted the dominant attitudes in the broader culture around them—"How could those kids handle this project when they're not even getting their regular work done?" "The better students deserve the recognition!"

One student, Ami, unwittingly revealed how the project had expanded her interests:

Ami: When I first found out about the project, I said I just wanted to do photography. It was great that they didn't force you, you weren't stuck doing this or that just because it was an assignment. I wanted to do what I was good at. . . . We also had a whole day at the library for each group. I liked the reading.

Visitor: Wait a minute. I thought you just wanted to take photographs. What did you read?

Ami: Well, art books, at first. I looked at a lot of pictures.

Visitor: What were you looking for?

Ami: I'm an artist. I want to do something different than other artists have done. That's the whole point. So I had to see what kinds of photographs had been taken. Everyone does these straight-on flat views of the fronts of buildings. So I lay down on the ground and pointed my camera up. It was great. I also read some history.

Visitor: History? Why history?

Ami: I had to know what pictures were needed to illustrate various points in the architectural development of the period. When you just walk into a building, you don't necessarily know what's important, what pictures will be meaningful. I needed to find out where I should point my camera. . . . I felt like I had the chance to be a real photographer, to find out what it would be like to really do it as a job.

And there were thoughts about time. Julia Heiden mused about the time students took finding a focus for their chemistry studies—how it was frustrating but necessary. "I always think I can do things faster than I really can. But in science, you need time to think and reflect. You realize solutions to problems at unexpected moments." Science to Julia Heiden is thinking and problem-solving, not just memorizing formulas. Regular classes and over-stuffed curricula don't easily allow for this; the project did. Ami, too, understood it:

> In this project you were given freedom. When we went to the site, instead of being led and told, 'Look here, now there,' you had three hours to wander around. I can walk right past something ten times and not realize it's there. Then finally I realize it. . . . So many things you find out about these old houses, things you never knew existed. . . . We've overlooked so much in Decatur. If you kill your history, what do you have left?

Works Cited

Anson, Chris M., ed. 1989. *Writing and Response: Theory, Practice, and Research.* Urbana, IL: National Council of Teachers of English.

Atwell, Nancie. 1987. *In the Middle: Writing, Reading, and Learning with Adolescents.* Portsmouth, NH: Boynton/Cook.

Calkins, Lucy. 1983. *The Art of Teaching Writing.* Portsmouth, NH: Heinemann Educational Books.

Freedman, Sarah Warshauer with Cynthia Greenleaf and Melanie Sperling. 1987. *Response to Student Writing—NCTE Research Report No. 23.* Urbana, IL: National Council of Teachers of English.

Gentry, Richard J. 1987. *Spel . . . Is a Four-Letter Word.* Portsmouth, NH: Heinemann Educational Books.

Graves, Donald H., ed. 1981. *A Case Study Observing the Development of Primary Children's Composing, Spelling, and Motor Behaviors During the Writing Process.* Durham, NH: University of New Hampshire.

————. 1983. *Writing: Teachers and Children at Work.* Portsmouth, NH: Heinemann Educational Books.

Harste, Jerome C. and Kathy Short, with Carolyn Burke. 1988. *Creating Classrooms for Authors.* Portsmouth, NH: Heinemann Educational Books.

Hillocks, George. 1986. *Research on Written Composition: New Directions for Teaching*. Urbana, IL: National Council of Teachers of English.

Newkirk, Thomas and Nancie Atwell, eds. 1988. *Understanding Writing: Ways of Observing, Learning, and Teaching K–8.*. Portsmouth, NH: Heinemann Educational Books.

Spear, Karen. 1988. *Sharing Writing: Peer Response Groups in English Classes.*. Portsmouth, NH: Boynton/Cook.

Stillman, Peter. 1989. *Families Writing*. Writer's Digest Books.

Zemelman, Steven and Harvey Daniels. 1988. *A Community of Writers: Teaching Writing in Junior and Senior High School.*. Portsmouth, NH: Heinemann Educational Books.

Suggested Further Readings

Elbow, Peter. 1973. *Writing Without Teachers*. New York: Oxford University Press.

Fulwiler, Toby, ed. 1987. *The Journal Book*. Portsmouth, NH: Boynton/Cook.

Gere, Anne Ruggles, ed. 1985. *Roots in the Sawdust: Writing to Learn Across the Disciplines*. Urbana, IL: National Council of Teachers of English.

Graves, Donald H. 1989. *Investigate Nonfiction*. Portsmouth, NH: Heinemann Educational Books.

Harris, Muriel. 1986. *Teaching One-to-One: The Writing Conference*. Urbana, IL: National Council of Teachers of English.

Johnson, Donna and Duane Roen. 1989. *Richness in Writing: Empowering ESL Students*. New York: Longman.

Macrorie, Ken. 1984. *The I-Search Paper*. Portsmouth, NH: Boynton/Cook.

Rhodes, Lynn K. and Curt Dudley-Marling. 1988. *Readers and Writers with a Difference: A Holistic Approach to Teaching Learning Disabled and Remedial Students.*. Portsmouth, NH: Heinemann Educational Books.

Rose, Mike. 1984. *Writer's Block: The Cognitive Dimension*. Carbondale, IL: Southern Illinois University Press.

Taylor, Denny and Catherine Dorsey-Gaines. 1988. *Growing Up Literate: Learning from Inner City Families*. Portsmouth, NH: Heinemann Educational Books.

BEST PRACTICE IN TEACHING WRITING

Increase	Decrease
Student ownership and responsibility by: —helping students choose their own topics & goals for improvement —using brief teacher-student conferences —teaching students to review their own progress	Teacher control of decision-making by: —teacher deciding on all writing topics —suggestions for improvement dictated by teacher —learning objectives determined by teacher alone —instruction given as whole-class activity
Class time spent on writing whole, original pieces, through: —establishing real purposes for writing, and students' involvement in the task —instruction in, and support for, all stages of writing process — pre-writing, drafting, revising, editing	Time spent on isolated drills on "subskills" of grammar, vocabulary, spelling, paragraphing, penmanship, etc Writing assignments given briefly, with no context or purpose, completed in one step
Teacher modeling writing—drafting, revising, sharing—as a fellow author, and as demonstrator of processes	Teacher talks about writing but never writes or shares own work
Learning of grammar and mechanics in context, at the editing stage, and as items are needed	Isolated grammar lessons, given in order determined by textbook, before writing is begun
Writing for real audiences, publishing for the class and for wider communities	Assignments read only by teacher
Making the classroom a supportive setting for shared learning, using: —active exchange and valuing of students' ideas —collaborative small group work —conferences and peer critiquing that give responsibility for improvement to authors	Devaluation of students' ideas through: —students viewed as lacking knowledge and language abilities —sense of class as competing individuals —work with fellow students viewed as cheating, disruptive
Writing across the curriculum as a tool for learning	Writing taught only during "language arts" period—i.e., infrequently
Constructive and efficient evaluation that involves: —brief informal oral responses as students work —thorough grading of just a few of student-selected, polished pieces —focus on a few errors at a time —cumulative view of growth and self-evaluation —encouragement of risktaking and honest expression	Evaluation as negative burden for teacher and student by: —marking all papers heavily for all errors, making teacher a bottleneck —teacher editing paper, and only after completed, rather than student making improvements —grading seen as punitive, focused on errors, not growth

4

Best Practice in Mathematics

The Way it Used to Be

Many adults believe they have a clear sense of what mathematics is and why they despise it. These thoughts and feelings have been slam-dunked into them by their years in school struggling with textbooks and teachers living a kind of mathematical mythology of memorizing math facts (orally and with flash cards); computing page after page of sums, differences, products, and quotients (with and without remainders); going to the chalkboard to work out the answer; trying to remember the rules and procedures such as "Write down the 2 and carry the 1" and "Invert and multiply;" and developing careful, step-by-step proofs (beyond a shadow of a doubt). These practices provide a continuing source of material for cartoonists and comedians. Even Pippi Longstockings derides the hated process of "pluttifikation."

Common myths about mathematics include a variant of the Marine Corps recruiting slogan: math is only for a few good men; most mere mortals (especially women) are not good at it. Other prevalent myths are: doing math means getting the one right answer, quickly; mathematics is a collection of rules, theorems, and procedures to be memorized (and you might get to use some of them later . . . maybe); math requires working with numbers, doing more and more complicated arithmetic. And finally, many parents and teachers assume that teaching math involves steadily working through the textbook, page by page, assigning sheets of drill exercises from workbooks or dittoed worksheets for practice.

These ideas are fundamentally wrong; teaching practices and textbooks that directly or subtly perpetuate them continue to delude the American public into maintaining the mythology. Perhaps the saddest outcome of this situation is that each year a significant percentage of children come to believe that they are incapable of doing math. Teaching the mathematics that was needed by shopkeepers of the nineteenth century through stultifying drill and memorization has caused anxiety and loathing in a large portion of schoolchildren. The successive elimination of children at each grade level from enjoying and understanding mathematics is like a strainer that allows only a few to continue with confidence and power. By high school, when students can start avoiding math courses, each year only about half continue. By college, just a trickle of those who began counting on their fingers in first grade take more mathematics than required and a mere drop of these students major in it.

It does not have to be this way. And in a growing number of class-rooms in the U.S. today, it isn't.

Teaching Mathematics the New Way: Five Teachers Show How

Sally Netherville

Sally Netherville's district has made a commitment to a hands-on approach to learning mathematics. She has no textbook, no workbooks; instead she has a truckload of specially designed "manipulatives," a vast assortment of colorful, durable plastic materials with accompanying teacher resource handbooks for suggested activities. The children usually work in pairs or groups of three with the manipulatives on a variety of tasks: counting; arranging materials in groups of 2, 3, 4, 5 or 10; sorting and categorizing in various ways (by shape, size, color). The children make designs and patterns with some materials. They are building a sense of the base ten number system by gathering some materials into groups of ten. When they get ten groups of ten, they trade them in to the teacher for a special "100 prize."

Most of these activities are suggested to the children by Sally, who carefully prepares bags and boxes of materials the night before, arranges the students in working groups for the activity, and explains the tasks for them to do. She supervises their work while walking around the room, occasionally stopping to provide a suggestion to a group. Frequently, the materials lend themselves to further exploration by the children and Sally encourages them to go beyond the task she has "choreographed," so they might discover facts, relationships, and patterns on their own.

Jan White

Jan White's school district has failed to pass a tax referendum for the past ten years. So, unlike Sally, Jan does not have a roomful of commercially produced materials for her first-graders. But both she and her principal believe they must provide students with hands-on experiences in counting, grouping, sorting, and the like. Jan rarely uses the outdated textbook provided by the district. Instead she has become the self-proclaimed "Queen" of recycling. She, the children, and their parents collect materials for their own manipulatives: plastic screw-on caps, pop top tabs, washers, nuts and bolts, ceramic tiles, and so forth. Jan hounds businesses in the community for donations of leftover materials and containers. She is vigilant at garage and alley sales for leftover toys, blocks, games that she can use. Often she buys odd lots of generic commodities and foods for manipulatives, such as dried beans, rice, and toothpicks.

Pam Hyde

Pam Hyde teaches third grade in a school whose principal has supported a lively, hands-on approach to teaching mathematics by purchasing extensive materials and encouraging teachers to share ideas and activities. For one typical lesson, Pam arranges six balance scales around her classroom, organizes the students into six cooperative groups, and gives each group a plastic Ziplock bag with four different brands of bubble gum. She asks the students about their experiences with bubble gum: How big can they make bubbles? How long do they chew it? What are its ingredients? Then the students must predict how much of the bubble gum is sugar. Is it more than half or less than half of the weight? She records their predictions.

The students then weigh each piece of gum in their bags with the two-pan balance scales by placing centimeter cubes that each weigh one gram into one pan and a single piece of gum in the other pan. They record how many grams each piece weighs. Next, each student chews a piece of gum for about five minutes and then weighs it. The resulting weight is always less than the original weight. Students record these data and Pam leads them in a discussion that compares the pre- and post-chewing weights for each brand. There are differences among the students for the same brand. She asks them to explain why this might be so. There are marked differences among brands. One of the brands was "sugar-free" and its post-chewing weight was more than half its original weight, but not by much. The brands with sugar show dramatic weight differences pre- to post-chewing, definitely less than half. Pam again asks the students to hypothesize what would account for these differences.

This is one of several activities from the AIMS Project (see resource list) that Pam and the third-grade teachers of her school use with the balance scales to give students a strong sense of quantity, gram weights, measuring, and the concept of half of a quantity. Students are also getting firsthand experience with doing science and mathematics together. In another version of this activity in the upper grades of the school, students use their data to calculate the specific *percentages* of sugar or sugar-substitute lost during the chewing. They will be more precise with the scientific experimentation, investigating the effects of different chewing times, and the like.

Pam also uses the balance scales for the students to determine what part of a one hundred gram bag of peanuts consists of shells. Students predict, remove the shells and return them to the Ziplock bag, and weigh the shells alone. They eat the peanuts. In this activity, the weight of the shells in grams (centimeter cubes) is compared to an initial total weight of one hundred. Pam uses this activity with others to help the children think in terms of parts of one hundred, building up experiences that will provide a foundation for concepts of two-place decimals and percentage. She will also have the students repeat this experiment with one hundred gram bags of various nuts to investigate differences among these foods. The upper grade teachers in her school have their students do analogous experiments with bananas and oranges, initially weighing the food intact and then weighing the peel or skin. Since the comparisons between these part and total weights involve "messy" numbers (because the total will not be one hundred grams), students use calculators to determine percentages.

Carole Malone

Carole Malone teaches mathematics to all ninety sixth graders at her school, using the textbook only two days per week. On other days, she uses activities from resource books that address the same topics and concepts as the text, but in ways she feels are better. One day each week, she arranges "Math Labs" in which small groups of students work on tasks, problems, or investigations designed to address major themes suggested by the National Council of Teachers of Mathematics (NCTM).

For instance, in a Measurement Lab, students were given a centimeter tape measure and a dozen or more cylinders of different sizes (e.g., soup can, hockey puck, plastic medicine bottle). Their task was to measure and compare the lengths across and around each cylinder. They made lists showing these two measurements for each cylinder (such as, 4.3 centimeters across and 13.7 centimeters around). Next, Carole asked them to estimate about how many times bigger the around measurement (the circumference) was than the across (diameter) this circular base of the cylinder. Students could readily see that it was a bit more than three times longer. With calculators students computed what three times as long would be. Then they divided the circumference by the diameter to see exactly what this ratio was for each cylinder. Because the measurements were in centimeters, students could enter these figures directly into the decimal-based calculator. The ratios didn't vary too much among the cylinders; they were between 3.1 and 3.2 (unless students had measured incorrectly). Students were surprised that no matter how much the cylinders differed in size, this ratio was always the same (except for approximations in measurement). They had empirically determined the nature of *pi*, the constant ratio of the circumference to the diameter of any circle.

Jerry Cummins

When Jerry Cummins's freshman math students at Lyons Township High School begin studying algebraic expressions, they do so through an energetic, collaborative process of writing-(and talking)-to-learn. Jerry usually starts things out by putting a board-game number-spinner in some student's hands and an expression on the board. Say the expression is $X + C$. Jerry asks the volunteer to spin the spinner, yielding a random number between one and nine. If the number is three, Jerry then fills in the variable $X + 3$. Now he asks a few volunteers to offer a verbal phrase, a statement of some real-world situation that this expression might refer to. A typical response might be "A person's age, three years from now" or "The number of kids in this school plus three transfers." Once students get the idea, Jerry wants them to have plenty of in-class practice, so he uses a structure called "Roundtable." He introduces another expression, say "$2X - B$" and fills in B with another random number from the spinner, to yield "$2X - 4$." Then each student is asked to write down on a sheet of paper a phrase to go with this expression. After a minute or two, each kid passes his or her paper to the left, where the next student reads the phrase and must generate another, unique phrase. Then everyone passes and writes again, and finally a fourth time.

The fun grows as students become increasingly involved and original, trying to top each other with the plausible and relevant phrases. $2X - 4$ becomes: "The promoter printed up twice the number of seats in the theater because the band was going to play two shows, minus four seats because the promoter was saving two seats for himself and his wife at each show."

Now it might be time to get teams of four students together to co-author phrases and share these with the whole group. Jerry puts "$BX + C$" on the board, spins random numbers for both B and C, and then gives the groups two or three minutes to collaboratively devise and write down the best phrase they can come up with. Then the groups pause to share, hearing a few other groups' phrases, and then they do another one. When everyone is warmed up, Jerry lets teams share with one other team, rather than with the whole group, so everyone gets the maximum "air time." Meanwhile, Jerry circulates through the room, observing, facilitating, and helping out.

Qualities of Best Practice in Teaching Mathematics

Although the words "reading" and "writing" invite images of people **doing** these actions, the analogous term, "mathematics," is oddly static. What is a truly comparable, dynamic word? "Mathing"? "Mathematizing"? Perhaps "problem solving" could carry the connotations of students actually doing mathematics, using mathematical knowledge, engaging in mathematical thinking, investigating situations with mathematics. The five teachers just described all have their students actively involved in doing mathematics so that they can build their understanding of mathematical ideas, see the power and usefulness of mathematics in their lives, and feel confident in their own capabilities as "problem solvers." These are key themes at the heart of two major reports from the National Council of Teachers of Mathematics (NCTM): *Professional Standards for Teaching Mathematics* (1991) and *Curriculum and Evaluation Standards for School Mathematics* (1989). The following are the important and interrelated characteristics of the best practices of teaching mathematics embodied in these reports.

The goal of teaching mathematics is to help all students develop mathematical power. Students should develop true understanding of mathematical concepts and procedures. Teachers must help students build up understanding and meaningfulness by using mathematical ideas and by thinking mathematically. They must come to see and believe that mathematics *makes sense*, that it is understandable and useful to them. In these ways, they can become more confident in their own use of mathematics. Teachers and students must both come to recognize that mathematical thinking is a normal part of everyone's mental ability, and not just confined to a gifted few. They can begin doing this by uncovering the prior knowledge and mathematical thought patterns that children bring to school from their home and play experiences.

Teaching for mathematical power requires providing experiences that stimulate students' curiosity and build confidence in investigating, problem solving, and communication. Students should be encouraged to formulate and solve problems directly related to the world around them so they can see the structures of mathematics in every aspect of their lives. Concrete experiences and materials provide the foundation for understanding concepts and *constructing* meaning. Students must truly create their own way of interpreting an idea, relating it to their own personal life experiences, seeing how it fits with what they already know, and how they are thinking about related ideas. In the process, they experience the enjoyment of a challenge, the excitement of success, and the development of a good self-image. Their curiosity, inventiveness, and willingness to persevere is increased in such an environment.

How well students come to understand mathematical ideas is far more important than how many skills they acquire. Teachers who help children become mathematically powerful devote less attention to telling students about mathematics, assigning worksheets for computational practice, and requiring rote memorization. Instead, they employ activities that promote the active involvement of their students in doing mathematics in authentic situations. Such teachers use concrete manipulative materials regularly to build understanding. They ask students questions that promote exploration, discussion, questioning, and explanations. Children also learn the best methods for knowing when and how to use a variety of computational techniques such as mental arithmetic, estimation, calculators, as well as reasonable paper and pencil procedures. When students possess such understanding, they are far more likely to study mathematics voluntarily and acquire further skills as they are needed.

Yes, but . . . Shouldn't students know the math facts? Won't students do poorly on standardized tests if they don't?

Versions of these questions are asked frequently. At issue is not if students should "know math facts," but what it means to *know*, how one comes to know (or learns), and when. For instance, children in kindergarten are capable of memorizing the multiplication tables, just as they can memorize the names of the Emperors of the Roman Empire. In what sense do they know or understand what they might repeat from memory? In what ways might they thoughtfully use this information? On the other hand, if children participate in activities that develop a strong sense of what is happening as quantities of objects are counted, sorted, grouped, regrouped, arranged, and arrayed, they can build up a profound understanding of number, operations, and computation. From such a foundation, remembering is not difficult at all. Memorizing without such experiences is dreadfully difficult.

Furthermore, through these active experiences the teacher can help children's understanding evolve into two different types of formal mathematical knowledge: procedural and conceptual. Procedures for working with symbols such as: "invert and multiply" can be learned without understanding the underlying concepts. However, knowing *when* (which situations) to use which procedure requires understanding the concepts. Both kinds of knowledge are extremely important to success on tests and in life. Understanding the concepts of multiplication and division, their various forms, and how to think about the real-life situations in which it would be appropriate to use them, is essential for learning many topics of higher mathematics. "Knowing" the math facts without true understanding of the underlying concepts guarantees serious problems with learning other concepts in the mathematics curriculum.

Mathematics is not a set of isolated topics, but an integrated whole. Mathematics is the science of patterns and relationships. Realizing, understanding, and using these patterns is a major part of mathematical power. Students need to see connections among concepts and applications of general principles to several areas. As they relate mathematical ideas to everyday experiences and real-world situations, students come to realize that these ideas are useful and powerful. Students' mathematical power increases as they see and understand how various representations (e.g., physical, verbal, numerical, pictorial, graphical) are interrelated; to do so, they need experiences with each and with how they are connected.

Problem solving is the focus of a curriculum that fosters the development of mathematical power. Problem solving, broadly defined, is an integral part of all mathematical activity. Rather than being considered a distinct topic, problem solving should be a process that permeates the curriculum and provides contexts in which concepts and skills are learned. Problem solving means far more than the narrow "word" problems or "story" problems of yesteryear. Instead, problem solving requires students to investigate questions, tasks, and situations that they and the teacher might suggest. They create and apply strategies to work on and solve problems.

Students need many opportunities to use language to communicate mathematical ideas. Discussing, writing, reading, and listening to mathematical ideas—all these ideas deepen students' understanding of mathematics. Students learn to communicate in a variety of ways by actively relating physical materials, pictures, and diagrams to mathematical ideas, by reflecting upon and clarifying their own thinking, by relating everyday language to mathematical ideas and symbols, and by discussing mathematical ideas with peers.

A major shift in mathematics teaching has occurred with helping students to work in small groups on projects collecting data, making graphs and charts of their findings, and solving problems. Giving students opportunities for *reflective* and *collaborative* work with others is a critical part of mathematics teaching. Mathematical ideas are constructed by humans; students need to experience the *social* interaction and construction of meaningful mathematical representations with their peers and with the teacher. In *democratic* fashion, the teacher is not the sole owner and transmitter of knowledge. Students and teachers are inquirers together. The students can and should initiate mathematical questions and investigations of interest and importance to them. Teachers need not always have "the answer" (for there may not be one). Teachers and students can investigate together without threat to the teachers' authority and control.

Reasoning is fundamental to knowing and doing mathematics. Students must come to believe that mathematics makes sense, that it is not just a set of rules and procedures to be memorized. Thus, they need experiences in explaining, justifying, and refining their own thinking, not merely repeating statements from a textbook. They need to make and defend their own conjectures by applying various reasoning processes and drawing logical conclusions.

Helping students to move among various ideas and their representations in meaningful steps is a major task of teachers. Facilitating students' growth in abstraction and generalization is best accomplished by fostering experiences and reflection, rather than by the teacher presenting and telling. For students to discuss, make conjectures, draw conclusions, defend their ideas, and write their conceptualizations are now seen as a vital part of doing mathematics.

Concepts of numbers, operations, and computation should be broadly defined, conceived, and applied. Real-world, authentic problems require a variety of tools for dealing with quantitative information. Students must have many experiences in order to develop an intuitive sense of numbers and operations, a "feel" for what is happening in the different situations in which various operations might be used. For instance, two different conceptions of subtraction are involved when asked (1) If I have ten marbles and give you two, how many will I retain? versus (2) If I have three marbles and you have seven, how many more marbles do you have than I do? Teachers cannot afford to gloss over the differences in these two situations by simply invoking the procedures of subtraction to "find the right answer."

The concepts of geometry and measurement are best learned through experiences that involve experimentation and the discovery of relationships with concrete materials. When students construct their own knowledge of geometry and measurement, they are more able to use their initial understandings in applied, real-world settings. They develop their spatial sense in two or three dimensions through explorations with real objects. Measurement concepts are best understood through actual experiences with measuring and estimating measures. Furthermore, such experiences are especially valuable for building number and operation sense.

The understanding of statistics, data, chance, and probability come from real-world applications. The need to make decisions based on numerical information permeates society and provides motivation for working with real data. Probability emerges from realistic considerations of risk, chance, and uncertainties. Students can develop mathematical power through problem formulation and solutions that involve decisions based on data collection, organization, representation (graphs and tables), and analysis.

Yes, but . . . What if the mathematics textbooks in the district don't support these new Best Practices? Isn't this teaching too hard for teachers? Won't they just fall back on the textbook?

There is no textbook series, nor single text at a particular grade level that adequately addresses the NCTM Standards. All publishers of mathematics texts have attempted to move toward the standards, but groups of authors (and their books) have different strengths and emphases, as well as drawbacks. Looking for the right or even the best text to adopt is not the most important task facing schools. The textbook should not define the curriculum. Instead, each teacher should have a clear sense of the concepts and thinking to be addressed during the year, how they fit together, how they build on what has been addressed in the prior year, and how they are likely to be addressed at the next grade level in the subsequent year. Each teacher should teach a curriculum of activities in which students are doing mathematics: estimating, measuring, manipulating objects, drawing pictures, making graphs and diagrams, collecting data, compiling lists and tables. The textbook should be a resource to the process.

Although this activity orientation may sound extreme, it is the only sensible direction because no textbook, being limited to the print medium, can provide all the stimulation required for mathematical learning. Even with a "good" text, each teacher must supplement the printed material with manipulatives and activities. To do so, teachers must realize what is lacking in the texts, what kinds of activities are best, and how to help students to do them. Though this is not easy, teachers are quite capable of learning these new approaches to curriculum and instruction with good staff development. And yes, without effective staff development and clear district expectations for this kind of teaching, many teachers will rely too heavily on imperfect texts and paper-and-pencil routine worksheets.

A major purpose of evaluation is to help teachers better understand what students know and make meaningful decisions about teaching and learning activities. A variety of assessment methods should be used to assess individual students, including written, oral, and demonstration formats, all of which must fit with the curriculum. All aspects of mathematical knowledge and its connections should be assessed and used to help the teacher organize teaching and learning activities. Standardized tests are better suited to evaluating programs than to assessing individual students.

Yes, but . . . Aren't these practices more appropriate for elementary schools than secondary schools?

These practices describe how humans learn, understand, and use mathematics; they apply, though in somewhat different ways, to learners of all ages and levels of development. In fact, the NCTM Standards (1989) on instructional practices for grades 9–12 are remarkably similar to those for grades K–4 and 5–8. However, these practices are decidedly less prevalent in high school mathematics classes today than in elementary school classrooms. There may be many reasons for this state of affairs. Secondary teachers are subject-matter specialists who tend to focus on content and the structure of knowledge in their field, rather than on the processes of helping students understand. As students move up the grade levels, teachers expect certain skills and content to have been mastered and assume increased capability to deal with concepts and symbols of greater abstraction. Therefore, many high school teachers emphasize (often to the exclusion of all else) formulas, equations, and paper-and-pencil manipulation of symbols from the textbook. Students who cannot handle the pace and the high level of abstraction are judged incapable of learning algebra, calculus, or other branches of "higher" mathematics.

However, research on cognition has made it quite clear that abstract symbols, with all their power and generalization, are best used when the concepts underlying the symbols are truly understood. This understanding requires many varied experiences with particular situations and concrete referents (such as physical models, manipulatives, and the like). Best Practice in mathematics applies equally to elementary and secondary school teachers. Unfortunately, we tend to see more of these practices in the elementary schools, particularly in the primary grades (K–2), than in secondary schools.

How Parents Can Help

Children have a great many opportunities to interact with older siblings, adults, and mathematical ideas before coming to school. In fact, research studies have repeatedly shown that young children begin schooling with some well-developed and effective problem-solving strategies. These processes help children figure out what they want to know *mathematically* about situations that mean something to them. For instance, they can often judge perceptually whether or not they received half of a candy bar (or at least, got about the same amount as their older brother). Also, many use their fingers to count, keep track of quantities, or calculate needed amounts. Such methods are natural, developmentally appropriate, cognitive devices that work because they make sense to children. Unfortunately, instead of building upon the homegrown strategies of five-year-olds, teachers often demand that the children abandon these devices in favor of more abstract manipulations of symbols on paper. The jump from working with fingers and concrete objects to symbol manipulation is often too great for children; it is a chasm they cannot bridge without some overlap.

The Best Practices in mathematics teaching and learning described above make frequent mention of manipulatives, concrete materials, and real-world situations for optimal learning. These are the contexts that make understanding of mathematical ideas possible and provide a bridge to the more abstract symbolism that has maximal power and usefulness. Parents and the home environment of children of all ages can provide the richness of materials and opportunities for latent mathematical thinking to flourish. Mathematics and mathematical patterns are all around us: floor tiles and wallpaper; paintings and sculpture; coins and paper money; heights, weights, and ages of family members; combination pizzas; toys, games, and puzzles; shopping lists and recipes. The possibilities are limited only by adults' perceptions, willingness, and understanding.

Family Math is an excellent project to help parents realize the myriad of simple, mathematically stimulating activities they can do with their children. This organization offers several publications, including a book *Family Math* (1986) by Stenmark, Thompson, and Cossey (available from the Lawrence Hall of Science, University of California, Berkeley, CA 94720).

In general, parents need only the desire to involve their children in talking and thinking about the meaningful and relevant mathematics they encounter each day. A good place to start is taking the time to figure out *together* how much of something is needed, rather than the adult doing all the thinking and then telling the child what "the answer" is. For instance, "How many days until my birthday?" should be an occasion for parent and child to look at the calendar together, count the days *in each intervening month*, and add them up, as well as simply counting each day, one at a time. Real-life, authentic questions and tasks should be seen as opportunities to work with mathematics. Occasions for counting, sorting, and measuring abound in our lives. Even though video games have held children's attention for a number of years, there are many excellent games, toys, and cards that break through the flashing lights of the TV monitor. In fact, many children enjoy the different stimulation that physical sports and games offer beyond the passivity of the video medium. However, some have to be cajoled into trying something old-fashioned like Monopoly or playing cards. The inherent mathematics of such pastimes may or may not be obvious. However, the incidental learning (especially the number and operation sense) that comes from playing such games is pronounced. When students have a strong need to understand what is happening mathematically, they will exert effort and attention to do so. It is likely that three generations of Americans built their basic sense of what percentage means from landing on the Income Tax square of the Monopoly board.

In an analogous fashion, how many architects and engineers had their spatial sense nourished by blocks, Tinkertoys, and other three-dimensional building toys? Probably the most famous example is Frank Lloyd Wright, whose mother gave him a special block set at an early age. Parents should encourage children to build, create, explore, and arrange whatever toys and materials they can provide for their children. There is no lack of inexpensive materials.

When adults state that they are not good at visualizing or have no sense of direction, how do they know this to be true? Perhaps they have had limited opportunities to work in relevant spatial mathematics. Even if there are inherent genetic differences in visual, perceptual, or spatial abilities, it is clear that experience, exposure, and practice with enjoyable, stimulating materials can enhance and develop anyone's capacity. In school, we have found that students who habitually do poorly at the drudgery of computational drill often excel with geometric and spatial manipulatives. They need to know that they are capable "mathematicians" in these legitimate areas of mathematics.

Our news media have repeatedly trumpeted the mathematical achievement and ability of Asians. Despite claims of genetic reasons for mathematical prowess, an inescapable conclusion has been drawn by many who have studied Asian families. In many Asian cultures, it is assumed that all children are inherently capable of learning and understanding mathematics. If they evidence a difficulty in understanding a concept, they are told, in effect: "You can understand it! Work harder! We will help you!" This message is fundamentally positive, self-affirming, and encouraging. "Mathematics is not so difficult that it is beyond you. It is within your grasp. You are capable!"

Contrast this message to the response of the typical American parents whose child comes home complaining about the difficulty of understanding the math topic of the day. "I never did understand this! I never was good at math! I guess you inherited my poor math ability! Call a friend and just write down the correct answer to your homework." Not only does the basic message tell a child that she or he is unlikely to ever be any good in mathematics, but it also lets the child off the hook. There is no need to try any more. "Give up, why bother?" In fact, it is socially acceptable in this country to say, "I'm no good at math. I can't balance my checkbook." Why is it socially acceptable to say such things while it is not okay to say, "I'm no good at reading; I can't make any sense out of the newspaper?"

Perhaps the best way for parents to help their children with mathematics is to send the clear message through their words and actions that mathematics is all around us, it is a vital part of our lives, and it is understandable with some effort. Let's do it together; it can be fun.

How Principals Can Support
Best Practice in Mathematics

There are several critical roles that a principal plays in the life of a school; each bears on the issue of supporting best practice in mathematics. The principal is the key figure in public relations for the school, the spokesperson for the school, and for its teachers and programs to the community and parents. Since new approaches to mathematics curriculum and teaching in many ways run contrary to conventional wisdom and popular beliefs in our society, the principal (and other district administrators) should be in the forefront, *actively promoting* Best Practice in mathematics. She can explain and demonstrate new methods and materials, counter misconceptions and myths, and help to build support at home for this new vision of mathematics.

Of course, the principal must educate herself to these monumental changes that are occurring in mathematics education. The NCTM reports and other related publications are an excellent source of information. These outline what the best minds in the country are saying about teaching mathematics so that students will learn with true understanding and capability. Administrators must read them, go to workshops to learn about them, visit classrooms where they are happening, and see for themselves what is possible and what must be done.

Many principals hold Parents' Nights to present new mathematics ideas, methods, and materials to parents. Some make videotapes of these presentations and send them home to parents who did not attend. Principals arrange for Family Math programs on evenings or Saturdays, at which teachers develop activities for parents and their children to do together. Then parents continue these activities and extensions of them at home. Teachers often train a small group of interested parents to take over this program, recapitulating the activities with another group of parents in a self-sustaining fashion. The principal provides a coordinating function: ensuring that announcements are made, the building is open, materials are available, and so forth. Thus, the principal sends a clear message that parents and teachers can work together on a vitally important area of children's experience.

The principal also sets a major tone in the life of the teachers, within school. We know many teachers who get excited about new ways of teaching mathematics by attending courses and workshops, only to return to a wholly unresponsive principal who neither understands nor values what they are trying. Students actively doing mathematics means increased discussion, movement, and noise. The principal must validate such dynamic activity as an essential part of doing mathematics.

Principals are often major determinors of budget priorities for the school and the district. The new approaches to mathematics require investments in people and materials. Staff development, courses, workshops and other opportunities for teachers to learn more about Best Practice are essential. In addition, the principal can often effectively rearrange the available time within the school calendar for teachers to collaborate on trying these new practices, planning, sharing ideas and materials, and helping one another.

Similarly, the principal should find funds for mathematics materials, manipulatives, and resource books. Some schools have deliberately refrained from purchasing textbooks in the early grades in order to purchase manipulatives and teachers' resource guides instead. Other schools no longer buy one mathematics textbook for each student, but rather buy one set for each two or three classrooms; the teachers can share the set of textbooks, because they are just one medium of many for mathematics learning. Principals play a coordinating role in ensuring the equitable and timely sharing of all materials. Some schools have a centralized location (e.g. the media center) for all mathematics materials that are checked out by teachers. Ideally, each teacher (or at least each grade level) should have the particular manipulatives needed to effectively teach the concepts of the curriculum; however, centralized arrangements are necessary when a school does not have sufficient manipulatives.

A final area in which the principal's leadership can be vitally important is assessment. If we believe the NCTM standards that assessment should primarily involve teachers' realizing what and how their students are truly understanding, principals and other administrators have a major job to do with the public and the boards of education. There must be a significant reorientation away from standardized achievement tests as the sole method of assessment (for grouping and placement of individual students, for evaluating schools and programs, and the like). Teachers must begin to use a host of alternatives to formal paper and pencil tests to determine how a child is conceiving of mathematical ideas. The principal's leadership can be invaluable in promoting the legitimacy of math journals and other written formats as well as demonstrations and other oral formats through which students can portray their understanding and teachers can infer what might occur next in students' activities. See the suggested handbook on mathematics assessment by Stenmark (1991).

EXEMPLARY PROGRAM
Math Stations in Second Grade

Mary Fencl

Beye School
Oak Park, Illinois

A visitor kneels next to Lamaya at the "tangrams" table in a second-grade classroom at Beye School. Lamaya and three other children are each trying to put together a puzzle consisting of various sized triangles and one small square. They are supposed to form a larger square, but the solution is elusive. This is the sixth and last day for working on this particular set of "stations," or math problems, and Lamaya states readily that she's been avoiding the Tangrams table because "It's hard!" The children know they're not supposed to peek at each other's work, and even though everything is out in open view, they follow the rules.

The teacher, Mary Fencl, tells the visitor she will offer hints to keep the children from becoming discouraged. But it's clear that in addition to acquaintance with geometrical shapes, one of her purposes for this table is to help children learn to be patient and to keep on experimenting. "Play around with the pieces in as many ways as you can," she urges them. Later, when Lamaya shows frustration, Mary gives her an interesting hint. She places the two largest triangles together and draws the rest of the boundary for the final square on the formica tabletop with a marker pen. Lamaya then continues trying out various arrangements with a clearer definition of where she's headed, so that she's still using the process of "playing around," but in a slightly more supportive situation. After one more hint, Lamaya solves the puzzle, the kids and adults who are observing all applaud, and Mary remarks, "See, if you stick with something, it works out." Mary tells the visitor later that Lamaya came to

83

the class from a more restrictive school and that while she's good at things like spelling, she has trouble taking initiative or being creative. Mary hopes that experiences like the tangrams table will help Lamaya learn to experiment and take risks.

There are six "math stations" in the room, and on each day that they're available, a different group of children works at each of them. The class has math stations two days a week, so after three weeks everyone has had a turn at every station and new ones are readied. Mary makes sure that several of the stations allow the children to review concepts they've studied earlier, several are focused on topics presently being explored, and several deal with future topics. During the other three days of each week, the present topics are covered in lessons from the textbook required by the district. However, the children especially enjoy the more unexpected activities on future topics, and Mary says she learns a great deal from these. She discovers what explanations the children will need, where they will have difficulties, and what concepts they are ready to tackle. And the children pick up the ideas through experience, so that the explanations will make more sense when they come.

Each day that math stations are scheduled, Mary reviews with the whole class the activities at the stations before the children begin to work, so they remember what to do. This preparation also serves as an efficient review lesson, and by the end of the cycle for a set of stations, she asks children to do most of the re-explaining. Those who have already been to a table readily describe it for those who haven't. For this three-week period, the stations are as follows:

1. A board game using a die that has geographical directions on it—N, S, E, W. The object is to see how many rolls it takes for each player to move from the center of the board to the edge, "out of the city." The children are adding and working with directionality, which is presently a topic in social studies as well as in math.

2. Tangrams, using the puzzle described above. When the children complete the puzzle they make a design with the same cutout shapes, to put up out in the hall.

3. Categorizing and Venn diagrams. Children think up their own categories for grouping cutout figures of fish, from a large and varying boxful. Then they lay two large wire loops on the floor with an overlapping area, to sort by categories that allow for some fish to fall into the mutually inclusive overlap (e.g., "spotted fish" and "fish with big fins," and then some that are both).

4. Averaging. The children carry out various timed activities— signing their names in cursive (helps with the recently begun

process of learning it), jumping rope in the hall, dropping clothespins in a bottle, adding numbers on flash cards. The kids count the number of times they each complete a given activity within a three- or four-minute period, and then average the scores for the group, for each activity. This is a challenging concept for second graders, but Mary wants to see how far they can go with it.

5. Figuring arrangements. Children work with three recipes—an ice cream sundae with three ingredients, a four-layer cake, and a pizza with five ingredients. Colored paper "layers" and cutouts represent the various ingredients. The object is to see how many different ways they can rearrange the ingredients to make each of the foods. For example, the sundae can have strawberry ice cream on top, chocolate in the middle, and fudge sauce on the bottom—or the fudge can go on top. They know there's a button on their calculators that will tell the answer (the factorial function), but they still need to write out all the permutations or combinations to see for themselves. Mary tells them that since the pizza can be arranged so many different ways (120), they'll need a "system" to get them all.

6. Lunch menus. Here, each child gets twenty dollars of play money and a copy of a restaurant menu. On a blank chart the child writes his or her name and the names of the others in the group, and decides what will be ordered for each. Then subtotals are to be added up on the calculators for main dishes, side orders, drinks, and desserts. Finally, the total bill must be tallied, and cannot be over twenty dollars for the whole group of diners.

Many of the activities are connected with other subjects the class is studying, or interests the children share. As we've already mentioned, compass directions had been a topic in social studies. Mary had noticed that the children struggled with translating physical orientation of one's body to lines and arrows on a map. The fish come from the "Lake Michigan" unit the class has been exploring in science. The food combinations turned into the making of real "pizza" (using English muffins) on a previous day. And the class *is* planning to go to the restaurant to celebrate the end of the school year, so each group will actually have to decide on their final choices for lunch.

As Mary reviews the stations with the children before each session, she urges the children to use a system for approaching each one, and offers a few hints about them—"Who used adding to figure out your restaurant bill as you went along? . . . Ok, did anyone use *subtracting*? How would you do that?" Mary also makes many other kinds of connections. When she gets to "Categorizing," Mary pauses to ask the class about comparisons they've been making with two books they've read. Some elements are unique to one book, some to the other, and some are common to both. This clarifies the Venn diagram concept, and also turns into a brief but spirited review of a couple of books the kids enjoyed.

When the review gets to the "arrangements" station, Dierdre volunteers to explain it, but then halts, laughs, and covers her face in embarrassment. "Did you do this station, Dierdre?" Mary asks. "Not yet, but I tried it at home after Everett told me," she answers. Dierdre seems slightly worried, thinking she has cheated somehow, but the teacher's smile reassures her that there's nothing wrong with growing interested in something and doing it on your own.

As children go to work at the stations, the teacher circulates around the room providing help. One group sorting the fish does fine, but another needs reminding to stay with the task. Some children using the calculators are confused because these calculators leave off final zeros that occur to the right of the decimal point. Since the kids are figuring dollars and cents, they don't realize at first that a total like "3.3" means "$3.30." The group working on averaging is so absorbed with the competition over who signed her name the most times in four minutes ("Ali" won with seventy-four, because she used the shortened version of "Alexandra") that they need reminding to continue with the next steps of adding and dividing. The kids at the tangram table need hints at the right moments so they don't give up. When the room gets *too* noisy, the teacher clicks off the lights and very calmly reminds the children to keep the sound to a reasonable level. But in fact the period goes very smoothly and most children finish their tasks.

It's interesting to notice that while some of the stations require cooperative work, others are individually focused. The Venn diagrams and permutations are cooperative. The lunch menus and tangrams are individualized. And the averaging and the directions game are actually mildly competitive.

Even though Mary is using two days out of every week for math stations and only three on the book, her class has no trouble keeping up with other second grade groups that spend the entire week on more traditional lessons and exercises. She finds the combination of textbook and activities handy, because the book organizes the topics, and she can work gradually on expanding her hands-on repertoire. One of the more complex issues in all of the curricular areas we've described is how to make the transition from textbook to active inquiry, and Mary has solved it deftly.

Later, the visitor asks Mary about how she groups the children and provides the training they need to ensure that they use time well. Mary points out that the children love the variety and challenge of the math stations, and so it doesn't take much warning for them to get back on track if they've strayed. One secret, she says, is to start with group work immediately, at the beginning of the year. "If I don't start something right away,

I'll never do it," she observes. The children were allowed to choose where they wanted to sit on the first day, and the groups that formed around the tables (desks are not separated or in rows) became their permanent groups. She found that the children quite naturally had formed groups with mixed ability levels, and over the course of the year only a few changes were needed to solve behavior problems or achieve a better ability mix.

Mary admits that she didn't always enjoy math—"As a student, I hit the wall, myself, at about seventh or eighth grade." As a result, she didn't enjoy teaching it, either. However, as a special education teacher, before she took on her present assignment, she was driven by the desire to find something that would work for the children, since it was clear that traditional approaches to math did not. When she returned to the regular classroom, she specifically chose as one of her supervisory evaluation goals to develop the "math stations" approach, to force herself to make it work. "Now," she says cheerily, "math is my favorite subject!"

In fact, Mary's enjoyment of helping her students to *do* mathematics has led her to become one of the staff development teacher-leaders in her school district. Her principal, Susan Gibson, has encouraged teachers at Beye School to share ideas for teaching at the regular Wednesday after-school meetings. Mrs. Gibson also arranged for eight teachers from Beye School (including Mary) to attend a district-sponsored staff development program in Mathematical Problem Solving that Arthur Hyde led. Since then, Mary has worked with other teachers to lead this program several times and frequently shares her methods and materials with teachers in her school and others in the district.

Works Cited

Curriculum and Evaluation Standards for School Mathematics. 1989. Reston, VA: National Council of Teachers of Mathematics.

Professional Standards for Teaching Mathematics. 1991. Reston, VA: National Council of Teachers of Mathematics.

Stenmark, J.K., ed. 1991. *Mathematics Assessment: Myths, Models, Good Questions, and Practical Suggestions*. Reston, VA: National Council of Teachers of Mathematics.

Stenmark, J.K., V. Thompson, and R. Cossey. 1986. *Family Math*. Berkeley, CA: University of California.

Suggested Further Readings

AIMS Newsletter. AIMS Educational Foundation, Box 8120, Fresno, CA, 93747.

Cooney, T.J., ed. 1990. *Teaching and Learning Mathematics in the 1990s*. Reston, VA: National Council of Teachers of Mathematics.

Hyde, Arthur A. and Pamela R. Hyde. 1991. *Mathwise*. Portsmouth, NH: Heinemann Educational Books.

Post, T.R., ed. 1988. *Teaching Mathematics in Grades K-8*. Boston, MA: Allyn and Bacon.

Reys, R.E., M.N. Suydam, and M.M. Lindquist. 1989. *Helping Children Learn Mathematics*. Englewood Cliffs, NJ: Prentice Hall.

Trafton, P.R., ed. 1989. *New Directions for Elementary School Mathematics*. Reston, VA: National Council of Teachers of Mathematics.

Whitin, David J., Heidi Mills, and Timothy O'Keefe. 1990. *Living and Learning Mathematics*. Portsmouth, NH: Heinemann Educational Books.

BEST PRACTICE IN TEACHING MATHEMATICS

Increase	Decrease
TEACHING PRACTICES	**TEACHING PRACTICES**
Use of manipulative materials	Rote practice
Cooperative group work	Rote memorization of rules and formulas
Discussion of mathematics	Single answers and single methods to find answers
Questioning and making conjectures	Use of drill worksheets
Justification of thinking	Repetitive written practice
Writing about mathematics	Teaching by telling
Problem-solving approach to instruction	Teaching computation out of context
Content integration	Stressing memorization
Use of calculators and computers	Testing for grades only
Being a facilitator of learning	Being the dispenser of knowledge
Assessing learning as an integral part of instruction	
MATHEMATICS AS PROBLEM SOLVING	**MATHEMATICS AS PROBLEM SOLVING**
Word problems with a variety of structures and solution paths	Use of cue words to determine operation to be used
Everyday problems and applications	Practicing routine, one-step problems
Problem-solving strategies	Practicing problems categorized by types
Open-ended problems and extended problem-solving projects	
Investigating and formulating questions from problem situations	
MATHEMATICS AS COMMUNICATION	**MATHEMATICS AS COMMUNICATION**
Discussing mathematics	Doing fill-in-the blank worksheets
Reading mathematics	Answering questions that need only yes or no responses
Writing mathematics	Answering questions that need only numerical responses
Listening to mathematical ideas	
MATHEMATICS AS REASONING	**MATHEMATICS AS REASONING**
Drawing logical conclusions	Relying on authorities (teacher, answer key)
Justifying answers and solution processes	
Reasoning inductively and deductively	
MATHEMATICAL CONNECTIONS	**MATHEMATICAL CONNECTIONS**
Connecting mathematics to other subjects and to the real world	Learning isolated topics
Connecting topics within mathematics	Developing skills out of context
Applying mathematics	

(continued on next page)

BEST PRACTICE IN TEACHING MATHEMATICS (continued)

Increase	Decrease
NUMBERS/OPERATIONS/COMPUTATION	**NUMBERS/OPERATIONS/COMPUTATION**
Developing number and operation sense	Early use of symbolic notation
Understanding the meaning of key concepts such as: place value, fractions, decimals, ratios, proportions, and percents	Complex and tedious paper and pencil computations
Various estimation strategies	Memorizing rules and procedures without understanding
Thinking strategies for basic facts	
Using calculators for complex calculation	
GEOMETRY/MEASUREMENT	**GEOMETRY/MEASUREMENT**
Developing spatial sense	Memorizing facts and relationships
Actual measuring and the concepts related to units of measure	Memorizing equivalencies between units of measure
Using geometry in problem solving	Memorizing geometric formulas
STATISTICS/PROBABILITY	**STATISTICS/PROBABILITY**
Collection and organization of data	Memorizing formulas
Using statistical methods to describe, analyze, evaluate, and make decisions	
PATTERNS/FUNCTIONS/ALGEBRA	**PATTERNS/FUNCTIONS/ALGEBRA**
Pattern recognition and description	Manipulating symbols
Identifying and using functional relationships	Memorizing procedures and drilling
Developing and using tables, graphs, and rules to describe situations	
Using variables to express relationships	
EVALUATION	**EVALUATION**
Having assessment be an integral part of teaching	Having assessment be simply counting correct answers on tests for the sole purpose of assigning grades
Focusing on a broad range of mathematical tasks and taking a holistic view of mathematics	Focusing on a large number of specific and isolated skills
Developing problem situations that require applications of a number of mathematical ideas.	Using exercises or word problems requiring only one or two skills
Using multiple assessment techniques, including written, oral, and demonstration formats	Using only written tests

5

Best Practice in Science

Teaching Science the New Way—Elementary

The fourth graders are working with "mystery powders" this month. Chris Davis first asks her class to recall times when they've happened upon some material and don't know what it is. The kids think of quite a few—containers in the cupboard or freezer that have lost their labels, old medicines left in the bathroom cabinet, a parent accidentally pouring spoonfuls of salt instead of sugar into the cake batter, the time when playmates dared them to eat strange berries growing in the empty lot. They talk also about the scientific method—how do you systematically find out what a substance is, or what it contains?

Chris doesn't just define the vocabulary terms, like "hypothesis" or "scientific method," but asks the class to predict what they think the terms mean. What prior knowledge do they have about what scientists do? They realize that on TV they've seen representations of scientists mixing things into liquids and heating them, and they talk about what might happen when substances are treated in such ways. Finally, they learn that they'll be testing five "mystery powders" to discover what they are, and they make more predictions about what these might turn out to be. The kids usually expect they'll be edible.

Now that the mental ground has been set, the children work in groups to identify their five powders. Dittoed guidesheets help them to keep on task and record their findings. They smell, touch, listen (as they stir the dry materials), look closely with magnifying glasses. They realize that while all the powders are "white," they don't really look the same up close. Some are crystalline, others not; some particles are larger, some finer. They try dissolving each in water, vegetable oil, and vinegar, and different things happen. Three disappear in the water. One fizzes in the vinegar. One mixture turns hard when left to stand for a while. They heat each powder and observe the results. They put a drop of iodine on each—

91

and one turns black as a result. It takes a week of entire afternoons to complete all the testing. The groups decide their own order for testing, based on whether some facilities (like the burners for heating) are occupied or not. Because the children have had plenty of experience working in groups, they proceed with minimal teacher direction.

Then comes write-up, discussion and comparison of their results, and the kids learn what the materials really are: sugar, salt, baking powder, cornstarch, and plaster of paris. After this, the kids get a new task: each group receives a bag of powder that is a *mixture* of the five substances and they must determine their particular constituents. The final write-ups follow a scientific protocol that the students try out by doing one collaboratively first. The write-up and revision work goes on during language-arts writing time.

The kids also write and share their reflections about what the unit has taught them. Chris is surprised and pleased when the children, on their own, talk about the value of working through a step-by-step procedure, and using a process of elimination. "We can use this for math, too," they say, "especially when we get stuck." Finally, they list the questions they realize were *not* answered during the activity: *Why* did the baking soda fizz in vinegar? Why *does* iodine make cornstarch turn black? What was happening when some of the powders burned during heating? These will become topics for successive units later in the year. Some of the kids also decide, during art or language-arts time, to make safety posters about not playing with unknown substances, to be put up in their kitchens for the benefit of younger brothers and sisters. Altogether, the unit takes a month to complete. The lab times are lengthy, but time is actually saved because the kids don't have to clean up and set up as many times as they would with shorter work periods.

Teaching Science the New Way—Secondary

In San Antonio, Roger Robison's biology class begins their study of genetics by reading several articles about teenagers suffering from some debilitating conditions—diabetes, sickle-cell anemia, and a rare liver disorder that claimed the life of a student from their own school. The students discuss the articles and list their questions about these diseases: If they're inherited, will every child of the same two parents get the illness? Why don't the parents have it too? Exactly how are the diseases passed from parent to child? Is there any way, short of going childless, to prevent them or to protect future generations?

With these kinds of questions in mind, the kids head to the lab for an experiment. Each group of three students receives a pair of dishes with fungi growing in them. The fungi in one dish have spores of one color, and those in the second dish have another. Each group talks over what they think will happen when they crossbreed their fungi. Will the spores from the next generation of fungi be brown? Gray? A color in between? Some of each? In what proportions? The groups write out their predictions and their reasoning, and then after a lesson on sterile technique (so the experiment will be accurate), they breed their two fungi in a third dish and examine them two days later. Of course, the teacher has set things up a bit. As a result, the groups get differing results, compare them, and write out their own guesses about what is going on. It is at this point that they are ready to learn Mendel's laws.

Class sessions now focus on reading and information-sharing on the principles of genetics that will explain the experimental results and also answer some of their questions about human genetic disorders. Student groups take turns studying sections of the textbook and then explaining them to the rest of the class. Roger provides additional explanatory and curiosity-provoking articles, plus suggestion sheets listing ways to promote class discussion, to help the groups plan their sessions. One important job for each group is to explain how their information helps answer one or more of the questions the class first posed.

The study moves on to population genetics. The class conducts surveys of their own genetic patterns. How many class members are left-handed? Which ones can taste the chemical PTC? How many have index fingers longer than their ring fingers? How many cannot see certain colors? These are all inherited traits. If the students haven't already stumbled on certain questions, Roger poses them for people to write about in an "admit slip" at the start of a class period: If sickle cell anemia is an inherited trait, why is it more common in the Black population? If most people with cystic fibrosis die as teens, before they can have children of their own, then why does the gene for it still occur? Answers are found by working through the text together.

While this whole-class study has been going on, the students also extend their initial discussion of genetic disorders by brainstorming and gathering information (through calls to hospitals, doctors, finding news articles, etc.) to identify other diseases and related genetics topics they might inquire about: Tay-Sachs disease, Down's syndrome, the work of genetics counselors at hospitals, purposes and problems of inbreeding pets and farm animals. Ultimately, everyone chooses a topic to investigate further, with most working in groups of three or four.

As their classroom study continues, the students carry out interviews to get information on the topics they've chosen to investigate. Students visit hospitals, interview patients who agree to cooperate, talk with March of Dimes officials. Then each group prepares an informational brochure about the disease they've studied. Finally, after reading each other's brochures (which will be displayed in the library, or at local hospitals), they list further questions they now have. These often prove to be questions that can be answered through study of succeeding text chapters. Rarely is anyone bored during the genetics unit.

Qualities of Best Practice in Teaching Science

National concern about Americans' ignorance of science has increased sharply in recent years. Several well-publicized reports, both national and international, have suggested the science achievement of our students may be far behind that of children in most industrialized nations, and even in some third-world countries. These results may exaggerate the problem a bit—U. S.-educated scientists still lead the world in most fields of basic research and many areas of technology, and continue to collect more prizes than their colleagues from other countries.

Yet the gap may be closing, and we certainly ought to pay attention. Whether it's a crisis or not, the happy fact is that we now have reports from several national bodies that agree on approaches, like those described above, that could make science education both more inviting and more effective. Among these sources, especially important ones are: *Science for All Americans*, by the American Association for the Advancement of Science; *Science and Technology Education for the Elementary Years* and *Science and Technology Education for the Middle Years*, from the National Center for Improving Science Education. These reports, drafted by scientists as well as science educators, are striking in their firm advocacy of the principles of progressive education that we've outlined earlier. They call for making science learning experiential instead of lecture-oriented, cognitive and constructivist rather than focused only on facts and formulas, social and collaborative rather than isolating students from one another. Now it happens that science educators have conducted fewer research and pedagogical studies than have reading and writing experts, and haven't yet worked out all the detailed applications of these principles for every science field at every grade level. The systematic development of teaching in this area is not yet as far advanced, and so fewer teachers are now teaching science the new way, compared to those working with "process writing" or "whole language." But the direction urged by the national science study groups is clear.

Students need opportunities to explore the significance of science in their lives. For both the students who will study and use science in their careers, and for all students, who need to be well-informed citizens, the broad goal of a school science program should be to foster understanding, interest, and appreciation of the world in which we live. Along with building a knowledge base, science education should encourage students' natural curiosity, develop procedural skills for investigating and problem-solving, consider the possibilities and limits of science and technology in human affairs, and build an understanding of the nature of science and technology as fields of inquiry themselves.

Science study should involve *doing* science, i.e., questioning and discovering, not just covering material.

> One San Antonio high school biology teacher begins the year by giving each student twenty-five acorns and asking students to observe everything they can about them. Then she asks if they float, something most didn't check. Some acorns float while others don't, and there are many possible reasons, so the students proceed to hypothesize about why. But this is only a prologue. Each student must then choose a topic to investigate, design his or her own data-gathering process, pursue it, and write up the results, a project that continues throughout the year while the rest of the biology study goes on.

While science has built a massive body of knowledge over the past few centuries, the essential spirit of science is one of *process*—of inquiry and questioning. Students can learn this spirit by engaging in it themselves. If they are asked only to memorize information that is presented as already known, they are not being exposed to this questioning side of the discipline.

What is more, science involves higher-order cognitive thinking, and comparison and connection of phenomena from a variety of settings. Therefore, as repeated research has shown, lecture, front-of-the-class demonstration, and rote memorization of explanations lead to very little long-term understanding or correction of misconceptions about the natural world. Much more effective is a "constructivist" approach, which means activating children's prior knowledge about a phenomenon, encouraging their questions about it, and helping them to gather information hands-on, and to build their own concepts.

It is important to understand that this approach does not negate or minimize the value of factual information in science. Rather, it seeks to ensure that students really understand and retain this knowledge, and that the information is seen in a larger context of thought and inquiry, since future scientific development may very well make particular explanations obsolete. In fact, if more students were involved in this stimulating and motivating kind of study, it's likely that more would be willing to continue with more demanding advanced courses and science careers.

However, not all hands-on laboratory activities present students with cognitive challenges. A "cookbook" approach can be as trivial as rote memorization of vocabulary lists. Therefore, teachers must organize and guide experiments so that the students engage in real problem solving—that is, they are helped to generate real questions, realize apparent contradictions between pieces of data, pose alternate hypotheses, gather information to test them, and analyze the meaning of the information.

Yes, but . . . Hands-on activities are time-consuming, and involve expensive materials and special expertise not all teachers have.

Most science educators already recognize the value of direct experimental activity, though many also acknowledge that they use it far less than they should. This approach does indeed take time, but science groups also urge that teachers shift to an in-depth exploration of fewer concepts, in order to allow a full process of inquiry to take place. We discuss this as a separate, major recommendation below. However, some steps, such as probing children's prior daily-life experience of a phenomenon and generating questions about it, or stopping to elicit alternate predictions or hypotheses about successive trials of an experiment comparing different materials, need not absorb large amounts of time. Even the simple addition of a few seconds of wait-time between a question asked and answers sought from the class has shown to increase students' learning significantly. The point of these steps is to help convert cookbook labs and class discussions into a real process of questioning and discovery.

For elementary teachers who are not experts in particular science areas, excellent resources are available that describe easy experiments using inexpensive, readily available, non-toxic materials (e.g., Vicki Cobb, *Science Experiments You Can Eat*, and *More Science Experiments You Can Eat*). The steps and objectives described in sections below help a teacher to guide classroom experiments so that they are productive. And once a teacher comprehends the essential investigating process, she or he needn't be an expert with all the answers, but can be a fellow experimenter with the students—i.e., a good *model* of scientific thinking.

Effective hands-on inquiry involves a series of steps that builds students' investigative skills. Scientific inquiry for learning, while open-ended and flexible in many ways, involves a number of distinct steps and helps children acquire a range of process skills. Thinking about these can help teachers organize and guide experimental activities to insure that in-depth learning takes place. The dividing lines within the process have been drawn differently by various science educators, but can be described generally as follows:

- **Questioning.** The teacher (and/or student) introduces a problem, incites curiosity, or invites recall of personal experience with a natural phenomenon. Students discuss and list what they know or think they know about it, and questions they have. Often a demonstration of contradictory or puzzling outcomes helps raise such questions.

- **Observation.** Students gather data, at first in an exploratory way to probe the question. They begin to propose hypotheses to explain variations they find. This leads to more focused observation to test the hypotheses.

- **Organizing data.** This may overlap with observation. It focuses on looking for patterns and differences.

- **Explanation.** Students may be able to discern a cause or theory to explain differences. With more complex phenomena, reading, textbooks, or a teacher's expert input will be needed—and by this stage welcomed.

- **Reflection.** Review of the process, obstacles, and how these were addressed them makes students aware of the concepts, problem solving, and thought processes they've learned in the course of the inquiry.

- **Taking action.** Some topics with technological implications can result in responsible action in the larger community. Others lead to further scientific questions the students realize remain unanswered, thus encouraging students to continue learning.

Just as with stages in the writing process (see pp. 51–52), these are not lock-step, one-after-the-other phases in some ideal "scientific method." A good teacher—or researcher—recognizes that at any stage, one may need to jump back to another, and that real science is a complex mixture of organized inquiry and intuitive playing around with ideas and possibilities. Students may realize their real questions or misconceptions only after they've begun to observe, or organize, or work out explanations for their data. By observing students carefully as an activity proceeds, a teacher can decide when to intervene to point out what has taken place thus far, when to guide students so they won't become bogged down, and when to stand aside so the students take more responsibility for their learning.

Instead of a single scientific method, science educators have come to realize that there are many process skills students learn as they carry out meaningful investigations (*Science for All Americans, 1989*):

- classifying data
- communicating
- controlling variables
- defining operationally
- designing experiments
- formulating models
- hypothesizing
- inferring
- interpreting
- measuring
- observing
- predicting

- questioning
- using numbers

- using space/time relationships

These thinking skills are extremely important for students' success in other school subjects, as well as in science. Teachers can use such a list to assess whether an activity they wish to employ will in fact give students a rich learning experience in science.

Meaningful science study will aim to develop thinking, problem solving, and attitudes of curiosity, healthy skepticism, and openness to modifying explanations. The National Center for Improving Science Education considers the following attitudes important:

- desiring knowledge
- being skeptical, willing to question self-evident truths
- relying on data, testing ideas rather than just accepting explanations
- accepting ambiguity, holding off on an answer if data isn't clear
- willing to modify explanations, being open to changing one's opinion
- cooperating in problem solving, working effectively in groups
- respecting reason, using logic to work out explanations
- being honest, presenting data observed, rather than cookbook expectations

Just as in the newer approaches to mathematics, good science teachers have recognized that attitudes toward—and learning good strategies for—problem solving are especially important to their teaching.

A start-of-the-year activity used by Jim Effinger at Naperville North High School illustrates just how a problem-solving approach can excite students about biology. Jim brings donuts to class and asks what sorts of things people might do before they eat their donuts. Possibilities include choosing and inspecting your donut, saying a prayer, and sooner or later someone mentions washing hands. "Why do that?" Jim asks. The students decide that *getting rid of germs* is the main purpose.

"How could we test to see if washing really does the job?" Jim asks. The kids agree to give this a try, and Jim brings out Petri dishes, soap, and pans of water. Each student touches one Petri dish, then washes up, and touches a second one. They inspect the dishes the next day, to see what has grown. Invariably, the results are:

- sixty to seventy percent of the dishes show **more** bacteria after washing than before
- ten to fifteen percent are the same before and after
- fifteen to thirty percent have fewer bacteria after washing

The students are surprised and confused, and begin to hypothesize about the cause of these results—old versus new bars of soap, drying or leaving hands wet, etc. They re-design their experiments, following rules they've decided on, in order to standardize their efforts and maximize the cleaning achieved and try again—only to get the same results!

The kids are now hooked, eager to discover what factor influences the difference in number of bacteria on their hands. But Jim tells them the experiment is taking too much class time. If they really want to continue, they'll have to come after school. They do, of course, and after trying out many variables (quick-thinking groups organize into cooperative teams, to try a number of factors at the same time) they finally discover the secret: *time*. A short scrub just loosens the bacteria, so that more end up on the dish. A long, eight-minute scrub (as doctors use) does indeed do the job. But far more than just finding an answer, the students have learned many important aspects of scientific thinking: to consider many possible causes for a phenomenon, to design ways to look for these causes, to plan and control their experiments so that additional variables are not introduced, and most importantly, to expect that their everyday beliefs and guesses may not always be correct.

More broadly, the national reports stress the value of encouraging students' natural curiosity, sense of self-esteem, and confidence in approaching science study. Students should see themselves as active, responsible citizens who use their knowledge to take an active part in public debate on the technological choices that always balance gains and liabilities as they are introduced into our surroundings. The AAAS report, *Project 2061—Science for All Americans* emphasizes overcoming student anxieties, associating science with positive learning experiences, and helping minority and female students to feel that science is an inviting field.

Science education can build a knowledge base focused on essential concepts, rather than disconnected topics or bits of information. The National Center for Improving Science Education, in its 1989 and 1990 reports on curriculum, states that most science curricula focus on discrete topics and present information, facts, and processes within these. Instead, these reports recommend that teaching be organized around broader themes, concepts, and kinds of thinking. They assert that nine essential approaches characterize the study of nature. These are:

- organization
- cause and effect
- systems
- change
- structure and function
- discontinuous and continuous properties
- models
- diversity
- scale

By organizing material into themes around one or several of these analytical approaches, teachers can focus more readily on thinking skills, make connections between various specific topics, and identify clear learning objectives within a number of inquiry activities, so that children can even choose which ones to carry out and still work through all the essential concepts. The themes also make it easier for teachers to integrate science with reading, writing, and math, and to explore technological implications of a science topic.

For example, an activity in which children collect seeds from nearby areas, examine them, and attempt to make them grow under varying conditions, could be used in a number of ways. It could fit within a unit on **structure and function** (the role of various parts of the seed), one on **cause and effect** (influence of light, water, and chemicals on germination and growth), or **change** (following the life cycle of the plant). Of course, the teacher would need to encourage observation, questions, and reflection to help make any of these themes explicit for the students. Then analogues for any of the concepts could be found elsewhere in the curriculum, in literature that the children read and the stories they write.

Students should explore fewer topics in depth, not skim many superficially. National panels on science education have, over the years, repeatedly stressed in-depth inquiry instead of wide coverage of science topics. According to the National Center for Improving Science Education,

> "Less is more" is a guiding principle, for the learning emphasis should be on quality rather than quantity, on understanding rather than memorization. The emphasis on teaching science in depth rather than quickly and topically recognizes the complex process of conceptual change, a process that requires that students may either have to relinquish prior knowledge or reorganize it so that their world view embodies new ideas.

The aim is for a larger number of educated citizens to be comfortable with science and scientific modes of thought, to be more personally involved with it, and thus more likely to continue studying it, either for career purposes or for informed decision-making in a world that is affected ever more deeply by scientific and technological choices. Achieving this attitudinal development requires sufficient time to focus on a continuing process in which students are deeply involved. The National Center ranks students' attitudes and investigative skills co-equally with conceptual and content knowledge in its framework for curriculum.

Some teachers, especially at the high school level, seek to cover lots of material because "These kids will probably never study biology again and this is their one chance to get it." Sadly, this becomes a self-fulfilling prophecy. Many students experience minimal engagement with the topic and so they discover little of its relevance to their lives or its ability to fascinate. Conversely, kids who are actively involved in an extended cycle of questioning, experiential data-gathering, group discussion and sharing of information will be engaged, will want to learn more, and will be motivated to do so later on, after the course is over.

Yes, but . . . What about the growing number of state competency tests, and the achievement tests for advanced students' college entrance? Don't the students need to cover a large number of science topics to do well on these?

Science education panels acknowledge that this is a problem, especially because the tests are focused on memorizing facts instead of learning scientific thinking. The panels have argued for shifts in district, state, and national testing, so that tests support the kind of science we ought to teach. Student performance on national tests and enrollment in science courses has been declining, and neither were strong in the first place, so for most students, there seems to be little to lose. If so many students don't fare well with superficial textbook and lecture study, a shift to in-depth learning may well result in *better* standardized test performance. In one classroom experiment that demonstrated this connection, a group of remedial students used ethnographic interviews of local farmers and gardeners to learn about factors that influenced plant growth. These remedial students, who had consistently failed in all subjects, scored higher than all other classes in their school on the related textbook chapter test on plant biology (Heath, 1983).

Students grow out of misconceptions and naive theories only by actively engaging in investigation. In our daily lives, all of us construct concepts that help us interpret familiar events. These ideas seem sensible, but with natural phenomena they are often incorrect. Because they appear reasonable to the student, such concepts are not readily changed, even when a more accurate scientific explanation is given by a teacher. Science teachers often have as objectives the clarification of such misconceptions. However, research studies show that much of the time students memorize a new explanation without truly understanding it and still retain their basic misconceptions. Usually, it is only through a process of active questioning, encountering contradictory data, and investigating it that students can internalize more accurate scientific concepts and perceive their plausibility and usefulness.

In one earth science class, for example, the teacher helps students undo their confusion about the phases of the moon by using two tennis balls, each one painted black on one side. Many high school students (and adults, no doubt) believe the moon's phases occur because the earth blocks sunlight, casting a shadow on the moon. The teacher hands each of two students a painted tennis ball, asks them to imagine one is the earth and one the moon, while a window in the classroom represents the sun. Now the two students decide how to move to represent the "moon" tennis ball orbiting the "earth," with the bright side of the "moon" always facing the "sun," where its light originates. At the same time, other students take turns observing, positioning one eye as close to the "earth" tennis ball as possible. They immediately see the growing and shrinking crescent that the "moon" displays to them. The earth's blockage of light, they later learn, is the cause of the much rarer lunar eclipses. This is not an expensive or complex experiment. But it is well understood and remembered by the students.

Learning science means integrating reading, writing, speaking, and math. When Georgeann Schulte's fourth graders study the desert, they use reading and writing in a wide variety of ways. They write letters to kids in Arizona, asking about how those children experience desert geography and desert life. They read *Desert Dog*, by Jim Kjelgaard. Georgeann reads aloud Bird Baylor's *I'm In Charge Of Celebrations*, which poetically celebrates the pleasures of closely observing in nature, and the children then find natural objects, creatures, and events to observe, after which they compose their own written celebrations.

It is not difficult to see how an effective science program involves a wide range of language and numeracy skills. Groups working on an investigation will use plenty of writing to list what they know, recall personal experience of the phenomenon, generate questions, keep track of data and variables in an experiment, compare hypotheses, plan presentations to the rest of the class, or write letters to outside authorities about technological implications of their learning. Students practice speaking skills when they work in groups, interview informants and visiting experts, and present results to the class. They read whenever they compare their written data and explanations. Once they are excited about a topic, students eagerly read and recount related information from textbooks, library materials, and news articles. Math is used in measuring, tallying, graphing, and averaging. Thus, teachers—especially those with self-contained classrooms—can readily integrate many parts of the curriculum in order to make time for extended science exploration.

Students need to consider issues of application of science and technology. As the reports by the NCISE emphasize, science education often neglects technology, or simply conflates it with science. However, technology addresses problems of human adaptation in the environment, while science attempts to answer questions about the natural world. Each, of course, influences the other. Students can be engaged in both these areas of thinking, and it is usually the technological questions that lead to major public issues—acid rain caused by industry and power plants; pollution in rivers, air, and food chains; depletion of natural resources; alternate energy sources, etc. All technologies involve both gains and environmental costs, and most present various alternatives for solving a given problem. These impact wider systems in the process. Students can be encouraged to weigh technological questions in these terms, rather than simply label a technological development "good" or "bad."

At present, many elementary teachers do conduct units on ecology and conservation, providing picture books and articles on preservation of rain forests and endangered species. However, few present these as controversies or introduce the arguments of competing interests. We do not mean to imply that we side with the timber industry against the spotted owl. However, if students don't get an opportunity, early on, to sort through a series of arguments and counter-arguments, which is usually what technological issues involve, they won't be able to effectively advocate for their ecological values later on. We've observed primary-level classrooms where children readily do this kind of thinking, if the teacher has encouraged thought and analysis rather than memorization.

Good science teaching involves facilitation, collaborative group work, and a limited, judicious use of information-giving. "Teaching related to scientific literacy needs to be consistent with the spirit and character of scientific inquiry, and with scientific values. This suggests such approaches as starting with questions about phenomena rather than with answers to be learned; engaging students actively in the use of hypotheses, the collection and use of evidence, and the design of investigations and processes; and placing a premium on students' curiosity and creativity" (AAAS, *Project 2061: Science for All Americans*).

When we consider the teacher's role in the science classroom, we must recognize that lecturing is not only unsupportive of hands-on investigation, but research shows that it is strikingly unsuccessful at influencing students' science concepts. The teacher needs to model the same kinds of questioning and problem solving that he or she wishes the class to learn. Fortunately, this means a teacher need not have all the answers or be an expert in all areas of science. Instead, teachers can facilitate learning in a number of ways. They can offer tantalizing natural situations and puzzles that invite children to question. Teachers can observe student groups carefully to see what kinds of help they need, and provide guidance and information when students become stuck or discouraged. Teachers can analyze the activities launched in the classroom to understand the concepts and process skills involved, so as to reinforce these during evaluation and reflection sessions. In other words, the teacher still has an important role as expert and information giver, but uses it more strategically to promote lasting learning, and holds back when it would short-circuit students' own initiative and investigation process.

As for students' classroom roles, real-world scientists frequently work in groups, and top science educators stress the importance of group work in school. They recognize that discussion promotes thinking and problem solving by leading students to compare alternate ideas and solutions. When differences of opinion occur in a group, the students are naturally forced to elaborate their explanations and reasonings, and so these are made more explicit and tested against opposing arguments. Thus students think out scientific explanations instead of just memorizing them. They realize the questions they have and are motivated to seek answers from the text or the teacher, because they desire to settle the passionate arguments that develop. As a result, they also remember a lot more of what they've studied. Group work need not be confined to lab periods. Students can work together throughout entire units, with each group investigating a different question under the same theme or topic, and then reporting its findings to the class.

Yes, but . . . Can teachers and students really adopt these teaching and learning approaches when they're so accustomed to the usual lectures, textbooks, memorizing and test-taking?

Fortunately, we have many more tools for applying new teaching methods than in the past. We needn't depend on intuitive trial-and-error approaches that can leave teachers and students floundering when they don't work well. For example, Johnson, Johnson, Holubec, and Roy provide very clear, practical, and effective methods for teaching children to work productively in small groups, in *Circles of Learning* (ASCD, 1984). This training takes time, of course, but as more and more teachers are using small group work in various subjects and grade levels, increasing numbers of students will arrive in science classes already equipped to do it well.

Teachers don't always have the time or expertise to design their own more experiential science investigation units. However, materials are also available to help with this—for example, Tik Liem's *Invitations to Science Inquiry* (1987) which presents four hundred activities based on discrepant events.

Meaningful assessment of students' learning in science must promote the objectives of a good science curriculum, and not undermine them. Testing in science classrooms often focuses on the body of knowledge in science, rather than the thinking and investigative processes or attitudes a student should acquire. If teachers are to promote experiential work and thinking skills in science, then assessment should stress these as well. Otherwise, teachers and students are being asked to do one thing, but being held accountable for another. While it may be difficult for formal pencil-and-paper tests to assess attitudes and thinking skills, informal but structured assessment based on teacher monitoring of group investigations can do this job very well. Teachers can use checklists to guide their observations, can have students fill out self-evaluation forms, and can, in brief conferences, ask questions about why individuals or groups are proceeding in a particular way. Even written tests can be designed so that they focus on the *process* of finding an answer, rather than just the answer itself. Some questions can be designed so that they have more than one right answer, so as to recognize creative thinking and problem-solving. Since assessment unavoidably influences curriculum, if we don't test for the real *doing* of science, our schools won't teach it.

How Parents Can Help

Kids are questioners. Every parent knows this, and we remind ourselves about it in endless cartoons and stories. Much as we can feel dogged by all the questions when the day has been long and dinner still isn't on the table, and much as we feel inadequate to answer them, we need to encourage children's questioning, for this is the real basis for scientific learning. Questions need not be viewed as a challenge to our parental authority, but as a chance to reinforce kids' natural desires to learn and to gain some control over the complex world around them.

Just as with teachers, parents don't need to be science experts, or to invest in expensive microscope kits to encourage their children's interest in science. They can read aloud from the steady stream of newspaper reports on science discoveries and technological problems and advances. The flow of new information about astronomy and the origins of the universe, genetic engineering and the curing of AIDS, pollution and global warming, and similar topics continues to challenge the very foundations of much scientific thought. If parents and children don't understand what some of it is about, they can head for the library, or ask a teacher to help the children decipher some of the mysteries.

Plenty of family activities can promote an interest in science— observing the habits of pet hamsters or guinea pigs, vacationing at the beach or the mountains, visiting zoos, museums, and special exhibits. As with all the curricular areas covered in this book, children's independent reading is especially important. When gift-giving time comes and parents are selecting books, fiction is not the only choice. Parents can choose some of the excellent (and not necessarily expensive) children's non-fiction books about nature, health, and technology. Among these are Ruth Heller's books on wildlife, David Macauley's splendid architecturally illustrated books on how things work, and Alfred A. Knopf's "Discovery" series, which covers everything from diamonds to dinosaurs. And we can avoid gender differences. If microscopes or computers *are* on the gift list, they should be given to girls as well as boys.

Parents should ask teachers and principals about how science is taught in their schools. Are there in-depth hands-on study units? Are the kids encouraged to ask questions, develop hypotheses, and interpret the data, or is the process primarily lecture, workbook pages, and cookbook experiments? What kinds of learning do the tests emphasize? Parents don't need to be scientists or education experts to ask these questions and to evaluate the answers they get. Communities tend to get the kind of education they demand.

What Principals Can Do

First and foremost, the principal can model an inquiring, problem-solving spirit in the school. When issues arise—rules of behavior, uses of space, etc.—he or she can distribute questionnaires to learn what is really happening, and can solicit suggestions from students. When unusual natural or biological events occur—violent storms, mold infestations, measles outbreaks—classes can be invited to investigate them and prepare explanatory displays. Anyone who's in charge of a building like a school, which depends for its proper function on many interlocking technological systems—heat, ventilation, electricity, roofing, insulation, traffic, communications, waste disposal, etc.—can always share experiences that involve "scientific" and technical decision-making.

Effective inservice training is vital for helping teachers, particularly those elementary teachers who have limited science backgrounds, to adopt meaningful, conceptually and experientially rich science explorations. Staff development can be provided not just in science itself, but also in connected areas like collaborative learning and writing across the curriculum. Teachers need help developing integrated curriculum activities that use time efficiently by connecting with all the subjects taught in the school day. Subject area specialists will, of course, need less help with the content of their teaching, but usually need support for adopting new classroom techniques, and need planning time in order to incorporate these appropriately into their teaching plans.

Developing extended thematic units takes hard work, and too few published materials are available to supply ready-made plans. Principals can work to gain resources for after-school and summer curriculum design time for teams of teachers. Teachers need to be given responsibility for inquiry and development if they are to encourage it in their students.

The principal can help build community understanding and support of kids' inquiries. School-wide science fairs often gain considerable community attention, although they also require plenty of planning and hard work by the staff. More daily on-going support can be developed through letters to parents, and contact with neighboring hospitals, industries, universities, botanical gardens, zoos, and other facilities that can provide visiting experts and data sources for inquiring kids.

Materials can be expensive. New computer "hypercard" programs are available that provide complex sets of data for students to explore, following their own lines of questioning—but good software is costly, and often creates the need for newer, more powerful hardware. At the elementary level, textbooks have been shown to be particularly ineffective in promoting science learning. If the district can afford extensive science materials, the principal should lobby for judicious selection, so that resources aren't wasted on systems that don't really teach much—especially when the same funds could be used for effective inservice training in active science inquiry methods, or for a good library of books for independent non-fiction reading. However, if the district cannot afford lots of new materials, the principal can seek help from community businesses and parents to obtain the simpler supplies that can support many excellent classroom experiments.

Testing is perhaps the issue on which principals feel most caught in the middle. Communities expect the kids to do well on standardized tests, and principals especially believe they are judged by performance on these. Principals can keep in mind, however, that American students are not, in general, performing very well on tests of science knowledge, anyway, and a more interactive curriculum is likely to promote a better understanding of science concepts than the more passive approaches. Further, faculties that are developing better science curricula can be asked to create assessment activities that reflect their goals, so that more meaningful information on students' learning is provided to the community, whatever the standardized tests show.

EXEMPLARY PROGRAM
Science Literature Circles in Intermediate Science

Jackie McWilliams
Carnegie School
Chicago, Illinois

Jackie McWilliams teaches a fourth/fifth grade "split" at Carnegie School on the South Side in Chicago. Carnegie is just south of the University of Chicago and the wide "Midway" that cuts an east-west swath across the area close to Lake Michigan. Most of the University and the professional-intellectual Hyde Park community lie North of the Midway; Carnegie serves the much poorer, racially segregated neighborhoods to the south. Jackie's students are full of energy and ideas, and she works gently but insistently to keep them on track, listening to one another, and using their time well.

Jackie's adaptation of literature circles to science takes a technique she originally employed for reading. This is especially efficient because the children have already learned how to use the activity in one setting and don't need separate training to employ it efficiently in another. The overlap also helps the children realize that effective group learning strategies can be extended to any sort of inquiry, and that the many subjects taught during the day are all interconnected. As we will see, Jackie uses topics and issues from throughout the curriculum to reinforce the principles involved in the cooperative work of literature circles. This unit not only integrates reading, writing, and science, but puts special emphasis on learning to generate questions that leads to further science study. We'll first describe the literature circle structure itself, and then explain how Jackie applies it to the study of biology.

Jackie learned about literature circles in her search for effective strategies to share as a staff development workshop leader. As Jerome Harste and his colleagues describe in *Creating Classrooms for Authors*, literature circles are small-group discussions of a book which all the group members have read. The teacher briefly reviews five or six books children may choose from, each child reads one book of his or her choice, and then joins a discussion group with others who chose the same book. Prior to the first time children try this, the teacher models her own questions and responses to the reading. She elicits initial reactions from the whole class, helps the group make a list of topics and issues, and asks lots of "why" questions—why characters act as they do, and why readers interpret passages a particular way—and encourages kids to do the same. In succeeding sessions, the children take over these leadership tasks themselves. By deciding at the end of each session on one issue to start the discussion at the next meeting, the group keeps thought and involvement going between sessions. We've described in more detail how this strategy works in practice in Marianne Flanagan's classroom, in Chapter 1.

Many teachers worry that their children "just don't work well in groups," and Jackie testifies that several background pieces are crucial to their success, in reading or in science. First, throughout the year she stresses with the children the importance of self-government, negotiation, and democratic problem-solving. When children come to her with a disagreement, she asks them to find a way to negotiate and work it out on their own. She asks students to divide up tasks or decide which groups will work with which books, and explains that if they don't reach compromises, the choice will revert to the teacher. Discipline problems with the groups are significantly reduced. "They come back to me later and brag about how they solved their problem," she says. The very content of the curriculum provides repeated occasions for stressing these values and processes. Every story has a conflict, Jackie points out; so that during discussions of literature, talk often centers on how conflicts get resolved in constructive ways. The neighborhood violence that frequently shows up in these kids' journal entries occasions yet more talk about alternate ways to solve problems.

The teacher must still work patiently on discipline as the children carry on their discussion groups. Talk, noise, and movement are natural parts of the process, and children need to learn boundaries between productive noise and distraction. Teachers unfamiliar with cooperative groups may envision only the extremes—complete control and silence, or letting kids go and watching the chaos. Instead, when the noise verges on the non-productive, Jackie reminds her children that the work is important and the aim is to learn together effectively. "You have to keep your eye on everything," she says, "but the kids really do keep working."

Now, for the science application of this strategy. Jackie used the science literature circles early in the fall, to generate science questions the children could pursue throughout the year. The focus was biology. Some hands-on experimentation established important concepts about scientific inquiry that would come up in the reading. In a short mini-lesson on the scientific method, Jackie introduced the concept of "hypothesis," using the verbal formula, "I believe that if I do X, Y will occur." The children then experimented with dried beans, employing an activity suggested by the science department head, Raymond Gardner. The kids used pins to test the permeability or brittleness of the beans, eventually discovering that the beans change when soaked in water. The children listed as many conclusions and further questions as they could, in light of their data. One obvious conclusion: if the beans were soaked in water, they could be penetrated. Other conclusions that began to reach farther afield:

- The longer a bean is soaked, the softer it gets.
- The bean has an outer membrane, which becomes wrinkled when soaked.

Questions the kids asked:

- Why do the beans get soft?
- Could the beans still grow after we've poked holes in them?
- Could just part of a bean grow into a plant?
- Does a bean have different parts inside?

Hypothesizing, posing questions, drawing inferences are then steps in scientific thinking the children will be encouraged to use as they read. Jackie explains how she developed the idea from here, using discussion circles for children to further their science study:

> I had some short (thirty pages) easy-reading, science-related books published by Troll Associates, and I chose five of them—*Ecosystems and Food Chains; Human Body; Birds; Fossils;* and *Plants, Seeds, and Flowers.* They weren't the most exciting science books, but they were what I had available, and they proved to be good enough, because the excitement came from the way the kids worked with them. We had been talking for months about eating healthy foods, and four of these books formed a nice sequence linking the natural world with children's health. I added the *Fossils* book as an alternative because I knew it would appeal to many of the children for a change-of-pace. I decided to name the activity "LSC" for "Literature, Science, and Children."
>
> Using the time period from 9:30 to 11:30 each morning, with a short break at 10:30, one full round of this LSC activity took about a week to complete. This represents a large chunk of the school day, but since we

were doing plenty of reading, writing, **and** science, while at the same time achieving a good, continuous stretch of concentration, I had no trouble justifying it in my own mind or with the principal. First, I asked the students to form groups based on their choices from among the five books. Each of the five groups that emerged then selected a method for reading the book, e.g., silent reading, taking turns with oral reading, choosing a leader to read to the group, etc. The only restriction was that the decision be collaborative.

After the initial reading of a book by each group, I visited each group and did a second reading of the book aloud to them. Then each member of the group developed questions about the book to ask the other group members orally. Most of the questions at this stage tended to be factual "review" questions about information found in the book, rather than higher level hypothesizing or inference questions. This was understandable, because the children were new to my approach and simply followed the questioning patterns they had absorbed in their previous years of school. Together, the children then worked on answers to their questions.

The next task was for a member from each of the five groups to explain his/her group's book to the entire class. After that, students responded in writing to the book read in their group, focusing on any aspect that caught their interest. They could choose to do this individually or collaboratively. Time was allotted for sharing those writings with the class and for classmates to respond.

Later, I rotated books so that eventually all five were studied by all five groups of students. The entire project covered a period of five weeks. This might seem like a lot of repetition, but the oral reports reflected children's differing styles, and emphasized different aspects of the books, each time around. And the repetition helped kids begin to grasp the larger science thought-processes I was teaching—problem-posing, hypothesizing, observing, using materials, drawing conclusions.

Since Jackie found that the children were not yet generating very thought-provoking questions, she added a step to help them learn this process more explicitly. Once they had finished all the books, she asked the groups to brainstorm new questions they had about health, growing plants, birds, ecosystems, and fossils. This took some work, because school had accustomed the children so thoroughly to considering only questions that could be answered by their reading selection. But after some modeling the groups worked intensely and produced a number of questions they wished to pursue further. Some could be answered through more reading:

• What is the oldest bird?

- How was the archaeopteryx discovered?
- How did the human body develop?

A few could be researched by classroom experiments:

- What are some relationships between plants and insects?
- How do muscles move the bones in your skeletal system?

And some were more about the nature of the concepts themselves:

- Why are there ecosystems and food chains?
- Why are we a part of the food chain?

All of these questions required elaboration, refinement, or narrowing of focus in order to become topics the kids could easily explore during the year. However, the children were now on their way to a more inquiring approach to science. Many completed special projects on their chosen topics during the course of the year.

After the circles project was finished Jackie noticed a marked effect on the students' general reading abilities and interests. The predictability and repetition helped children become comfortable with the words and ideas. A number of her kids began meeting at the library to do further reading about the topics together after school—in a neighborhood where such a step is nearly unheard of. When the children reflected on the value of working in groups, they remarked: "It helped me remember a lot of the information." "I liked asking questions." And especially gratifying: "I felt good because I realized some of my questions didn't have answers in the book, and some of the other kids had the same questions!"

Works Cited

Bybee, Rodger W., et al. 1989. *Science and Technology Education for the Elementary Years: Frameworks for Curriculum and Instruction*. Andover, MA: National Center for Improving Science Education.

———. 1991. *Science and Technology Education for the Middle Years: Frameworks for Curriculum and Instruction*. Andover, MA: National Center for Improving Science Education.

Harlen, Wynne and Sheila Jelly. 1990. *Developing Science in the Primary Classroom*. Portsmouth, NH: Heinemann Educational Books.

Harste, Jerome C., Kathy Short, with Carolyn Burke. 1988. *Creating Classrooms for Authors*. Portsmouth, NH: Heinemann Educational Books.

Heath, Shirley Brice. 1983. *Ways with Words: Language, Life,and Work in Communities and Classrooms*. New York: Cambridge UP.

Hyde, Arthur and Marilyn Bizar. 1989. *Thinking in Context*. New York: Longman.

Johnson, David W., Roger T. Johnson, Edythe Holubec, and Patricia Roy. 1984. *Circles of Learning: Cooperation in the Classroom*. Washington D.C.: Association for Supervision and Curriculum Development.

Liem, Tik. 1987. *Invitations to Science Inquiry*. Lexington, MA: Ginn Press.

Osbourne, Roger and Peter Freyberg. 1985. *Learning in Science*. Portsmouth, NH: Heinemann Educational Books.

Science For All Americans: a Project 2061 Report on Literacy Goals in Science, mathematics, and Technology. 1989. Washington, D.C.: American Association for the Advancement of Science.

Suggested Further Readings

Driver, R., E. Guesne, and A. Tiberghien. 1985. *Children's Ideas in Science*. Philadelphia, PA: Open University Press.

Hewson, P.W. and M.G. Hewson. An Appropriate Conception of Teaching Science: A View from Studies of Science Learning. *Science Education* 25 (3): 185–199.

Sprung, B., M. Froschl, and P.B. Campbell. 1985. *What Will Happen If . . . Young Children and the Scientific Method*. Educational Equity Concepts, Inc.

BEST PRACTICE IN TEACHING SCIENCE

Increase	Decrease
Hands-on activities that include: —students identifying their own real questions about natural phenomena —observation activity, often designed by students, aimed at real discovery, employing a wide range of process skills —students hypothesizing to explain data —information provided to explain data only after students have engaged in investigation process —students' reflection to realize concepts and processes learned —application, either to social issues or further scientific questions	Instruction based mainly on lecture and information-giving Dependence on textbooks and lock-step patterns of instruction Cookbook labs in which students follow steps without a purpose or question of their own Questions, concepts, and answers provided only by the teacher Students treated as if they have no prior knowledge or investigative abilities
Focus on underlying concepts about how natural phenomena are explained	Memorizing detailed vocabulary, definitions, and explanations without thorough connection to broader ideas
Questioning, thinking, and problem solving, especially: —being skeptical, willing to question common beliefs —accepting ambiguity when data isn't decisive —willing to modify explanations, open to changing one's opinion —using logic, planning inquiry, hypothesizing, inferring	Science approached as a set body of knowledge with all answers and information already known Attempts to correct student misconceptions by direct instruction
Active application of science learning to contemporary technological issues and social choices	Isolation of science from the rest of students' lives
In-depth study of a few important thematic topics	Superficial coverage of many topics according to an abstract scope-and-sequence
Curiosity about nature and positive attitudes toward science for all students, including females and members of minority groups	Sense that only a few brilliant "nerds" can enjoy or succeed in science study
Integration of reading, writing, and math in science unit.	Activity limited to texts, lectures, and multiple-choice quizzes
Collaborative small-group work, with training to ensure it is efficient and includes learning for all group members	Students working individually, competitively
Teacher facilitating students' investigative steps	Teacher only as expert in subject matter
Evaluation that focuses on scientific concepts, processes, and attitudes	Testing focused only on memorization of detail, ignoring thinking skills, process skills, attitudes

6

Best Practice in Social Studies

Social Studies a New Way: Post-Holes in History

In the usual American high school, the task of drawing on many parts of the curriculum for holistic learning activities presents a much greater challenge than in the lower grades, because subjects are departmentalized and the day divided into short, discontinuous pieces, while at the same time teachers feel pressed to "cover" an impossible range of knowledge. Here is how one high school teacher strives to overcome these limitations, to turn his classroom into an active place where students take responsibility and make choices about topics they will study in greater depth.

It's Wednesday, and Wayne Mraz's U. S. History class at Stagg High School is in the library to begin research for group reports on the 1960s and the Vietnam War. Some groups are clear about their topics and have begun looking for books and articles. Others are still struggling to understand what they're really after. One pair, Greg and Jim, has chosen the phrase, "Guns versus butter," that labeled the 1960s debate over use of resources for war or for domestic social needs. Wayne conferences with them for a few minutes. What are their reactions to what they've learned about the Vietnam War? "My father was there," Jim muses. "He says it was just a huge waste. It didn't do any good for anyone, and a lot of his friends got killed." The boys decide they want to focus just on weapons, literally the "guns" side of the equation. "So how do you relate your basic feeling about the war to the weapons?" Wayne asks. Gradually they begin to list some issues—the cost of the weapons, the situational advantages held by the Viet Cong, the limitations on what the military was permitted to do, the problematic nature of the most powerful unused weapon, The Bomb—all items mentioned in the textbook, but not really thought through in the students' heads until now. On a scrap of paper, the students begin drawing a cluster to see how the issues are connected and Wayne moves on.

Why does Wayne call his course "Post-Holes"? He explains that instead of a myriad of dates, names, and events, he wants students to grasp a limited, carefully chosen set of major issues and turning points upon which they can construct in their own minds an understanding of United States history. If they've got the post-holes, they can build the rest of the structure themselves. Wayne rarely gives a lecture. Instead, most of the turning points, or "post-holes" are explored in two-week units, each of which builds up to and centers around reports by collaborative groups. By the time the students reach the 1960s unit in May, they're well practiced at working together, using clustering or timelines as visual guides for presenting ideas, and teaching and learning with one another.

Wayne takes several days at the beginning of the unit to start the students exploring the period and considering possible topics for their investigations. The first day typically begins with an "admit slip." The students have been asked to read sections on the sixties and the war in their regular textbook, and they are to identify ten key words on a slip of paper in order to get in the door of the classroom. In September, some kids end up sitting on the hallway floor to fill out their admit slips, but by now everyone knows and follows the routine. Wayne checks the slips for interesting highlights to share with the class, and goes on to list and talk through some possible topics for reports. Typical topics for the sixties:

- guns vs. butter—the "Great Society"
- the 1968 Democratic Convention
- the Civil Rights movement
- the U.S. military doctrine of "flexible response"
- tensions between domestic and foreign policy
- the return of Richard Nixon

Students add topics of their own, such as "Music of the Sixties," or "Films About Vietnam." Within several days, the groups will have to choose their topics, but right now there's time to think and explore.

The next day, everyone brings in a seventy-five word summary of an article from the library about the sixties, or of one written in that period if they can get to the microfilm collection at the nearby community college. Again, highlights are shared. Working in their groups of three, students make charts listing things they think they know about the period and questions they have. These lists will give direction to their reading and perhaps spark some particular interest or curiosity that will influence the groups' choices of report topics.

The rest of the hour is spent watching portions of a video, "Homefront During the Vietnam War." Wayne doesn't sit passively and let the students snooze while the VCR runs, however. Every few minutes, he pauses the tape and poses a question or points out a connection with what they're watching and something else that has come up during these first two days of the unit. The period concludes with the groups quickly filling out a form to reflect on what has taken place thus far in the unit, and how the groups are working.

For a few minutes of the third day, the introductory activities continue as before. The students arrive to hear a Simon and Garfunkel tape bringing them sounds of the sixties. They complete short summaries of articles of their choice from a collection that Wayne has handed out, and then watch and talk through a few more minutes of the videotape that was begun the day before. Then it's off to the library to begin researching possible report topics. As Wayne circulates among the groups while they sift through articles and information banks, he learns which groups have settled on their topics and which ones need help. By the end of the period, all the groups have usually focused on something. They know they'll need to work outside class to do most of the research, but ordinarily one more class period is spent in the library with Wayne's guidance as the groups work.

A few of the groups are ready to give their reports on Friday, and the weekend provides time for the rest to get finished. Monday and Tuesday are devoted to the balance of the presentations. An observer might wonder what leads the students to draft their reports so quickly, and whether such promptness allows for sufficient thought and learning to go into them. But Wayne has done much to ensure that the reports are productive for both authors and listeners. The entire first week of the year is spent on thinking strategies and logical problem solving. Wayne believes this is most crucial. Then there's the regular practice: this is not a once or twice per year exercise. By the time the class reaches the 1960s, everyone has completed and presented at least a dozen reports. In addition, he finds that having students frequently prepare visuals—clusters, timelines, flow-charts—gets the groups into the habit of organizing their thinking. Teachers also worry about covering the material required by district curriculum guides; but Wayne estimates that eighty-five percent of the major events and concepts he would have discussed in more conventional lecture format are dealt with in the reports. And, of course, students remember the material more permanently because the reports are their own.

Wednesday is test day. Each group has already prepared one essay question and five multiple-choice questions on their own group's topic. Wayne circulates among the groups, helping them craft fair and interesting questions. For the test, each group draws an essay question out of a hat (though of course if they get their own, they must draw again). All the students in a group thus get the same question, but work on their answers separately. Everyone answers all the multiple-choice questions, plus one or two items Wayne adds in. The group that originated a given essay question are the people who grade it. As homework, each student must not only evaluate the essay of one other, but must also provide a written rationale for the grade awarded. Wayne adjudicates discrepancies and unfair evaluations, and on the final day of the unit the evaluating groups meet with the corresponding essay writers to discuss the evaluations.

Wayne has discovered that this approach to testing results in a great deal of learning. Students feel responsibility to listen to the reports, since they will have to answer questions on one of them. Much thinking goes into the question-drafting, evaluation, and rationale-writing. The students hold conferences with one another after the test, to go over their answers and their reasons for grading each other as they did. Students who find it hard to accept a teacher's response about an unclear explanation give much more credulity to their peers' observations about the same problem. Sometimes it takes several periods just for the groups to talk through their evaluations with one another.

What does a pair-conference on test results look like, when it's going well? On one particular day, two students in the basic-level class, Rob and Javier, were observed talking over Javier's test.

Rob: Where was your theme—you know, where you come out and explain what you are really . . .

Jav (discouraged) : I guess I didn't have one.

Rob: Yes, wait a minute, you did, look right here!

Jav: I guess it's just a little spread out.

The boys then proceeded to open several books to compare Javier's answers with the texts and with the cluster-chart left on the wall from the group's presentation. But it doesn't take long for them to become re-engaged in the actual topic:

Jav: Yours was pretty good . . . If I had more time, I would have put down more information.

Rob: Well, there was more about Martin Luther King, anyway. (*Jav laughs as he notices numerous spots where he scratched out words.*)

Rob: When you're writing, you get all excited, and you get into it, and you don't realize.

Jav: (*re-reading his paper*) I got the wrong date for when Malcolm X was assassinated. You know, one big difference was that even when they bombed his [King's] house, he didn't get angry.

A Perspective on the Field

As in the other major school subjects, good social studies teachers have long used creative and powerful strategies to make topics come alive for kids, and national commissions and task forces have repeatedly drafted recommendations for reform of less successful classrooms. Unlike the other subject areas, however, the direction and philosophy behind these recommendations have been matters of sharp debate. Professional groups like the National Council for the Social Studies have shown tremendous ambivalence, even within a single report, about the very nature of the goals and tasks for their field. Various commissions and reports have differed considerably in their approaches. A unanimous progressive consensus, in other words, has not emerged in the social studies to the degree that it has in science, math, and literacy. So before we proceed with any recommendations for best practice, we need to examine this debate and some of its roots.

The main issues have been listed fairly well in one of the field's well-known reports, "Building a History Curriculum," by the Bradley Commission on History in Schools (1988):

- Should history be taught as activity, as "something you do," or as cultural heritage?

- Should the history curriculum be driven by our cultural diversity as Americans, or by our common, mainly Western, political heritage?

- Should social history, concerned with the ordinary people and daily issues, play the primary role, or should political history, concerned with "elites" and decision-making?

- Should we stress facts or concepts? Chronology or case studies? Narrative or thematic history?

These questions are posed only for history, not the other social sciences, and the report, while claiming that the questions represent false dichotomies, goes ahead to take implicit stands on them. Still, the list suggests the key ambivalences that afflict social scientists.

All the social science fields worry about content versus process. Some reports, such as the "Guidelines for Geographic Education" (1984), prepared by the National Council for Geographic Education and the Association of American Geographers, stress coverage of content, and consist mainly of lists of things students should "know" or "appreciate." Others, like Michael Hartoonian and Margaret Laughlin's "Designing a Social Studies Scope and Sequence for the 21st Century," (one of *three* different frameworks offered by the National Council for the Social Studies in

1989) stress "habits of mind," broad unifying themes, or processes of student learning and thinking.

Another important question centers around the value of controversy and commitment itself. The Bradley Commission report argues that "By its nature, history is not wishful, or partisan, or proselytizing," but provides the facts for informed decision-making. In contrast, "Lessons From History" (Crabtree, et al.), the 1992 document from the National Center for History in the Schools, sees history as teaching very distinct social and political lessons vital for American citizenship:

> In observing the origins, struggles, and achievements of free societies, past and present, students should consider how democratic ideas have been turned into practice, and how they have been strengthened, violated, or defeated altogether. . . . Such knowledge empowers people to . . . understand the passion for reform in American history, and in the history of many other societies, as continuing struggles they themselves may join to bring reality closer to aspiration.

It is understandable why social studies has experienced more overt conflict than other fields. While all of public schooling in this country has been used as a vehicle for promoting social stability and obedient citizenship, social studies offers the main occasion for explicitly instructing children in traditional social values and behaviors. At the same time, it also offers the best opportunity in the curriculum for questioning those values, making people aware of the ways our society has failed to live up to its principles, and preparing future citizens to work for change. Thus, as at least some of the reports acknowledge, the subject is bound to engender debate.

The debate is especially harsh and repressive at this time, however, particularly because the most outspoken voices are those of conservatives who have been able to attract media attention—the Gablers in Texas, Phyllis Schlafly in the Midwest, and Diane Ravitch and William Bennett in Washington, D. C. Such educational reactionaries are often catered to. The NCSS report, *Charting a Course: Social Studies for the 21st Century* (1989), attacks "inquiry" strategies developed in the sixties, arguing that their stress on "relevance" made them anti-historical. Later, while endorsing the importance of student discussion, the report clearly rejects the idea of "letting students set the agenda." These assertions appear to ignore the importance of higher order thinking skills, student involvement, and modeling of the democratic ideals that American social studies ought to inculcate. Some educators respond to the political pressure by puritanically avoiding any serious examination of the more painful chapters in our national history. Others attempt to give equal time to all points of view in each dispute and to claim that their teaching embodies no particular social values. Unfortunately this eviscerates the material, leaving it lifeless and unengaging.

We'll be up front about where we stand in this debate. While disagreement is no doubt unavoidable and not to be squelched, the harshness of the conservative attacks have made advancement in the teaching of social studies far more difficult to attain. The reports all claim that many Americans don't know the history, geography, and economics they need for making informed decisions, and some authors even recognize that American kids find these topics thoroughly unengaging. But rather than address the need to involve students more actively, many writers simply call for more "coverage," more content, more time spent on their subject. It's the safest possible approach to reform—"let's just do more of the same thing that isn't working." Yes, there is lip service paid to "active learning," but when "Lessons From History" devotes only one page to methodology, compared with two hundred and fifty for the content to be covered in U. S. and world history courses, it's clear what matters most.

Yet the argument for more time to cover all those listed subtopics ultimately leads nowhere. "Take time away from literature, or math, and then emphasize 'my' field above any of the other social sciences," each of the commissions seems to imply. However, each also goes on to acknowledge that world history, or American history, or any of the other social science areas, in itself can't possibly be "covered" in a semester, or a year, or whatever time might be allotted. Furthermore, the reports admit, real understanding of a field requires in-depth exploration of at least some selected topics. And so the discussion goes round in an impossible circle.

The reports never seem to recognize an essential that educators in other fields have come to understand, namely that teaching must strive to promote life-long learners, students who continue reading and writing and observing on their own, to fill in the inevitable gaps left in *each* of the subjects in school. Particularly in social studies, without this life-long result, we haven't prepared the informed, responsible citizens that the field's experts say we need. And even the students who dutifully memorize all the assigned content in all the grades, outlined on all the scope and sequence charts, will soon need to inquire further on their own, for the particular embodiments of American social concern inevitably shift from decade to decade.

As the "Lessons From History" report admits, panels have been advocating more "active learning" for the social studies since the Committee of Ten recommendations on American education in 1892—over one hundred years ago! But we won't achieve this kind of goal by simply re-shuffling the scope and sequence charts. Students don't become life-long, self-motivated learners by listening to civics lectures for twelve years. They do it by *regularly* practicing the kind of inquiry, evaluation, decision-making, and action they'll be called upon to exercise later.

Fortunately, the debate among social studies educators is not all on one side. Within almost every report there are bright spots of real reform, applications of newer thinking about how students learn and practical ways that teachers can more creatively and effectively help. For example, *Charting a Course: Social Studies for the 21st Century* may take swipes at the sixties and spend many pages dutifully listing topics that "must" be covered in every grade, but seven of its ten overall guiding "characteristics" focus on learning processes and integrating with more global views and with other subject areas. This report also includes a separate "research" section that stresses students' prior knowledge as the base for building social studies understanding—a cornerstone of constructivist thinking about education.

Of the three alternate curriculum "frameworks" offered by the National Council for the Social Studies, only one lists topics for each grade, while a second is organized around a progression of thinking skills, and a third focuses on major themes that are the centers of most human controversy. And the most recent of the reports, "Lessons From History," provides, along with a brief summary of each historical period, a list of "major themes," "essential understandings," and "habits of mind"—approaches that move well beyond the simple march of historical facts. The first two categories aim to give coherence and meaning to the historical events. The "habits of mind" sections offer not only analyses, but probing questions about the many contradictions and unresolved issues contained within each historical development. For example, under the Civil War, some questions raised are:

> How much change and how much continuity was there in the lives of the freed slaves? How much did war and the Reconstruction accomplish for them and how much was unfinished? Students should confront and discuss de Tocqueville's grim prediction of 30 years before, observing that though slavery might be abolished, "the prejudice to which it has given birth is immovable." Perhaps the most significant of the issues that students should examine is how the hopes of black Americans for full equality, constitutionally raised with the 13th, 14th, and 15th Amendments to the Constitution, were subsequently undermined by the courts and by political interests, and so remained the unfinished business of the nation for another hundred years.

What we shall do, then, in our recommendations for best practice in this chapter, is to draw on the most forward-looking ideas and arguments in the recent national reports on teaching in social studies, those most in touch with the research about children's learning and constructivist teaching. We exercise our own judgment—but we do so guided by the thinking and demonstrations and achievements we've encountered in outstanding social studies classrooms and in every other major subject area of the school curriculum.

Recommendations for Best Practice in Teaching Social Studies

Students of social studies need regular opportunities to investigate topics in depth, and to participate in the choosing of these topics. Complete "coverage" in social studies inevitably results in superficial and unengaging teaching, like painting a room—plenty of square feet, but only one thousandth of an inch thick. Thus every one of the national reports recognizes that real learning involves in-depth understanding of the complexities of human existence. *Charting a Course* asserts:

> The core of essential knowledge to be incorporated in the instructional program at every level must be selective enough to provide time for extended in-depth study and must be directed toward the end goals of social studies education—the development of thoughtful Americans who have the capacities for living effective personal and public lives.

The National Center for History in the Schools' "Lessons from History" also emphasizes this need:

> Historical understanding cannot do without the broad perspectives gained from chronological narrative. But neither can it ignore the complexities and consequences of critical moments and places examined in depth. Innumerable, and memorable, insights are to be gained from longer, closer looks at selected episodes, and all the more so by the deft use of primary sources, which have the power to draw students into the historical moment itself. There they find the particularity of events, how none quite resembles any other, and each draws its particular character from its time and place, and personalities.

Yet there are many separate social studies fields—history, geography, sociology, anthropology, psychology; and each field includes many topics, all of which seem important. Therefore, teachers of social studies have no choice but to accept the fact that under *either* approach—thin coverage on everything or depth for a few areas—students won't really learn it all in twelve years of public schooling. Covering less in more depth not only ensures better understanding but increases the likelihood that students will pursue further inquiry of their own at later times.

It is also vital that students participate in choosing the topics they explore more deeply. This is a concept that *Charting a Course* actually rejects and the other reports seem to studiously avoid—and yet every report also asserts that social studies is meant to prepare students for *democratic* citizenship, and that active engagement is necessary to a good classroom. The role of student choice and ownership is so central to excellent practice in fields like reading and writing that it is impossible to ignore here. Social studies teachers can learn that student choice need not mean chaos, or an impossible paper load, or avoidance of important content. Good teachers often lay out lists of significant topics to choose from, give mini-lessons on how to make intelligent choices of what to study, and conduct brief negotiating conferences with groups of students as they design and focus their topics. This not only increases students' engagement, but teaches them an important academic skill needed for doing research projects in upper grades and in college—the skill of judicious choosing of topics for reports and papers.

Social studies teaching should involve exploration of open questions that challenge students' thinking. Along with more time and detail on a topic, in-depth study means going beyond the learning of information to consider some of the hard but meaningful questions brought up by just about any study of human social existence. *Charting a Course* puts it this way:

> Content knowledge from the social studies should not be treated merely as received knowledge to be accepted and memorized, but as the means through which open and vital questions may be explored and confronted. Students must be made aware that just as contemporary events have been shaped by actions taken by people in the past, they themselves have the capacity to shape the future.

Reports and panels have been recommending this approach for many years, but abstract and brief prescriptions are not enough to help teachers change—just as they aren't enough to help students learn. To enact this principle, teachers need to learn how to generate questions that invite discussion, rather than those that merely check to see if students read the chapter, *or* those that just lead the class to the teacher's own chosen conclusions. One of the virtues of the "Lessons from History" report—a virtue to which the authors do not themselves call enough attention—is the fund of important, open historical questions found in some of the "Habits of Mind" sections of the report.

Another teaching skill needed for this exploratory, open approach is conducting constructive group discussion. Teachers can learn to use brief learning-log jotting and small-group preparatory tasks so that students are ready to contribute to a larger class session. Climate-setting activities are essential, so that students learn to respect one another's differing opinions and to trust that their ideas will not be ridiculed when expressed openly. After a good discussion, student-made follow-up reports and wall-charts—or at the very least, end-of-class reflective log entries—can solidify learning, so that the ideas shared do not simply evaporate when class ends.

To make real the concepts being taught, social studies must involve students in active participation in the classroom and the wider community. This can be thought of as yet another way to achieve depth. "Charting a Course" makes this need clear in the very first of its ten characteristics of a good social studies curriculum:

> A well-developed social studies curriculum must instill a clear understanding of the roles of citizens in a democracy and provide opportunities for active, engaged participation in civic, cultural and volunteer activities designed to enhance the quality of life in the community and the nation.

However, because social studies groups and educators also agonize so extensively about covering every historical period or field sub-topic, and because district curriculum guides are so equally overstuffed, teachers often despair at finding time to organize and include such activity.

Yet the task need not be seen as overwhelming. Many of the concepts in sociology, economics, and politics have obvious embodiments right in the individual school building—issues of personal freedom versus the good of the community, relations between various cultural groups, questions of governance, authority, and decision-making. Children of most ages can debate an issue, draft letters and proposals, seek actual changes in school procedures or set up committees to accomplish some new goal. Wide student participation in these matters will, as an additional benefit, contribute to the social health of the school.

Active involvement can easily reach outside the school walls as well. For information-gathering, representatives of many social and governmental organizations are happy to visit classrooms to talk about their work. Parents who work in relevant fields make willing resource people. Genuine responses from community leaders to students' letters, proposals on community projects, and real advocacy are usually long-remembered by students as rich and exciting learning experiences.

Yes, but . . . How can a teacher find the time to prepare such projects if individuals or groups of students are to be working on different issues and there's no textbook for any of them?

A thematic approach, as outlined in Michael Hartoonian and Margaret Laughlin's "Designing a Social Studies Scope and Sequence for the 21st Century" (1989) certainly makes student participation easier to include in the curriculum. Walter C.Parker, in *Renewing the*

Social Studies Curriculum (1991) recommends a number of programs and units that provide teachers with workable materials and directions for participatory activities. Many are described in the October 1989 issue of *Social Education*. The National Issues Forum in the Classroom offers nine units on current topics such as immigration and AIDS. They include materials, suggestions for activities, and guides for research and thinking. When teachers take a thematic approach to the subject, they find that many of the concepts, skills, and topics listed in their social studies curriculum guides are automatically covered.

Social studies should involve students both in independent inquiry and cooperative learning, to build skills and habits needed for lifelong, responsible learning. Once significant topics are chosen, social studies classes can most easily generate active participation if projects use cooperative learning. Children who have not had previous experience with small-group learning will need training in how to work collaboratively and productively. However, this in itself is a significant social studies topic worth exploring, and the training will be valuable for students throughout their schooling and in their adult working lives.

It is wise to establish a balance between individual and group work. Some children learn more readily in one setting, some in another, and so variety helps reach them all. Children need skills and confidence for pursuing topics on their own, as well. A "classroom workshop" structure, in which students research topics of their own choosing while the teacher holds brief one-to-one conferences, is a highly efficient way of immersing the children in individual study. These two organizational structures—cooperative small groups and classroom workshop—are also essential tools for making a non-tracked, heterogeneous classroom work.

Social studies should involve students in reading, writing, observing, discussing, and debating to ensure their active participation in learning. Reports and studies all recommend active learning, but teachers and planners often expect writing, discussion, or group work will be time-consuming add-ons to the material that is supposed to be covered. They imagine essays that take days for kids to write and nights for teachers to grade. But many valuable activities can be brief and informal, moments to help students focus, consider a problem, or reflect on the meaning of the material. Students can write for two minutes at the beginning of the period to recollect main points from the last night's homework or the ideas covered the day before. They can stop in the middle of the class to talk for five minutes in pairs or threes about possible solutions to a particular problem. They can reflect on a notecard what they've learned or still have questions about at the end of class and turn in their responses so the teacher can see what's getting through and what isn't. Integrating other modes besides lecturing and quizzes means using those modes as tools for learning, to advance the subject matter itself.

Social studies learning should be built upon students' prior knowledge of their lives and communities, rather than assuming they know nothing about the subject. It is usual media practice to bash schools and students by periodically running features on how little geography or history kids know, or parading the bloopers they may write for short-answer quizzes (never mind the vagueness or lack of thought in some of the quiz questions). Yet young children constantly listen far more closely to adult conversation than adults like to acknowledge, and they sense the problems, issues, and paradoxes in the community, the school, and their families much more sharply than we realize. When we do take notice, many of us find this phenomenon alternately cute and threatening.

We do far better to find out just how much children *do* know about the social world around them and build our teaching on that. By drawing out and then building on this prior knowledge that children bring to school, we can help them discover how social studies concepts are close to, and relevant to their lives, and not just abstract words to memorize.

Of course, it is common sense to expect that children grasp more social studies concepts as they move up the grades, since older children are more sensitive to social interactions around them, and more aware of a wider world with all its complexities. Traditional social studies curricula have followed an "expanding environments" formula for elementary grades, starting with the family and working outward. More recently, however, educators have sought ways to introduce young children to history, geography, and other topics in forms they could grasp—see, for example, John Hoge and Claudia Crump, *Teaching History in the Elementary School*, 1988. The thoughtful "Research Base" section of "Charting a Course: Social Studies for the 21st Century" endorses an approach built upon recognition and use of children's prior knowledge:

> First, students at all ages know more about the world than is readily apparent. Much of that knowledge represents out-of-school learning. . . . Quite young students have rudimentary concepts of some of the critical ideas in social studies: spatial and temporal ordering, authority and power, the nature of groups, cultural differences, scarcity and many others. . . . In particular, the notion that students cannot deal with social studies abstractions until grade 4 is clearly discredited. These comments will seem like truisms to experienced teachers, but much of the supposed "boringness" of social studies, especially in the earlier grades, stems from the use of methods and lesson plans that do not permit teachers to act on this knowledge.

Social studies should explore a full variety of the cultures found in America, including students' own backgrounds and understanding of other cultures' approaches to various social studies concepts. "Lessons from History" explains the "full variety" side of this need very clearly:

> Students can genuinely comprehend the processes of history only if they understand the roles played by the many different people and constituent groups of the society under study. Without knowing them all, and how they interacted, students will understand none very well and will misconstrue both social and political history. What is needed is the effective integration into the historical narrative of men and women from all classes and conditions, ethnic and racial origins, national and religious backgrounds. . . . Many texts, both at school and college level, tack [these] on in brief sketches, sidebars, and tail-ends of paragraphs that are awkward and condescending. The realities of history are obscured, and its interest for students dimmed, when the role of diverse groups is slighted or presented in a disjointed way.

It is also essential to explore the cultures of the children who are present in the classroom, particularly because children of minority backgrounds so often see school subjects as disconnected from their own lives and worlds. We believe that the acrimonious debate over "our common heritage" versus study of individual ethnic groups has sadly obscured much of the real meaning in the latter option. First of all, minority children are not the only ones who have been cut off from their own history. Most students in any age group or social stratum know very little of the various historical and political developments that have affected their own families and forbearers. History, politics, economics, culture, folklore, all could become more meaningful to students through interviews about events and experiences in the past, with parents, grandparents, neighbors, and other adults they know.

What is especially crucial is *how* these things are studied. We've observed children enduring profound boredom as a teacher lectured and demanded memorization on the principle grain crops exported from various African countries. Such methods do not reconnect children with their own history but simply alienate them from it once again. In contrast, when students can make choices, discover facts that they find significant in their own family backgrounds, and share and contrast them with mutual respect, they will not only feel pride in their own heritages. They will also become more excited about history and geography and culture in general—and perhaps even be able to critique and evaluate aspects of their own past, as well as to honor them.

Social studies should eschew tracking of students because it deprives various groups of the knowledge essential to their citizenship. The "Lessons from History" report is eloquent on this matter:

A reformed social studies curriculum should be required of all students in common, regardless of their "track" or further vocational and educational plans. Only such a common core is democratic, because wherever the curriculum in history and ideas is truncated or optional, the students' right to know is violated and democracy is wanting. Something is wrong when the learning often considered necessary and appropriate for university-bound students is treated as unnecessary or irrelevant for the others. . . . A curriculum that is trivial, optional, or differentiated according to track produces a class system of education, no matter how innovative the methods or how many students receive a diploma.

More and more educators and school systems are now contemplating the social and racial implications of tracking and realizing that they must find alternatives. Research studies indicate that tracked classes really do not even benefit high-track students as much as once claimed, but they do systematically discourage and slow down the lower achieving ones. Particularly in social studies (though this thinking applies to many other subject areas as well), students of various backgrounds can benefit by hearing from one another.

Yes, but . . . how can a good classroom simultaneously meet the needs of students with differing achievement levels, particularly as students move up the grades?

The answer is to be found in how the classroom is organized. Traditional lectures and quizzes are the least adaptable to heterogeneous grouping because the teacher can offer only one version of the material for everyone. Small group work, with children of differing levels in each group, is much more successful, as long as children are trained to take an active role. When small groups are working, the teacher isn't "delivering" information to the unenlightened. Instead, kids talk through and argue over the ideas, which results in better learning. The teaching that the stronger students provide for the less prepared benefits them both—the old saw being quite true, that the teacher of a subject often learns more than his or her students.

The other effective structure for a part of each day or week in a non-tracked setting is the "classroom workshop." This structure has been most thoroughly described for literature and writing, but it's important to consider here, as a way to make non-tracked social studies classes work in the upper grades. In a classroom workshop, every student has a list of topics he or she is interested in reading and/or writing about, worked up through individual and group brainstorming, and negotiation or encouragement by the teacher. At the start of workshop time, each student reports in a phrase what he or she will be working on—a verbal contract that commits the student and tells the teacher who is on track and who needs some help. Students can sign up for conferences, and once the class gets down to work, the teacher circulates around the room for *brief* one-to-one sessions. In these, the teacher leads the student to solve his or her own problem rather than simply giving directions or answers. Brief moments can be taken at the beginning or end of the session to conduct "mini-lessons" on concepts or processes for getting work done, based on what the teacher observes the class or sub-groups may need. Near the end of the period, one or two individuals share something they've done, and every few weeks everyone turns in a written product. Student folders allow the teacher to survey students' work-in-progress regularly and quickly.

This may sound like a complex structure, and it does take training, both for teachers and kids. But it uses time very efficiently, allows students to work at their own levels and to make choices according to special interests, and teaches them responsibility, something surprisingly missing from traditional classroom structures. Teachers at all grade levels, in every socio-economic setting, have found the classroom workshop highly effective. Once again, not every historical period or geographical location can be covered— and indeed the teacher may not use workshop every day. But students' commitment becomes very strong, the learning acquires depth, and all the students in the room can be challenged and helped, whatever their achievement level. We describe this strategy in some detail because we recognize that only when decision-makers can begin to visualize a workable approach will they be ready to support the changes needed to achieve a non-tracked classroom for social studies or any other subject area.

Social studies evaluation must reflect the importance of students' thinking, and their preparation to be life-long responsible citizens, rather than rewarding memorization of decontextualized facts. In the history class described at the start of this chapter, Wayne Mraz has each small group of students compose a test question, evaluate the answers written by individual students from another group, and then review the answers with the test takers, one-to-one. This may take longer than a traditional quiz, but a tremendous amount of learning goes on. Evaluation in Mraz's classes is not just time spent checking on students; it's another occasion for learning.

Since the stated goal of social studies education in every one of the national reports is not just acquisition of information but preparation for democratic citizenship, it's pretty obvious that evaluation in social studies should serve that goal. The "Lessons from History" report goes back to the 1892 Committee of Ten for what we should seek from students, and the words speak to what ought to be truly *valued*—and thus evaluated— in their work:

> In 1892, the Committee of Ten strongly recommended active learning, in saying that students should always read more than one account of important events, should employ original documents, frame questions for discussion and debate, write and speak their own minds frequently on significant topics.

How, then, can evaluation in social studies encourage this, recognize it when present, and help students reflect on their own progress toward doing it well?

Given the goal, it seems that evaluation in social studies, perhaps more than in any other subject, must involve reflective **dialogue** between teacher and student. Yes, we can ask students to show they have inquired deeply into a subject, through detailed sharing of their knowledge. But on every occasion for evaluation, there should also be questions about what the student considers to *be* a good historian (or history book, or student of geography, or observer of folk traditions), questions on *how* one learns about families or governments or economic systems, and questions on the significance, the implications, the human issues within the material studied. The answers to these questions need to be valued by extending discussion out from them, rather than leaving them as final statements that are graded and then forgotten.

However, if students are to feel truly free to speak their minds, we must have many occasions when their thoughts and ideas are *not* evaluated, along with the times when they are. Students should be able to select some of the essays and products they will submit for evaluation, out of a larger portfolio, so that they have some zone of safety for expression that may seem risky, tentative, or unresolved.

Finally, to mirror the democracy that social studies aims to prepare our population for, students can participate in setting the standards by talking together about what makes a good paper/answer/project and how to evaluate it. In fact, the issue of meaningful evaluation of students' education is a very worthy social studies topic in itself!

How Parents Can Help

Because we are all social beings, helping children to learn about social studies at home is especially easy and natural. The most effective approach is to model social involvement. If a parent participates in community activity of some kind, even for small time periods, children will come to see such activity is important. They'll be curious and will naturally begin to learn about how things work, and what the problems are, in the community. Also valuable for learning about the nature of the community, as well as for fun and togetherness in a family, are trips to museums, historical societies, ethnic fairs, interesting neighborhoods, and historically or culturally significant sites in the surrounding regions.

For awareness of national politics, social issues, and history, it's important to subscribe to or bring home newspapers and news magazines. Parents and kids can read articles together and then discuss them, with the parents encouraging children to talk first so your adult opinions don't overpower them before they begin to consider an issue.

On a more immediate level, parents can share family history, memories, and customs to help children value heritage and to realize how the family's experiences are a part of the history, geography, and culture of the world that surrounds it. Visits to other places family members live or originated from can help to make this realization vivid. To help make the economic world more understandable, adults can share with children the satisfactions, problems, and issues involved in work lives. Of course, these are all forms of knowledge that also help make a family close-knit and supportive of one another.

In relation to formal school social studies, parents can let teachers know that they're available, to the extent that time permits, to share with students your experiences with work, community groups, political efforts, etc. Teachers need connections with the larger school community in order to illustrate for students the reality of the social studies material they are exploring in class. It's also especially important for parents to let school officials know they support the concept of mixed ability levels in social studies courses (and other areas, too). School staff often worry that the public won't understand if the school begins to adopt a more equal and interactive approach to learning.

What Principals Can Do

Given the pressure for wide coverage in areas like history and geography, and the unfortunate lack of real learning that occurs when teachers give in to this pressure, it is especially important for the principal to step in and help by lobbying for more meaningful curriculum guides at the district level. Also, encouraging teachers to sort through the many topics and parts of the social studies curriculum, to select a few for focused study—either for individual classrooms, or grade-level or school-wide special units—can help move them toward Best Practice in social studies. The principal can also support meaningful classroom learning by building confidence among teachers that if they encourage children to think honestly about real social concerns in class, he or she as principal will help the community to value and appreciate the effort.

Best Practice in social studies calls not just for classroom activity, but for development of the entire school community. If students learn about democracy, government, relations among social groups, etc., in the classroom, but find their lessons irrelevant or contradicted in their own surroundings, then they're likely to regard their learning as pointless. Therefore, the principal must help teachers build the school into a model community—not "model" in the sense of "perfect," but as an example, a school in which students can actively participate in decision-making, in developing norms and expectations, and in planning special study units and other school-wide learning activities. Teachers and kids can be encouraged not just to participate, but to reflect on what takes place and find connections with the topics they've studied in classes. This way, kids can see how the social structures, issues, and interactions they study are reenacted in the microcosm of their own locale.

It's particularly valuable, both for modeling group interaction and for the health of the school itself, to develop mechanisms to help social and ethnic groups relate positively in the school. In many communities, it may be important to develop mechanisms by which students can help arbitrate conflicts or deal with tensions or misunderstandings that may arise between individuals or groups.

Principals can use their influence to help move a school or district away from the tracking that separates social groups and deprives some students of experience and learning that would benefit them. This means not just working for policy change, but providing staff development so that teachers can learn how to individualize learning through classroom-workshop activities and through collaborative learning.

EXEMPLARY PROGRAM
Getting to Know You Culturally

Yolanda Simmons
King High School
Chicago

Pat Bearden
Metcalfe Magnet School
Chicago

Our colleagues, Pat Bearden and Yolanda Simmons are sisters who teach in two different Chicago schools. They have designed a multicultural cross-disciplinary unit that they conduct in very similar ways for three different audiences—Pat's third graders, Yolanda's high schoolers and groups of teachers in inservice programs. The students at all three levels find it involving and rewarding. The biggest difference in the activity between the three groups is simply the time allotment—high schoolers work longer on the whole project than either the younger kids or the adults. We'll describe the activity as it plays out in a high school classroom.

Day One. Students choose partners and conduct three-minute interviews with one another, taking notes on the following questions:

- Where were you born?
- Who were you named after, and what does your name mean?
- Where do your ancestors come from within the United States? Where do they come from outside the United States?
- Have you or anyone in your family researched your family history?

134

While the students are working, Simmons circulates around the room taking polaroid pictures of each kid. She also makes sure she has a bit of information of her own about at least one student. Students then take a minute or two to review and select from their notes, in preparation for oral presentations.

Next, each student introduces his or her partner "culturally." Simmons provides a model by doing the first introduction, giving some of the information briefly:

> This is John. He was born here in Chicago on the South Side, and he was named after his great uncle. His family comes from Macon, Georgia, where he used to visit every summer when he was small. He loved his grandmother's cooking, but hated the farm work he had to do. He doesn't know anything about where his family came from before that, but he wishes he did. Mee-ee-eet John Coleman!

Everyone applauds. As the introductions proceed, Simmons records the place-of-family-origin information in two columns—origins inside the U.S. and origins outside the U.S.—using newsprint paper on the wall.

Day Two. The students complete and edit one-page written versions of their interviews, with space left on each page for a photograph. These are pasted on, and someone with artistic talent is drafted to make a cover. Overnight, Yolanda photocopies the interviews to produce a class book, and everyone receives a copy the next day. The kids immediately check their own photographs and moan that they don't do the owner justice. But they save and browse through this information about their peers for weeks.

Day Three. The students come in to class to find newsprint sheets taped to the walls, with the headings, "English," "Language Arts," "Math," "Social Studies," "Science," "Phys. Ed.," plus a few blank sheets. Students are told to gather next to the sheets according to their strongest interests, with the option of also using the blank sheets to create their own categories—often "Dance," "Music," and "Home Economics/Foods." Their task is now to brainstorm and list questions for researching information about some of the locations on the "Origins" chart for their chosen subject area. The students especially warm to this work, no doubt because it offers a rare opportunity to share in control of the curriculum. Simmons remarks that no subject area seems to go without a few devotees in each class. Some typical questions the kids put on their charts:

- English—Who were some famous authors from this place, and what did they write?
- Language Arts—What are some slang terms teenagers use in this area?

- Social Studies—What is the student drop-out rate in this city?
- Science—What are some of the diseases that occur especially in this area, and what are their causes?
- Math—What are the population statistics, comparisons among them, and trends, for various ethnic groups in this area?

Days Four and Five. These are spent in the library. Each group chooses one of the research questions listed on their chart (the charts are brought to the library before hand and hung up so the students can consult them), and looks for answers to that question for each place of family origin in the U.S., in their particular group. The kids work on their research with help from Simmons and the librarian. Yolanda has been delighted to see even the low-achieving students working intently in their groups, and skipping lunch to continue their search.

Day Six. The students bring in their research reports and each group compiles an information book on their subject area. These books are kept as references in the classroom, reading material that the students can study on other occasions when they do reading of their own choice.

Days Seven and Eight. Each group gives an oral report to the class, sharing some of the knowledge they've gained on their particular aspect of the locations of the family origins.

Day Nine. At the end—and also at various points all along—the students "debrief" their research work in short discussion sessions. Among the important questions Yolanda poses are "How did you feel when you were doing _____ ?" and "Why do you think we included that step?" The students especially enjoy this reflecting, and find the latter question most thought-provoking. Such reflection adds to students' sense of ownership of the curriculum because they are asked to evaluate it. It also strengthens their learning by making them aware of the processes they've learned that lead to success in school. Many go on to write up their thoughts on these reflection questions as extra work on their own.

Clearly, this unit of study starts students thinking about multicultural issues, but it also does much more. It integrates all of the subject areas of school, and applies them to topics of real interest in the students' lives. It involves interviewing, writing, researching, working individually, in pairs and small groups, and giving oral reports to the whole class. It honors students' own knowledge and backgrounds, but also helps them discover much that they did not know about their own past, in aspects of geography and history that are actually quite traditional academically. It builds a classroom rapport that helps the students become a serious community of learners as well as a class that achieves a level of inter-group understanding that is sorely needed in many locales. It requires an extended piece of time—two weeks—but provides a powerful springboard to many other social studies topics, either in traditional areas or further afield.

Works Cited

Building a History Curriculum: Guidelines for Teaching History in Schools. 1988. The Bradley Commission on History in Schools.

Charting a Course: Social Studies for the Twenty-first Century. 1989. Washington D.C.: National Commission on Social Studies in the Schools. [Joint project of American Historical Association, Carnegie Foundation for the Advancement of Teaching, National Council for the Social Studies, and Organization of American Historians.]

Crabtree, Charlotte, Gary B. Nash, Paul Gagnon, and Scott Waugh, eds. 1992. *Lessons from History: Essential Understandings and Historical Perspectives Students Should Acquire*. Los Angeles, CA: The National Center for History in the Schools.

Hartoonian, Michael H. and Margaret A. Laughlin. 1989. Designing a Social Studies Scope and Sequence for the 21st Century. *Social Education* (October): 388–98.

Hoge, John D. and Claudia Crump. 1988. *Teaching History in the Elementary School*. Bloomington, IN: ERIC Clearinghouse for Social Studies and Social Science Education.

Kemball, Walter G., et al. 1987. *K–6 Geography: Themes, Key Ideas, and Learning Opportunities*. Washington, D.C.: Geographic Education National Implementation Project. [Joint project of The American Geographical Society, The Association of American Geographers, The National Council for Geographic Education, and The National Geographic Society.]

Kniep, Willard M. 1989. Social Studies Within a Global Education. *Social Education* (October): 399–403.

National Council for the Social Studies Task Force on Scope and Sequence. 1989. In Search of a Scope and Sequence for Social Studies. *Social Education* (October): 376–87.

Natoli, Salvatore J., Richard G. Boehm, James B. Kracht, David A. Lanegran, Janice J. Monk, and Robert W. Morrill. 1984. *Guidelines for Geographic Education: Elementary and Secondary Schools*. Washington, D.C.: National Council for Geographic Education. (Indiana, PA: Association of American Geographers.)

Parker, Walter C. 1991. *Renewing Social Studies Curriculum*. Washington, D.C.: Association for Supervision and Curriculum Development.

BEST PRACTICE IN SOCIAL STUDIES

Increase	Decrease
In-depth study of topics in each social studies field, in which students make choices about what to study, and discover the complexities of human interaction	Cursory coverage of a lock-step curriculum that includes everything but allows no time for deeper understanding of topics
Emphasis on activities that engage students in inquiry and problem solving about significant human issues	Memorization of isolated facts in textbooks
Student decision-making and participation in wider social, political, and economic affairs, so that they share a sense of responsibility for the welfare of their school and community	Isolation from the actual exercise of responsible citizenship; emphasis only on reading about citizenship or future participation in the larger social and political world
Participation in interactive and co-operative classroom study processes that bring together students of all ability levels	Lecture classes in which students sit passively: Classes in which students of lower ability levels are deprived of the knowledge and learning opportunities that other students receive.
Integration of social studies with other areas of the curriculum	Narrowing social studies activity to include only textbook-reading and test-taking
Richer content in elementary grades, building on the prior knowledge children bring to social studies topics: This includes study of concepts from psychology, sociology, economics, and political science, as well as history and geography. Students of all ages can understand, within their experience, American social institutions, issues for social groups, and problems of everyday living.	Assumption that students are ignorant or uninterested in issues raised in social studies
	Postponement of significant curriculum until secondary grades
Students' valuing, and sense of connection with, American and global history, the history and culture of diverse social groups, and the environment that surrounds them	Use of curriculum restricted to only one, dominant cultural heritage
Students' inquiry about the cultural groups they belong to, and others represented in their school and community, to promote students' sense of ownership in the social studies curriculum	Use of curriculum that leaves students disconnected from, and unexcited about social studies topics
Use of evaluation that involves further learning and that promotes responsible citizenship and open expression of ideas	Assessments only at the end of a unit or grading period; assessments that test only factual knowledge or memorization of textbook information

7

Classroom Structures for Integrating Curriculum

Over the past five chapters, we have presented dozens of recommendations from important national bodies and shared stories from many exemplary classrooms. Now the question arises: what holds all these recommendations and classrooms together? What's happening in common among all those teachers from Lynn Cherkasky-Davis to Wayne Mraz, from kindergarten to high school, from rural to inner city schools? What's the same about Best Practice, whether in reading, writing, math, science, or social studies? Is there a short list of fundamental classroom activities or structures that characterize the new, integrated model across all boundaries?

We've already asserted that one common ingredient of Best Practice is a **philosophy**; a set of harmonious and interlocking **theories about learning**. Whether consciously or intuitively (or a little of both), all the teachers we have visited in this book subscribe to a coherent philosophy of learning that's child-centered, experiential, reflective, authentic, holistic, social, collaborative, democratic, cognitive, developmental, constructivist, psycholinguistic, and challenging. Similarly, the professional societies and research centers whose reports we have summarized here subscribe to the same fundamental views of learning and teaching.

So all these teachers and organizations believe something in common. But what are these practitioners *doing* with children that brings the philosophy alive? How do teachers enact, implement, and live out their theory? Though the classrooms we've described so far may look quite diverse, under their varied surfaces are a few recurrent structures, basic ways of organizing kids, time, materials, space, and help. Actually, these exemplary teachers often are orchestrating a surprisingly *small* number of key activities in their search to embody Best Practice. Among these basic structures are:

- Thematic Studies
- Curriculum Jigsawing
- Collaborative Group Activities
- Learning Logs
- Classroom Workshop
- Conferences
- Centers
- Authentic Assessment

Most of these structures are simple, familiar, and well-proven. While these special activities can profoundly shift the classroom balance from teacher-directed to student-centered learning, many of them are actually quite easy to implement; they are easy to begin, easy to slot into the existing teaching day, easy to experiment with incrementally. Indeed, far from requiring teachers to master a huge inventory of newfangled, technical instructional methods, Best Practice largely means returning to some old, perhaps prematurely discarded approaches, and fine-tuning them until they work. But these simple activities are also very powerful: They can effectively take the teacher off stage, decentralize the classroom, and transfer responsibility for active learning to the students in any subject.

These eight key structures each contain within their design the management features necessary to make them work. But many of them also require careful training of students, and the more complex a structure is, the more time and training it will take—happily, of course, the learning and social skills acquired with this training are valuable in themselves. Many of these key structures are the subject of recent articles or whole books that explain in detail how they can be adapted for different subjects and grade levels. At the moment, some of these structures have been more fully developed in reading and writing than in other subjects, since literacy seems to be the cutting-edge field in the integrated education movement. In the next few pages, we'll offer a few comments on each structure; between the sources listed here and the recommended readings in Chapter 9, we point the way to detailed information and guidance about many of these structures.

Thematic Studies

From the earliest days of elementary school to the waning moments of high school, American children typically study a sadly disconnected assortment of facts, ideas, and skills. In the typical first-grade reading program, children are presented with a year-long series of reading "stories" sequenced according to the supposed reading skills that they teach, rather than their meaning or theme. This means that kids may jump from a basal story about fairies in a castle, to one about Daniel Boone on the frontier, to another about talking robots in outer space, without any sense of order, connection, or transition among them. At the other end of the educational system, secondary schools are *designed* for incoherence: students' days are chopped into seven or eight segments guaranteed to be discontinuous with each other. A kid may start the day with forty minutes of Greek history in social studies class, then move to English to read some modern American poems, then shuffle off to science where the refraction of light is presented, and then move along to math to do problems which are connected to no aspect of life whatsoever.

In Best Practice schools and classrooms, teachers refuse to accept this randomness. They believe that content does matter, and that for school to work it must make sense to students—ideally, make sense all day long. Therefore, these teachers identify a few big subjects of significance to children and then build extended units around those topics. In elementary grades, we know teachers who've built multi-week chunks of curriculum around topics such as Exploring, Bears, Castles, Australia, Fairy Tales, or Homes. In the Bears unit, for example, the children read (and hear read aloud) lots of different bear stories, build a library of favorite bear books, do bear readers' theater, study the biology of bears, work in research teams to investigate different kinds of bears (polar, grizzly, panda, etc.), go to the zoo and see real bears (noting details in their journals), write bear stories and bear reports, do bear mathematics (calculating the days of hibernation, the number of blueberries a bear could eat, etc.), and, of course, do plenty of bear art. When teachers design such thematically coherent activities, they usually find that they can quite easily fit in many of the old, mandated curriculum elements; these topics simply come up in a different way, at a different time, and in a different order. But the main benefit of such teaching is that it provides children with the continuity, order, and challenge they need, both to enjoy school and to stay engaged with the work.

Curriculum integration is often possible in elementary schools, where teachers may have the same thirty kids all day. Aside from district rules and controls (which may present formidable obstacles), if a self-contained elementary teacher decides to start integrating the curriculum, her or his own good will and resolve can actually get it done. Perhaps this is why some elementary teachers have always taught thematically, and this approach is now growing so rapidly as part of the burgeoning Whole Language movement. But in high school, things are a little tougher. Creating a truly integrated curriculum for any one student would require the cooperation of six or seven teachers who have no mandate to cooperate nor history of doing so, who have no common planning time, and who each still have on their desks a weighty scope-and-sequence document for their own segment of the school day—a curriculum that they have probably spent many increasingly comfortable years delivering. In Chapter 3, we described this struggle at Eisenhower High School in Decatur, including both the structural obstacles to building integrated curriculum, and the excitement of overcoming them.

Still, in high schools there are many ways teachers can move toward integrated, thematic instruction. If schools are ready to make moderate institutional reform, they can follow the pattern of Wasson High School in Colorado, where students now take four classes a day instead of eight, allowing kids and teachers to focus more carefully and deeply during ninety-minute class periods. Even where there's no such school-wide sanction, teachers still can reform their own forty-five-minute slice of the school day, reorganizing material into more meaningful, coherent chunks. If the textbook presents a jumbled or arbitrary sequence of materials, the teachers can rearrange it, finding and identifying organizing themes that the curriculum writers didn't notice or mention. Teachers can help kids by identifying and stressing the few "big ideas" that strand through the welter of seemingly disparate material often presented to students.

For example, at Stagg High School, which we discussed in Chapter 6, the history teachers decided that the old curriculum presented far too many disparate facts, and so the department went on a two-day retreat to hammer out a limited number of major themes in U. S. history. As the teachers now testify, this was one of the longest and loudest weekends of their professional lives, but they came back with a list of sixteen themes, (they called them "postholes of history") for a whole year's course. This provided every teacher with about two and a half weeks to approach each of the themes in a way that worked for their own students, even though everyone was still operating within the old bell schedule and framework. The Stagg faculty simply insisted that history make sense to their students.

Sometimes, two secondary teachers can get together to provide integration across more than one period of the day. For years, this has been done in American Studies programs, in which history and literature are taught in a combined, two-period, team-taught class. As a next step, several schools we've worked with have begun projects where a group of seventy-five kids and three teachers get a half-day together to pursue a big topic: at Stagg High School, one pilot group studied U. S. History, Literature, and German—an approach which, among other things, highlighted the often overlooked Germanic origins of American colonial culture. Although curriculum integration in high schools is especially problematic, there's increasing hope as schools around the country break down the barriers of student and teacher scheduling, departmental boundaries, ability-grouping, and subservience to standardized test scores.

Curriculum Jigsawing

As helpful as a thematic approach to curriculum can be, it is not enough to recast the customary curriculum into more meaningful themes and sequences. There's simply too much material for anyone to learn in any deep or significant way. Indeed, one of the most counterproductive elements of traditional American schooling has been its relentless emphasis on "covering the material" in a prescribed curriculum guide. Typically, such a mandated curriculum is an overstuffed compendium of facts, dates, concepts, books, persons, and ideas—a volume of material so enormous that no one thing in it can ever be understood if all of it must be mentioned. There's simply not enough time for deep study, and so each ingredient in the curriculum can only be "covered" in the sense that a wall is covered with a microscopically thin layer of paint. Among the many manifestations of the "coverage curriculum" are lecture-style classes, with emphasis on student notetaking, followed by multiple-choice tests stressing temporary memorization and factual recall.

In Best Practice classrooms, teachers realize that every child needn't study every possible topic, and that not everyone has to study all the same topics. Indeed, it is good educational practice (and solid preparation for adult life) to be part of a community where tasks and topics are parceled out to work groups, task forces, teams, or committees. When teachers jigsaw the curriculum, they seek natural ways to divide a given topic, assigning small groups of students to investigate the different parts, each team bringing back its piece of the puzzle to the whole group later on. In American History, for example, not every student needs to learn about every Civil War battle. (Indeed, if everyone had to study every battle, the only choice would be for the teacher to simply talk as fast as she could.) Instead, a Best Practice teacher might let groups of kids each pick a single battle to study—Antietam for one group, Gettysburg to another, Bull Run for a third, and so on. Then the kids' job is to really dig in with reading and researching and talking, taking time to carefully explore and grasp the events involved, pursuing a deep understanding of their particular battle. Later, when the class comes back together, each group has a responsibility to share a few key concepts or highlights that have emerged from their study. To pull the whole experience together, the teacher helps students find the similarities, differences, connections, and key concepts in the sub-topics all have studied. In following this procedure, everyone learns one subject in detail, while still gaining a familiarity with related topics by way of reports from other classmates.

A final comment: The old "coverage curriculum" dies hard. Because the rote memorization of multiplicitous facts was so much a part of every American adult's education, many grownups still confuse factual recall with a good education. This craving for coverage has even given rise to a cottage industry; under the banner of "cultural literacy," E. D. Hirsch and his collaborators have given the parents of America a series of books that lists "What Your First (Second, Third, or Fourth) Grader Needs to Know." These sad handbooks reiterate what the old school curriculum used to say: that everyone should study the same things at the same time, and that a satisfactory outcome of schooling is the mere recognition of certain key words.

The durability, indeed, the marketability, of this "curriculum of superficiality" is a real challenge to school reformers. The bung-full curriculum has many defenders who use words like "rigor" and "standards" when they defend their view. Yet this advocacy of comprehensive coverage by self-appointed cultural guardians is deeply ironic, since their model of curriculum actually breeds disrespect for learning. After all, everyone involved in traditional schooling, teachers and students alike, will testify with remarkably little embarrassment that students normally forget virtually everything they "learned" in school. Yet we who want to *raise the standards of learning* by insisting that students study a smaller number of topics in much greater depth are labeled permissivists. This is clearly a long and deeply rooted cultural struggle, one that won't be settled for generations—but it is wise for school reformers to be aware of its dynamic.

Collaborative Group Activities

Best Practice means big changes in the way classrooms operate. Across all content areas, the new curriculum calls for much less teacher presentation and domination, far more active student learning, and constantly shifting groupings. If teachers are going to successfully implement all these promising new student-centered activities, their first task will be to create a productive, interdependent, cooperative classroom group. It is a *sine qua non* of Best Practice that teachers must nurture student sharing, responsibility, and independence. If the climate isn't right, instruction will inevitably regress toward the old teacher-centered, lecture-test model. Further, as we will argue in detail in Chapter 9, these classroom communities must not be tracked, leveled, or ability-grouped: if we want a rich education in a genuinely democratic society, school groupings must enact pluralism and welcome diversity.

At the whole-class level, teachers must help students to join in effective, democratic meetings during which the group can brainstorm ideas, set goals, make plans, learn new structures for working, solve problems, and evaluate their own work. While this kind of session may sound routine, most teachers are experienced in giving whole-class presentations and instructions, not in chairing meetings that invite genuine interchange and decision-making by the students. William Glasser (in Joyce, 1986) has outlined a recurrent cycle of classroom meetings that builds both content learning and democratic involvement. The class 1) meets regularly to talk about its own learning activities and social processes; 2) identifies learning goals or group problems; 3) prioritizes its goals or problems; 4) proposes and discusses alternative courses of action; 5) makes a formal, group commitment to action; 6) regularly meets to share and review the outcomes of group decisions. While this pattern of whole-class meetings can obviously nurture the socioemotional development of the classroom community, its academic uses are just as vital: at these meetings, students decide what to study, divide into working groups, plan how and when to report their learnings with others, and more.

If students have difficulty functioning in a participatory whole-group democracy, teachers need artful strategies to build comfort, familiarity, and fluency with the procedures. For sessions when a class is planning a project or investigation, the teacher can use brainstorming, asking people to call out options or stages in the work, listing them all, and then having the class order or prioritize them afterward—a simple, well-known, but underutilized strategy. If participation isn't proving sufficiently widespread, a resourceful teacher will ask students to talk in pairs for a minute to make their own lists and then request one idea from each person. Meaningful discussions of a topic in any course can be started effectively by having students write brief "learning log" entries on an open-ended question such as: "What do you think was going through the character's mind when he said that?" "What are some of the pros and cons President Lincoln might have considered as he thought over his decision about emancipation?"

Whole-class meetings are also important for sharing completed work that students are proud of or that they want more input on, to help them revise further. Many elementary teachers end their daily writing workshop time with ten minutes for a few students to occupy the "author's chair," read their work aloud, and call on peers who ask questions, offer specific praise, or explain where they felt confused. A whole class can profitably talk through the qualities that characterize an effective lab explanation, report, or small-group presentation—so that the class participates in setting criteria for meaningful evaluation. And when a unit or project is finished, a science teacher can help the class internalize the underlying concepts and become more effective learners by outlining together not only the major ideas explored, but also the activities the class used, and how people overcame various obstacles and solved problems in the course of their learning.

However, genuine whole-classroom participation is only one part of the new dynamic. Best Practice classrooms cannot succeed unless kids can work together effectively in small groups—in pairs, threes, *ad hoc* groups, and long-term teams—without constant teacher supervision. Happily, this crucial piece of the reform puzzle has fallen into place over the past few years. Teachers all across the country have been discovering and adapting the powerful versions of collaborative learning described by William Glasser (1990), David and Roger Johnson (1984), Robert Slavin (1985), and others. They have been reassured and excited by research showing that, even using the customary standardized measures, students of all grade levels show significant achievement gains across the curriculum when they are organized into collaborative groupings and projects. It works.

But we must be sure to apply these effective collaborative structures to an elevated conception of curriculum. So far, too many cooperative learning applications have been essentially study teams—harnessing the power of social learning to help kids memorize the same old curriculum content. In fact, kids *can* teach each other dates and facts and formulas quite effectively when they study as a group, but why bother? Far more powerful and appropriate uses of collaboration occur when students read and discuss novels in literature circles, or generate their own crafted pieces of writing through the input of peer response and editing groups. Below are listed a few structures for collaborative learning that move kids toward higher order thinking.

Partner/Buddy Reading

Paired reading activities with many variations. Two students may take turns reading aloud to each other from a story or textbook, either passing a single book back and forth, or with the listener following the text in her or his own copy. Pairs can read the same section outside of class and join to discuss the reading, or they can jigsaw the text, reading different sections and sharing their respective pieces of the puzzle.

Peer Response and Editing

Ongoing groups in which students give diplomatic and critical feedback on drafts of each other's writings. Training students to help each other with their work requires both management tools (such as how to talk quietly, developing a "twelve-inch voice" so that everyone in the room can hear their own partners) and process skills (how to pose questions that help authors make their own decisions, instead of just being criticized).

Literature Circles/Text Sets

Groups of four or five students choose and read the same article, book, or novel. After doing their reading outside of class, they prepare to play one of several specific discussion roles, and come to the group with notes to help them take that job. Circles have regular meetings, with discussion roles rotating each session. When they finish a book, the circle may report briefly to the whole class; then they trade members with other finishing groups, select more reading, and move into a new cycle.

Study Teams

Where it is necessary for kids to memorize voluminous or complex material, Slavin's "Team Games Tournament" and related strategies help students bring energy to the task. These structures help kids form interdependent groups that parcel out tasks, share the work, stop to help members who fall behind, and provide an interlocking reward system where everyone gets maximum benefits if everyone in the group succeeds. (One caution: if such team strategies merely harness collaborative learning to an archaic, irrelevant, teacher-dominated curriculum, they are a corruption of Best Practice.)

Group Investigations

One useful legacy of the 1960s is the wide assortment of group inquiry models developed in different fields, including the Biological Science Curriculum Study, the Social Science Curriculum Project, and the Group Investigation Model (all described in Joyce, 1986). In the common structure of these models, a learning cycle begins when the class encounters or identifies a problem for study. As a first step, the whole class discusses the topic, shares its prior knowledge, generates hypotheses, poses questions, sets goals, and makes a plan for studying the topic. Roles and tasks are parceled out to different groups of students, based upon their curiosities and skills. Then the inquiry proceeds in the small groups, with the teacher serving as facilitator and resource along the way. When the investigations are completed, the teams reconvene to share and discuss their findings.

Learning Logs

One way to overcome the passivity of the traditional classroom, to make students more active and responsible for their own learning, is to use learning logs across the curriculum (Fulwiler, 1987). When teachers adopt this kind of writing-to-learn, students regularly do short, spontaneous, exploratory, personal pieces of writing about the content they are studying. Instead of filling in blanks in worksheets and jotting short answers to textbook study questions, students respond to fewer, broader, more open-ended prompts: What would have changed if Lincoln were shot six months earlier? What are the advantages of an indicator over a meter? What are three questions from last night's reading that we ought to discuss in class today? In logs, teachers ask students to react, record, speculate, compare, analyze, or synthesize the ideas in the curriculum. Students aren't writing to be graded on spelling and grammar, but to pursue ideas and try out thoughts. Journals are a way of running your mind, monitoring your thinking, of making reflection habitual and concrete. This is writing for thinking, not for creating a polished product.

As a cognitive tool, learning logs can help learners in any content field. After all, whatever the subject matter, learners can always jot down their responses, record their own prior knowledge, probe their own thinking patterns, make predictions and seek connections, or sketch plans for what to do next. When they are shared, journals also open a private channel of communication between the teacher and each student. In learning logs, teachers report, students will often say things that they would never announce out loud, thus providing teachers a new and valuable kind of feedback.

Teachers also use student writings-to-learn in class, reading them aloud, feeding them into group discussions, parceling them out to teams for review or action. Many teachers, like our friend Wayne Mraz, assign "admit slips" and "exit slips," short bits of writing that are used to start and end a class. Others run classroom conversations about a topic—a poem or a civil war battle or a chemical process—conducted entirely in notes that students pass back and forth, formally called "dialogue journals." For teachers who use these writing-to-learn strategies regularly, the compiled entries become an increasingly thick record of what each student has done and learned. One of the surprising and reassuring side effects of writing-to-learn is that the classroom is *quiet*. While many people anticipate chaos in progressive classrooms, the opposite is often the case. If you visit the kind of reading workshop described by Nancie Atwell (1987) and implemented by teachers around the country, what you will typically find is a room full of teenagers working quietly, without overt supervision, for forty-five minutes at a stretch. Students will be reading novels of their own choice, which they will occasionally put aside at a good stopping place to write a "literature letter" to the teacher or to a designated student partner. Or they may jot a note in response to a "lit letter" received from their partner. In this quiet but hardworking classroom, the teacher and the students are all industriously (but often quietly) reading books and using a special kind of writing to channel their responses and enhance their comprehension.

Although learning logs are often called journals, they are not diaries. Some teachers are wary of trying journals because of the confessional connotations of the word, but academic journaling (which we've labeled learning logs) is expressly for recording and advancing subject-matter learning in school. Other teachers worry about implementation problems; perhaps they have seen too many ill-advised English teachers trudging home from school on Friday afternoon, lugging a sky-high stack of student spirals that they "have to" respond to over the weekend. But learning logs needn't increase the workload of either students or teachers. These writings are supposed to *replace* textbook study questions, ditto sheets, or other low-level, memorization-oriented activities. Students should spend the same amount of time working, and teachers the same amount of time responding, with everyone engaged in higher-order, more valuable thinking. In fact, many teachers find that when the students' writing-to-learn pieces are used as the starting point for class activities and discussions, they don't even need to collect and read the work separately: hearing the ideas discussed aloud provides plenty of feedback about what kids are thinking.

Some teachers wonder whether their content is too technical or their students are too young for journals to work. We have seen learning logs effectively integrated into everything from preschool classes where kids draw their entries, to animal husbandry courses at a technical college. Other teachers worry that if students are assigned learning logs in all school subjects, they will either become confused or will "burn out" from the overuse of this teaching novelty. One answer to this: in Terrie Bridgman's first-grade class at Baker Demonstration School in Evanston, Illinois, the six-year-olds are keeping a math journal, a reading journal, and a personal "news" journal within the first few days school, with gusto and without any confusion. On a deep level, treating writing-to-learn as a gimmick makes no more sense than labeling *reading* in every class a fad. Effective teachers, as well as theorists, are finally recognizing that writing is the rightful bookend to reading, a too-neglected tool that helps students actively process their encounter with ideas, to deepen their engagement with the curriculum.

Classroom Workshop

Undoubtedly the single most important new strategy in literacy education is the reading-writing workshop. As Donald Graves, Nancie Atwell, Lucy Calkins, Linda Rief, Tom Romano, and others have explained, students in a workshop classroom choose their own topics for writing and books for reading, using large scheduled chunks of classroom time for doing their own reading and writing. They collaborate freely with classmates, keep their own records, and self-evaluate. Teachers take new roles, too, modeling their own reading and writing processes, conferring with students one-to-one, and offering well-timed, compact mini-lessons as students work. In the mature workshop classroom, teachers don't wait around for "teachable moments" to occur—they make them happen every day.

The workshop model is simple and powerful. It derives from the insight that children learn to read by reading and write by writing, and that schools in the past have simply failed to provide enough guided practice. It recognizes that kids need less telling and more showing, that they need more time to *do* literacy, and less time hearing about what reading and writing might be like if you ever did them. Even the term "workshop" harks back to the ancient crafts-place, where not only did products get produced, but education went on as the master craftsman coached apprentices.

In school, a workshop is a long, regularly scheduled, recurrent chunk of time (thirty minutes to an hour or more) during which the main activity is to do a subject: reading, writing, math, history, or science. Workshops meet regularly, at least once a week; in many classrooms, students have workshop time every day. A defining element of a true workshop is *choice*: individual students choose their own books for reading, projects for investigating, topics for writing. They follow a set of carefully inculcated norms for exercising that choice during the workshop period. They learn that all workshop time must be used on some aspect of working, so when they complete a product, a piece, or a phase, they aren't "done" for the day: instead, kids must begin something new, based on an idea from their own running list of tasks and topics, or seek a conference with the teacher. While there are regular, structured opportunities for sharing and collaborating in a workshop, students also spend much time working alone; there are other times of the day when teachers set up collaborative group or team activities.

Today, pathfinding teachers are beginning to extend the workshop model outward from reading and writing, where many have already found success, into other parts of the curriculum—establishing math workshops, science workshops, history workshops. They do this because whatever the content, deep immersion is the key to mastery: teachers want kids to *do* history, *do* science, *do* math.

Below is a generic schedule for a single forty-five-minute workshop session that could happen in any subject, just to show one way that teachers commonly manage time and activity.

> **Five Minutes: Status of the Class Conference** Each student announces in a few words what she will work on this session.
>
> **Thirty Minutes: Work Time/Conferences** Students work according to their plan. Depending upon the rules and norms, this may include reading or writing, talking or working with other students, going to the library, making phone calls, using manipulatives or microscopes, etc. The teacher's roles during this time are several. For the first few minutes, the teacher will probably experiment, read, or write herself, to model the activity. Then the teacher may manage a bit, skimming through the room to solve simple problems and make sure everyone is working productively. Then the teacher shifts to her main workshop activity: conducting one-to-one or small-group conferences with kids about their work, either following a preset schedule or based on student

sign-ups for that day. The teacher's role in these conferences is as a sounding-board, facilitator, and coach—rarely as critic or instructor.

Ten Minutes: Sharing In many workshop sessions, teachers save the last few minutes for students to discuss what they have done that day. Writers may read a piece of work aloud, readers may offer a capsule book review, math students show how they applied a concept to a real-world situation, scientists demonstrate a chemical reaction, social studies teams report the results of their opinion survey.

Obviously, the workshop classroom is not an entirely new phenomenon. Its decentralized, hands-on pattern, with kids "doing" the subject rather than just hearing about it, is familiar to teachers of art, science, home economics, physical education, and other "doable" subjects. Of these fields, however, only art has traditionally allowed for any measure of student choice in the work. The commitment to student autonomy and responsibility is rooted more in experiments with independent study, classroom contracting, the open classroom, and learning laboratories. This new vehicle for student-centered learning—the workshop classroom —works because it addresses the shortcomings of prior experiments: it gives both students and teachers clear-cut roles to perform, it provides for careful balancing of social and solitary activities, and it respects the necessity of detailed training for students to work purposefully in this decentralized format.

Still, implementing the workshop classroom is a real challenge for teachers. The structure itself violates the expectations of many students, administrators, and parents, it competes for time with the official curriculum, and it often contradicts teachers' professional training and their own childhood experience in school. Nor do students always take smoothly and effortlessly to the workshop model: on the contrary, implementation can be bumpy, tricky, and slow, even for dedicated teachers in progressive districts. Yet, when the workshop starts to work, it turns the traditional transmission-model classroom upside down: students become active, responsible, self-motivating, and self-evaluating learners, while the teacher drops the talking-head role in favor of more powerful functions as model, coach, and collaborator.

Conferences

Conferences between teachers and students are one of the most effective and underutilized strategies in American classrooms. In spite of decades of research confirming the impact of one-to-one conversations— from Jerome Bruner's scaffolding research in the 1960s to this year's headlines about "Reading Recovery" tutoring—most American students still spend their school day deployed in groups of thirty, listening to the teacher or doing seatwork. Ironically, most teachers will readily agree that a one-minute private conversation with a child, timed at just the right moment and targeted precisely to that kid's own work, is often more effective than hours of whole-class instruction. But still, too few teachers are reorganizing their day to make more one-to-one exchanges happen.

Why haven't conferences caught on more widely? There are several sticking points. Tradition, as usual, provides a first layer of resistance. Teachers' formal training, as well as their own experience as students, strongly conditions them to think of teaching as a one-on-thirty, rather than a one-on-one, activity. Experienced teachers already possess banks of lesson plans, some of them developed and polished over years, for teacher-centered classroom activities that seem to work. These treasured whole-class lessons are ready to use, and they don't carry the risks and uncertainties that are inevitably part of anything new.

The second level of reluctance involves classroom management: teachers worry about "what to do with the other twenty-nine kids" while they hold conferences with individual pupils. This is a reasonable concern: Until teachers can get a classroom of students working productively without constant monitoring, they won't feel clear to introduce decentralized activities like conferences. This, of course, is one of the main reasons why it is so important to establish the workshop structure described above—not only does it provide practice time in key curriculum areas, but it also creates the basic frame within which conferences can occur. And, working further backward, building a productive workshop depends upon the initial climate-setting, group-building activities we talked about earlier.

The other worry of teachers is that they won't know what to say to a child in a conference. Many think that in order to have an effective conference they must first study the learner's work and then ask "the right questions"—or have the right advice ready to give. For teachers just starting to consider instituting such one-to-one conversations, this sounds like a lot of work. But good conferences do not necessarily require extensive teacher preparation. In writing instruction, for example, we have found that kids who have regular three-minute "process conferences" with their teachers will gain significantly in writing achievement, even when the teacher does not read the papers or give advice in those conferences.

So what kinds of things can the teacher say? Three simple questions can start a conference in any subject: 1) What are you working on? 2) How is it going? 3) What do you plan to do next? For each of these key questions, teachers will gradually develop some sub-prompts or helping questions, but the three basic queries serve just fine for starters. In such a process conference, it is not the teacher's job to tell or teach or offer instruction; the tasks are to help the student talk and to listen. In fact, such process conferences can actually help teachers avoid one conferencing problem that they may not worry about, but should: dominating the student. Too many teachers, when they first begin conferencing, simply offer a kind of knee-to-knee lecture, talking at the student for three or four minutes. The simple, three-question process conference transfers the conversational responsibility from teacher to student, providing the teacher with a good implicit reminder to keep quiet.

How do such short "content free" conferences actually promote the learning of content? Process conferences work because they teach a habit of mind. They help students learn how to reflect on their own work, to review their own progress, to identify their own problems, set their own goals, and make plans and promises to themselves about steps they are going to take. As we regularly hold conferences with students, leading them through the pattern of where-am-I-and-where-do-I-want-to-go, we are truly modeling a way of thinking for themselves; we are holding out-loud conversations with kids that they can gradually internalize and have with themselves.

All of teachers' questions about conferences, from management to content, are answered by teacher-authors like Nancie Atwell, Donald Graves, Linda Rief, Lucy Calkins, and Tom Romano. These are many of the same people who have written about the workshop classroom, where conferences are integral to the program.

Centers

One of the key structures of the now-discarded "open classroom" experiment was the idea of centers—learning stations or labs set up by the teacher around a classroom, which students visit and explore in some organized sequence. Centers were meant to replace passive whole-class presentations with active exploration by individual kids and small groups, and even included an element of student choice, in that kids could decide when to visit each center, traffic permitting. However, in schools where centers were supposed to be the main teaching device, teachers often imploded from stress. They were required to "teach" kids all day by setting up independent-learning centers that were engaging and active, that somehow covered the curriculum, that coordinated with each other, that kept kids busy for roughly the same amount of time each, that allowed for record-keeping and grading, and that didn't make too big a mess.

Today we still recognize the importance of a decentralized classroom, but balance is our watchword: We know that kids learn best across a school day that provides a rich mixture of different activities, from quiet individual work to energetic collaboration. Centers still have a place, not as the main vehicle for instruction for most of the day, but as a natural element of differentiated classroom space and a varied schedule. We know many elementary teachers—like Lynn Cherkasky-Davis whom we visited in Chapter 2 and Mary Fencl in Chapter 3—who routinely have four or five centers in their room, rotating in new ones periodically, and who schedule between forty-five minutes and one and a half hours a day of "center time" when kids can explore these. We also know some high school teachers who don't think centers are just for the little kids, who believe that creating some functional sub-areas around the room makes an ideal environment for teenagers who welcome settings where they can work alone or with a few friends. In a high school classroom, a computer can be a kind of center; so is the table at which writers meet to conference over their work or where teams meet to work on their research.

As teachers set up an environment in the classroom, differentiated space is needed both to create some nooks for privacy and some areas defined by purpose; some are temporary, and some are permanent. Good centers should be natural. A writing center might be mainly a supply depot with a variety of paper, pens, markers, tape, white-out, and a table for editing. A reading center would include a classroom library of enticing books of various levels of difficulty, hand-published books by other students, comfortable corners for reading, and a table and chairs for quiet group discussion. Listening centers, with a couple of tape recorders and a good collection of tapes, offer kids a chance to listen to books read aloud (either familiar ones or ones they can't yet handle independently), or to hear interviews with favorite authors. Math centers can present a variety of manipulatives and problem-solving activities, so that as students cycle through all of them over a period of weeks, they are involved in a variety of tasks—required to do some review of previously taught ideas, some work with topics presently being discussed, and some challenging inquiry into more advanced concepts. A science center might be the location where a classroom pet is kept, along with books about that creature, and a set of observational activities to be recorded in each child's learning log. A room with centers offers kids variety in the day, a chance to engage content actively, natural occasions for quiet talk, opportunities for ad hoc collaboration, and the responsibility for making choices. Centers also put the teacher in a helper-observer role, providing a splendid time to give help to kids who need it, and to observe carefully the ways in which different kids approach the work of different centers.

Authentic Assessment

In Best Practice classrooms, teachers don't just make up tests and put grades on report cards. They are less interested in measuring students' recall of individual facts or use of certain subskills, than in how they perform the authentic, complete, higher-order activities that school aims for: reading whole books, drafting and editing stories or articles, conducting and reporting a scientific inquiry, applying math to real problem solving.

Because progressive teachers want deeper and more practical information about children's learning, they monitor students' growth in richer and more sophisticated ways. More and more, teachers are adopting and adapting the tools of ethnographic, qualitative research: observation, interviews, questionnaires, collecting and interpreting artifacts and performances. They use information from these sources not mainly to "justify" marks on a report card, but to guide instruction, to make crucial daily decisions about helping students grow.

Many teachers now keep anecdotal, observational records, saving a few minutes each day to jot notes about students in their classes—some call this "kidwatching." Instead of numbers, letters, or symbols, teachers create written descriptions of what students are doing and saying. Some teachers put these observations on a schedule, tracking five particular kids on Monday, another five on Tuesday, and so forth. Some watch just one kid per day, some simply jot notes on any kids who show noteworthy growth, thinking, problems, or concerns on a given day, while other teachers prefer to record observations of the class as a community. The common feature of these observational records is that teachers save time for regularly recording them, they develop a format that works for them, and they consistently use these notes both to guide their instruction and to communicate with parents and others about children's progress.

Teachers are also beginning to use students themselves as self-observers in increasingly powerful ways. In face-to-face interviews, written questionnaires, or in learning logs, teachers ask kids to record and reflect upon their own work (books read, experiments conducted, etc.). In Best Practice classrooms, it is common for students to have periodic "evaluation conferences" with their teachers, where both parties use their notes to review the child's achievements and problems over a span of time, and then set goals for the upcoming weeks or months. In a curriculum that values higher-order thinking as well as individual responsibility, such self-evaluation teaches multiple important lessons.

One of the most promising mechanisms for authentic evaluation is the student portfolio, a folder in which students save selected samples of their best work in a given subject. The practice of keeping such cumulative records has many benefits. First, of course, it provides actual evidence of what the child can do with writing, math, art, or science, instead of a mark in a grade book—which represents, after all, nothing more than a teacher-mediated symbolic record of a long-discarded piece of real work. These portfolio artifacts also invite all sorts of valuable conversations between the child and the teacher, children and peers, or kids and parents: How did you get interested in this? How did you feel while you were working on this? How did you solve the problems you encountered? What would you tell another student about this subject? What are you going to do next? The process of selecting and polishing items for inclusion in the portfolio invites students to become increasingly reflective about their own work and more skillful at self-evaluation.

In order to add these new, more productive forms of evaluation to their classrooms, teachers need to subtract something else—they need to reclaim some time and energy by terminating any forms of evaluation that don't usefully steer instruction, advance kids' learning, or produce artifacts worth saving. For many teachers, this means assigning and grading far less busy-work, dittos, workbook pages, study questions, and worksheets. Instead of spending their time tabulating the errors in stacks of identical fill-in-the-blank worksheets, teachers instead spend their precious evaluation time responding to each kid's whole original reports or stories, perhaps writing a personal note of response that gives guidance as well as modeling solid adult writing. This means teachers are making a time trade: They're not spending any less time on evaluation, but they're also not spending more. They're differentiating their assessment efforts, looking at children's growth in wider variety of ways. They are committed to the principle that the most valuable assessment activities are **formative**, aimed at understanding a child's development and making instructional decisions about that child. **Summative** evaluation, the process of converting kids' achievements into some kind of ranked, ordinal system that compares children to each other, needs to happen far less often, if at all.

Can Teachers Still Teach?

All of the above activities have one thing in common: They take the teacher off stage. They do not cast the teacher in the familiar role of information-dispenser, font-of-wisdom, expert/presenter/lecturer. In each of these key classroom structures, the teacher is somewhere further in the background, acting as a moderator, facilitator, coach, scribe, designer, observer, model—everything *but* the standard, normal, stereotypical, conception of the teacher as . . . well, as a *teacher*. What gives? Does this mean that in the idealized, progressive Best Practice classroom the teacher never "teaches" in the old-fashioned sense of the word?

Not at all. But once again, balance is the key. It is fine for teachers to conduct whole-class presentations, to give information, to share and tell and even lecture—*some of the time*. But time-sharing is the key. In the traditional curriculum, we have catastrophically neglected the student-centered side of the "airtime" equation. Indeed, one of the key findings from classroom research across subjects is that students don't get enough time to try out, practice, and apply what teachers are talking about. Kids never get to do any science or any writing or any math, because the teacher is so busy *talking* that there is never any time to practice the target activity.

Because it is so deeply ingrained in our culture that teaching means talking at other people who are silent and inactive, we all must police ourselves very closely to make sure we don't regress to that old transmission model. That's one reason why this chapter may seem so unbalanced, giving almost all of its attention to the structures for student-centered classroom time. But teachers already know how to conduct whole-class presentations, probably all too well. It was highlighted in their professional training, it was the core of their personal experience as students, and it probably predominates in their on-the-job experience. Most American teachers simply don't need as much help conducting whole-class presentations as they do with, for example, facilitating a collaborative workshop. So teachers need to fill this gap, to correct this imbalance in their professional repertoire by equipping themselves with all the classroom structures they need to comfortably and safely get off stage, to provide and manage plenty of kid-centered time for practice and exploration.

With this extended disclaimer in place, we can return to the subject of whole-class, teacher-directed activities and see what's valuable about them. There are at least three reasons why teacher-centered whole-class instruction can and should remain part of the school day. First and most important, teachers have great things to teach—they have knowledge, wisdom, experience, ideas, content that can be shared through whole class presentations they design. All of us who teach have developed great units, favorite sequences of activities which engage students, year after year. We have worked to design and refine and enrich these units; they are our treasures, and we're not about to give them up. We also realize that as we present these favorite lessons, we are modeling for students our own passion for the material. Even if they don't understand or remember everything, we hope they'll catch our excitement about ideas.

On a more pragmatic level, some teacher-directed lessons are still necessary because most teachers work within a mandated curriculum. They are responsible for students learning (or at least briefly remembering) many required elements of an official syllabus of content. We've argued earlier that some ingredients of the typical school curriculum can be learned incidentally, amid innovative, student-centered techniques. For example, kids who have regular writing workshops will acquire many English spelling and editing skills even though they are not taught them directly in teacher presentations or workbook drills. However, the average school curriculum still contains much other material which isn't learned collaterally through applied experience in the subject. In language arts, for example, all the writing workshops in the world will not teach students the names of the parts of speech. If kids and teachers are to be held accountable for learning about gerunds, subordinate clauses, and the like, the teacher will probably have to take the initiative to conduct such lessons.

Thirdly, as learners and as people, teachers deserve to feel safe and comfortable in school, too. They need the security of doing something familiar for some of the day: we cannot expect teachers who have been trained and socialized to think of teaching as presenting to suddenly cast aside that whole model for the entire six-hour day. The fact is that teachers *will* continue to present whole-class lessons; the point is for them to get better at it and at the same time start doing it less.

Ways to Improve Teacher-Directed Lessons

Because good teachers have been creating dramatic and effective individual performances for years, we'll just mention a few valuable examples here. One presentational activity that is especially powerful, but mistakenly neglected above the primary grades, is **reading aloud**. Great writers in every field and subject have hypnotized readers for as long as there has been print. Many of their writings were the very sources that inspired some teachers to enter the profession in the first place. So reading great writing aloud can be one of the most captivating and motivating presentational techniques a teacher can use. Quality children's literature new and old, primary source documents, insightful historical essays, passionate political arguments, biographical and autobiographical accounts of key discoveries in math and science—all are capable of mesmerizing children, adolescents, and adults and drawing them into real engagement with the subject matter. National recommendations on teaching reading advise plenty of reading aloud by the teacher at all levels.

Another strategic way to think about direct teaching is the **mini-lesson**—a very brief explanation or demonstration aimed to help students with a skill or concept about which the teacher has observed many students having difficulties, at a time when they actually need it. For example, children who are writing plays may need to understand quotation marks and paragraphing to separate characters' speeches from each other and from stage directions.

Mini-lessons can be given to a whole class before, during, or after more active, experiential activities—or offered to small, selected groups of students as others continue their work. Indeed, one of the fundamental insights of mini-lessons is that teachers' old-style presentations—we might call them maxi-lessons—often were simply too long and too overloaded to be effective. We now find that teachers can convey key content more effectively when they are very selective and provide quicker, smaller bites. Mini-lessons are an integral feature of the workshop classroom; teachers can draw out small groups of students who are struggling with a particular skill or topic, sit them at a table in the back of the room, and give a compact, focused five or six-minute lesson—and send them directly back to work, where they will be immediately applying the concepts taught. This mini-lesson strategy obviously requires that the teacher be a sharp observer—but handily, the workshop structure itself provides the teacher with the time and the responsibility to monitor students' work closely through conferences and constant observation.

Demonstrations are a closely allied technique, and they are useful in plenty of situations beyond the science lab. A good writing teacher may revise a piece of his own work before the eyes of the whole class, using an overhead projector. Kids can ask questions about his choices as he works. Most students have never watched a competent adult at work on a piece of writing and all too often their only visual image of the process is from some melodramatic movie in which a struggling poet rips pages out of a typewriter, crumples them, and shoots them despondently toward the waste basket. Teachers can profitably demonstrate how they go about brainstorming a new writing topic or choosing an appropriate book to read, how they figure out the meaning of a new word from context clues, or mentally sort through likely possibilities while working on a geometry proof.

In truly interactive classrooms, many teacher presentations become hybrids. Teachers invite questions and suggestions as the session proceeds. Students know their ideas are valued and they don't hesitate to take part. Teachers decide to offer an explanation to just the half or third of the class who need it, while others who don't can continue with more appropriate activities.

When we talk about the balancing between teacher-directed and student-centered activities, it always boils down to how *time* is spent. Teachers must design days, weeks, years that provide kids a rich alternation between different configurations, groupings, and activities. The schedule must be predictable so students can prepare, mentally and even unconsciously, for what is coming up. This predictability is especially important for poor children who may lack continuity elsewhere in their life. The balance in a day's or week's activities must also include things that make teachers reasonably comfortable, and yet teachers need to be growing and challenging themselves, too. In the end, school is more satisfying when everyone is growing and stretching themselves every day.

To work toward the goal of Best Practice, to embody the changes recommended in the curriculum reports we have cited, most teachers need to enrich their classroom repertoire in two directions: 1) setting aside time and building classroom structures that support more *student-directed activity*, using the eight key structures outlined in the past few pages; and 2) making their *teacher-directed* activities both less predominant and more effective. We've seen that when teachers learn practical strategies to manage both of these modes of instruction, the curricular improvements they desire begin to take hold.

Works Cited

Atwell, Nancie. 1987. *In The Middle: Writing, Reading, and Learning with Adolescents*. Portsmouth, NH: Boynton/Cook.

Calkins, Lucy. 1986. *The Art of Teaching Writing*. Portsmouth, NH: Heinemann Educational Books.

Fulwiler, Toby. 1987. *The Journal Book*. Portsmouth, NH: Heinemann Educational Books.

Glasser, Willam. 1990. *The Quality School*. New York: Harper.

Graves, Donald. 1983. *Writing: Teachers and Children at Work.*. Portsmouth, NH: Heinemann Educational Books.

Johnson, David W., Roger T. Johnson, Edythe Holubec, and Patricia Roy. 1984. *Circles of Learning: Cooperation in the Classroom*. Alexandria, VA: Association for Supervision and Curriculum Development.

Joyce, Bruce and Marsha Weil. 1986. *Models of Teaching*. Englewood Cliffs, NJ: Prentice-Hall.

Rief, Linda. 1992. *Seeking Diversity: Language Arts with Adolescents.*. Portsmouth, NH: Heinemann Educational Books.

Romano, Tom. 1987. *Clearing the Way: Working with Teenage Writers*. Portsmouth, NH: Heinemann Educational Books.

Slavin, Robert, Sharon Schlomo, Karen Spencer, Clark Webb, and Robert Schmuck. 1985. *Learning to Cooperate, Cooperating to Learn*. New York: Plenum Press.

8

Making the Transition

Jan calls Steve one night to talk. She's been teaching many years, but suddenly it's all new. "You won't believe what's happening in my classroom! Since the books I ordered didn't arrive on time, I started with something else. We interviewed each other, just like you had always been telling me we could. It was unbelievable. We told stories about ourselves and our families, and everyone loved it. When the book did arrive, I couldn't even *pretend* I knew any more than the students did, since it was just published and I hadn't had a chance to read it myself. So we're reading and talking over each chapter together, instead of my telling them what they're supposed to get from it. They're thinking about it a lot more that way. We're trying out those notebooks Lucy Calkins said would work so well. The other day, one of the students started crying, and the rest of us just had to comfort her. Everything seems to really matter in that room."

Jan had been reading and working on a more student-centered, Whole Language curriculum for a long time. She'd been comparing ideas with Steve, and he'd appreciated her basic caring for her students and her openness to good teaching ideas. He had visited her class, modeled a few strategies, and suggested others. But he'd also wondered why the process she talked about wasn't as fully enacted as it might be, in her own teaching. Now suddenly she was ready to take some risks when the opportunity presented itself, and to help her students do so, too. For Steve, it had been difficult to be patient, to accept the best in Jan and not press too quickly for her to do more. He could tell in discussions when he'd gone too far, when the possibilities didn't connect with her own thoughts, or put her on the defensive. Now, the waiting paid off, and Jan had made her discovery on her own. She also knew Steve had been waiting. "You've probably been doing this stuff all along, haven't you?" she remarked sheepishly.

Why Change Is Difficult

Teachers, students, parents, and principals must go through many learning steps to make new approaches work. They need time and positive support

161

as they grow. They need organizational structures and relationships that provide this support. And they have many questions that must be respected: *"What about the math facts?" "Can children really help each other and collaborate in small groups?" "How do we evaluate children's progress with this kind of teaching?"* If change is forced on them, not only will they rebel, but the act of force will contradict the very spirit of the change. The educational strategies described in this book are all based on helping children make their own choices, ask their own questions, and become invested in their own learning. *Forcing* teachers to adopt a new pedagogy with this approach, but without teachers' ownership, is indeed a disturbing contradiction. People always recognize this kind of discord at some deep level, even when they're not conscious of it, and resent its hypocrisy.

Many other complexities make educational change a tricky business. Much has been written about how the "culture" in a school building—as in most complex organizations—can support or discourage the kind of change Jan experienced. Sociological studies of teachers, such as Dan Lortie's *Schoolteacher* (1972), reveal how they spend most of their careers in cellular classrooms, isolated from one another and from administrators. The trial-by-fire initiation into teaching, the lack of time for interchange among staff, the sense of being "evaluated" rather than helped to develop—all lead teachers toward a protective isolation and defensiveness. Principals have the authority to mandate classroom actions, but their power to reward and punish can undermine the chance to nurture and coach. A principal's suggestions can easily appear to be critical, or teachers can feel threatened when a colleague tries something new: "Does this mean they think *my* way is old fashioned? Will they become obnoxious with missionary zeal and try to force it on me?" This is not meant as an indictment. Each person becomes caught up in this system and is hard put to change without great effort and practice at new kinds of communication.

Mass testing is a typically problematic school structure that reinforces the status quo. Much recent school reform has mandated tests to supposedly enforce standards for student performance and pressure teachers to do a better job. However, as any good teacher will testify, tests force teachers to drill students for the tests, which is not the same as really *doing* science, or history, or writing. When teachers are held accountable purely for students' scores, then the most engaging questions kids bring up spontaneously—"teachable moments"—become annoyances. Even the news media have begun to critique standardized tests that simply don't, *and cannot,* test the learning we know is most important. Indeed, the public scrutiny of standardized testing reached a new level with the January 1990 cover story in *Newsweek* titled, "Not as Easy as A, B, C." Many educators have read the articles and heard the research, but are reluctant to abandon the tests because of political pressures: "Isn't this accountability what the community demands? Will they understand if we try to explain that it's more complicated?"

Or consider textbooks. They've gotten their share of casual bashing, but sit on a district committee deciding whether to purchase a new volume or to abandon textbooks in favor of real literature or real science inquiry. Some committee members will recognize that most publishers embrace new approaches only as camouflage for the same old ineffective strategies. However, the realists on the panel may ask, "What about the traditional teachers unprepared to go without a book?" Perhaps they know the district won't spend enough money on staff development to support the textless teachers. Perhaps they fear a backlash from more traditional teachers or administrators who are just waiting to capitalize on any disorganization that comes with change. Maybe the committee is even sensitive about forcing change on teachers involuntarily. But they also know that when they do choose a book, it will become one more limit which only the more adventuresome teachers will be willing to overcome. What should they do?

Achieving real change in the interlocking structure of a school district is a complex process, not readily accomplished by a few pronouncements, or fancy new curriculum plans. Systemic change seems like the hardest of all tasks in education. We're up against all the roadblocks of organizational and psychological inertia, and we're trying to use roadmaps that are newer, less familiar, and that don't always show us the entrance ramps or tell us where to watch out for potholes or falling rock.

The Key: Teacher Empowerment

At least we've begun to learn from past experience. In many failed efforts such as "new math," teachers were the last to hear of the experiment, and the only change they were asked to make was in "content." An official goal of "new math" was for kids to become excited about mathematics and to develop understanding that would entice further learning, rather than create blockages and dislike of the subject. However, as critics pointed out, in many locations teachers were introduced to the program only at a final training and "delivery" stage. This left them uncommitted, feeling inadequate about the concepts, and they proceeded to deliver the material in a self-defeating way to children—and ultimately nothing changed. To bring true reform to learning, we must involve teachers from the beginning, not just hand them new curriculum as a last step.

Teachers need to be involved in decision-making and to re-create their own understandings of how learning can work for children. There are a host of reasons why this ownership is vital, and plenty of literature, including books about change in the corporate business world, to explain them. Why is it so crucial for teachers to "buy in" in order for change to take root?

1. The teacher working with students daily knows best what the specific needs, conditions, and obstacles are.

2. No matter what changes are prescribed from the outside, their success in the classroom depends on teachers' own choices and interpretations as they move through the school day. So if choice isn't involved sooner, it will inevitably come later, with less likelihood of positive commitment.

3. The most important changes needed in education are not superficial, but involve the teacher's deeply held beliefs, expectations, and relationships.

4. Many key changes involve giving responsibility and ownership to children, which will be undermined if ownership is not there for teachers.

The centrality of teachers' role in decision-making is gradually being recognized by those researching and experimenting with school change. Ann Lieberman and Lynn Miller (1988, 1990) have written strong statements about collaborative leadership that redefines the relationship between teachers and principals. Henry Levin's (1988) "Accelerated Schools" concept features school-based governance with input from all parties—teachers, students, parents, administrators—and uses the strengths of the particular teachers who work in a building. John Goodlad (1988) describes the need for faculty dialogue and organizational "health" if schools are to escape from passive, uninspired classroom experience.

Considering the many school reform experiments now taking place, we can't prescribe one right structure, or one best starting point. But perhaps, based on our own work with many schools large and small, urban, suburban, and rural, we can identify some ingredients for promoting change. Because the teacher is in a pivotal but too often neglected position, we shall focus on what can help a teacher improve instruction; but through this lens we can also see what is needed in the broader school setting.

How One Teacher Changed

To help us think about what strategies will encourage the kinds of teaching and learning described in this book, and to keep from getting discouraged by the many obstacles, here's one success story in detail. This tale is not over yet; many things aren't settled or solved. But it's a story of real hope and excitement.

Delois Strickland teaches second-grade in an inner-city building with housing projects on one side and empty lots on the other, left from apartments burned or razed twenty-five years ago. She's no charismatic heroine of some pious movie about the valiant inner-city miracle worker who triumphs over all. She's also not the long-suffering, ineffectual martyr, the well-meaning but hopeless urban educator pictured by Tracy Kidder in *Among Schoolchildren*. Lois is quiet, calm, loves children, and desires continually to improve her teaching. She's not burning herself out with overwork, but enjoys her profession. Like most good teachers, Lois can do at least three things at once. When a visitor joins her at lunchtime, she sits at her desk and chats uninterrupted while simultaneously preparing materials for an afternoon activity, receiving a steady flow of office messengers, and coping with the kids who insist on hanging around.

Lois attended a thirty-hour workshop on teaching writing one fall and experienced many new possibilities. The teachers in the workshop interviewed one another and compiled a book of their portraits. They wrote about significant personal moments and shared autobiographical writing in small groups. They talked about journals where children could write what they chose without fear of being judged. They explored strategies for small group work, practiced teacher-student conferences, debated about when grammar work obstructs children's writing and when it's more effective. They shared food, gossip, disagreements, frustrations, laughs, hopes. After eight weeks, they went off to apply what they had learned.

Lois tentatively started putting one or two new ideas to work. Her actions were courageous, considering the conservative tone in the building. Her first experiment was with children's journals. Lois understood that these special writings belonged to the children and were not to be graded. Her seven-year-old inner-city kids enjoyed the writing, were prolific and proud of their work, but there never seemed to be enough time in the day to fit journal writing in. A few enthusiastic weeks passed, and then she began to feel pressure to produce the formal essays the principal periodically collected from every class. Lois felt it was possible to do writing for only two forty-five-minute periods per week at most, so after an initial burst of success, the journals languished on a shelf under the windows.

Lois's next step was to introduce an interviewing activity like the one teachers had enjoyed in the workshop. The children were to interview one another and write portraits to be accompanied by photographs and hung on the bulletin boards. At this point a grant project staffer asked if he could visit as a participant observer. His main contribution at first was simply to encourage Lois and to help individual kids as they worked. Lois was very organized, helping the children brainstorm questions to ask one another and copying the list so everyone could reconnect after a two or three-day interruption. The children followed the question list slavishly — but they were writing and having a grand time.

Lois wanted these papers to look good, particularly because other teachers in the building were watching her conduct what seemed to them a fairly radical experiment. She therefore decided to try individual conferences to help the children revise and polish their interviews. These second-grade interviewers had naturally tended to write down literal first-person answers the interviewees gave to their questions:

I like ice cream.

I have two sisters.

I will go to college.

At first, Lois patiently explained to each child how to restate such sentences in the form, "Tyree likes ice cream." The consultant realized that the kids had conflicting ideas about *whose* paper it was. Was the interviewer an author or a transcriber?—an understandable, in fact a very thoughtful, confusion for second-graders. Meanwhile, kids waited impatiently in line to have their paper "checked," or fiddled in their seats if Lois shooed the line away. Finally, Lois asked the consultant to intervene more actively to conduct a brief whole-class lesson on how to translate statements into indirect quotations. He also set up a conferencing sign-up list on the chalkboard and urged children to work on their journals if they were waiting for a conference.

Lois welcomed these refinements. Still, her conferences consisted essentially of proofreading, and so the mood was dogged—kids would go back to their seats to try again and return once more to the teacher, hoping for deliverance. The papers were gradually cleaned up, but the tedious work spread out over several weeks and seemed to involve little learning. Wouldn't it be better to have less revising and get on to some new writing topics and new skills? But the observer let this be. Perhaps, he thought, Lois had enough new ideas to digest for one year. Perhaps with the other teachers and the principal looking over her shoulder, this was as far as she could go right now.

Lois learned other valuable lessons that spring. Kids began very naturally to help one another. Lois tried a persuasive writing task and most children chose to write letters to their parents pleading for new bikes or other toys. Pieces grew longer. Slower children made surprising advances. Writing seemed to be a positive, enjoyable activity. But how much, the observer wondered, did this depend on having a regular visitor in the room, an extra hand to provide lots of individual help? The children were hungry for attention and could easily have benefitted from twice as much. His presence was a luxury most classrooms couldn't afford.

The next fall, Lois requested help from another outsider, a consultant from a literacy program at Chicago's Erikson Institute who was already working in the building. She had heard that this consultant could help her reorganize and better use the materials in her classroom. By winter, the whole room looked different. On one side next to the windows was a large rug where small groups of children could be found quietly playing math games. Many new children's books occupied one set of shelves. The writing center desks were cleared of old dust-gathering projects and restored to active use. Kids were industriously working on various tasks in small clusters everywhere. "My room used to be so disorganized that my children could never use what we had," Lois explained.

The consultant convinced her to bring in her own children's books, which were much more interesting than the hand-me-downs crowding the shelves. The consultant argued that if Lois were clear about rules and responsibilities, the children would treat the books with respect. A mobile now hanging next to the bookshelves stated on its dangling parts the rules about caring for books. Children took turns serving as classroom librarian. "They're reading much more and enjoying it more," Lois reported, "And they take good care of these books."

The consultant also modeled good teacher-student conferences. Lois handed her returning visitor an article about using conferences to help children take responsibility for writing instead of simply executing the teacher's corrections. "You ought to have teachers read this in your workshops," she urged. The visitor smiled, knowing the very same ideas had been suggested in last year's sessions. Clearly, Lois wasn't ready to absorb those ideas then, but had made them her own now. She had even added the skillful variation of conducting conferences with groups of four or five children looking on, so they could learn more. The visitor asked, with a tinge of guilt, whether it would have been helpful to provide more forceful modeling the previous year. "No," she said. "I needed to feel my way. I was just starting, then."

The children are writing far more now—four to five days per week. "If you only write once a week you don't really get into it," Lois says. "But if you enjoy it as a teacher, you'll do it more." Old restrictions and pressures simply don't stop her. Still another improvement: the teacher's aide in the room is now involved. Last year, the aide usually sat off to the side, doing busy work and occasionally scolding an overactive child. Lois and the Erikson consultant had arranged for the aide to get some training, and now she too was helping with conferences. Lois felt the aides should be included in all workshops for city teachers.

Where is Lois headed next? She'll use interviewing at the beginning of the year, instead of waiting until winter. "That way, they'll get to know one another better right at the start," she explained—a good refinement, making the assignment more purposeful and natural. She wants to start group conferences earlier, too, because these build children's excitement about one another's writing. The logistics of journals need to be handled better. Kids spend too much time stapling paper into the folders, and so she plans to purchase spiral notebooks. Every little physical adjustment means better use of time. Reading remains a frustration. The children read more, enjoy it more, and even do better on practice tests. But they still fall apart on the official sub-skills-oriented reading tests. "I guess I'm not a miracle-worker," Lois sighs.

The visitor asks one last question: When will Lois join with the Writing Project as a leader so she can share her struggles and discoveries with colleagues from around the city? She says she isn't ready yet. She wants to learn more and polish what she's doing in the classroom. But a few years down the road . . .

What Helps a Teacher?

What are some conditions that facilitate the kind of evolution we've seen in Lois Strickland's teaching, and that help change spread to teachers throughout a school system? At first Lois was intimidated by pressures from standardized tests and administrators. Later, she felt freer to follow her own judgment. How do we engender ownership and initiative in a setting that emphasizes authority? In working with schools and teachers, we've found that the following conditions and approaches help teachers grow and change. We'll describe them briefly, and then return to each one to list specific ways to turn it into a reality. The first three categories focus on the external structural conditions in the school, and the second three on the internal consciousness of individual teachers, though of course each aspect, internal and external, is really a manifestation of the other.

1) **Teachers need regular time together**—to talk, encourage, compare ideas, trouble-shoot when things don't go as expected, and organize cooperation between classrooms. Unlike other professions, where planning meetings, "staffings," and conferences at fancy resorts, are regular activities, teaching as it is organized in this country has shockingly little room for professional conversation. And since teachers' work is carried out almost entirely out of contact with colleagues, there's little daily time for informal exchange. Parents and community members who, at their workplaces, spend many hours in cooperative tasks, in department and committee meetings, don't realize how little of this connectedness teachers enjoy.

Achieving real instructional change calls for more than brief "inoculation" sessions for teachers once or twice a year. Deep inquiry into reading or math or science in an inservice program requires time to build group trust, experience model activities, discuss, disagree, re-think, and work out classroom applications. Teachers new to process approaches usually try one thing at a time and gain confidence before moving on to another, so change requires several school years. It takes time to extend a new concept to all of one's teaching.

2) Especially because teaching involves so much day-to-day isolation from fellow professionals, it's important that **teacher change efforts be collaborative, social experiences.** Collaborative work among teachers on tasks that have concrete results in classrooms builds supportive bonds. However, collaboration does not have to mean conformity. Nor does real teacher leadership and decision-making mean that a few senior teachers are virtually promoted to become new supervisors. Rather, it's important to find a complementary role for each of the different abilities and interests in a group of teachers.

3) When Lois Strickland was trying out an interviewing activity with her second-graders, many worked diligently, but some grew noisy as she circulated to help individuals and pairs. What would the principal think if she walked by at that transitional moment? And with upcoming standardized tests, was it really acceptable to take so much time for writing while the other teachers were drilling their students for the big tests? Last year's scores were discouraging, and the stakes are high. Lois needs to know where her principal stands.

This requirement may seem simple and obvious. Yet, it really asserts two seemingly contradictory things at once—that is, **significant change needs leadership from the top, even *while* the support itself emphasizes teachers decision-making and initiative.** To be realistic, we are trying to introduce democratic and collaborative elements in organizations that will remain pyramidal. We can try to alter the underlying style of operation in a school, but at base we are working with contradictions. And so the best staff development effort in the world can fail if school leaders do not consistently support the changes.

Perhaps this need for administrative support is especially strong in urban schools, where chaotic conditions make it extra difficult for a teacher to carry out classroom changes. When the classroom population turns over because families are regularly forced to move, when books and materials don't arrive for months because of bureaucratic delays, when distant administrative offices announce sudden new requirements for testing or reporting every day—teachers need protection and help so they can feel safe to experiment. In this situation, a strong, encouraging principal who knows curriculum, welcomes innovation, and believes in teachers, and who does not impose sudden arbitrary requirements, is vital.

4) If teachers are to take more decision-making roles, we need to **support and strengthen teachers' latent professionalism.** Such attitudes include:

- viewing teaching approaches not just as private preferences or personality traits, but as strategies to be compared, analyzed, and then adapted to one's own style
- regarding a school staff more as a community and less as a hierarchy of leaders and led, senior people and junior, etc.
- seeking improvement not because we are "deficient," but because in our work there's always more to learn, and that's what keeps us fresh and energized for our kids

Most teachers originally entered the profession with enthusiasm and a desire to do something of value with their lives, and they are regularly reminded of that desire by the children sitting in front of them. So the internal impetus toward more professional attitudes is usually there, waiting to be re-ignited.

5) In our observation, both the strengthening of professional commitment and the initiation of new classroom strategies is most effectively initiated by inservice programs **using concrete experiential activities**, rather than starting with educational philosophy or research data. In the chapters on each of the curriculum areas, we outlined how experts in every field have found that children's learning must be experiential and authentic, reflective and constructivist. Teachers need these ingredients just like kids do. Powerful experiential activities are not merely "demonstrations;" they immerse participants in fresh alternatives instead of just initiating debate about them.

To say that experiential learning is important for teachers is actually a controversial assertion. Much of the literature about school change comes from university academics, whose own careers have required them to stress theory and research. But classroom teachers' mental constructs, though often implicit and unconscious, must stand up to the rigorous test of everyday application. And so teachers especially need to directly experience models for what is possible in the classroom, to end the isolation that cuts them off from alternatives, and to help them work out the many details that go into a new classroom approach.

6) After experiencing new classroom strategies, **teachers need to reflect, to analyze, to compare—to build knowledge and theoretical understanding**. Of course, within book covers the knowledge has been there for years—shelves full of reports about classrooms that work, and research about what doesn't. However, because academic research is so often used in the educational world to prove one person's status higher than another's, rather than to really improve schools, teachers often view "theory" with well-justified suspicion. This is just one more reason why teachers appreciate experiential activity first, as an inductive approach to theory. Yet when a teacher's natural curiosity has been tapped and when

she is ready to digest and use the ideas, it's hard to stop her. Lois Strickland showed *us* the article about conferencing, because the information became meaningful to her.

Getting Down to Business

Following are some ways in which schools and reform programs have created conditions to help teachers improve children's learning. Because schools are such complicated social structures, and because many of the elements are extensive and intricate, we can only sketch some of the issues that must be addressed to make programs succeed. Those interested in a particular program will want to consult the more detailed literature on it. We'll describe these efforts according to the six needs outlined above, that teachers have as they attempt to change.

1. Time to Explore and Plan

Make a "concerns" list with any group of teachers, and what invariably comes at the top? Time. Teachers need significant chunks of time with their peers if they are to plan serious changes in curriculum or school structure. The school system that fails to provide this time sends a clear signal that teacher participation is not really important. The few days before school begins in August are hectic with preparation, not a good time for reflection. Two or three inservice days scattered through the year, even on the same topic, amount to only a gesture. Brief before-school meetings do not permit concentration. More extended workshops are often held during the summer or after school hours when teachers must fight weariness after the day's work.

Find time creatively. In several buildings in Chicago, the staff has restructured the school day. Children arrive fifteen minutes earlier to school each day, and are then dismissed 1 1/4 hour early one afternoon a week, to gain cooperative work time for teachers. It works out that kids and teachers still spend the same total amount time in school as before. In another school, the PTA parents—totally illegally—cover classes one half-day each week so teachers can meet in curriculum workshops.

Another part of coping is finding funds to pay for extra committee work, consultants, or after-school inservice time. While schools everywhere are always short of cash, it's surprising how much money can be available if decision-makers are clear about priorities. In Chicago Public Schools, for example, as much as twenty-five percent of a school's budget is actually discretionary. While there are other legitimate needs to be met in each building, devoting some funds to pay for teacher planning time is certainly possible.

Take time for the long view. Finding time means planning—easy to say, not always in evidence. Making "science" this year's theme for two inservice days doesn't do the job. The essential steps:

- organizing to study an issue
- conducting a needs assessment, and finding internal or outside help
- building interest
- providing in-depth workshops
- identifying and training teacher-leaders
- sharing, through follow-up sessions and informal peer support
- repeating the inservice and follow-up cycle to gradually spread the new approaches to more teachers
- revision of formal structures (report cards, for example) to support the changes
- continuing support of teacher-leaders

All this can take three to five years in a school or district. But if it includes teachers in the decision-making, it makes change broad and deep.

Taking time, in the long-range sense of coming to new realizations, sometimes means having patience. This is hard. A school may not be ready for change, perhaps because not enough teachers really seek it or the administration is ambivalent. An enthusiastic advocate can burn out in frustration, and needs to know when it is better—at least temporarily—to focus on her or his own classroom and share ideas just with a few sympathetic friends. The effort to change ought not destroy the people initiating it. And sometimes it pays to wait. Many a principal or department chair has been known to come back a year or two later and ask blithely for help—because the problem, of course, hadn't really gone away.

2. Collaboration and Peer Leadership

It's easy to forget what social creatures we are, or how discouraging it is to be a lone risk-taker. Most people would rather go along, or at least keep their differences quiet rather than bear the group's disapproval. The "far-out" character who advertises his stance gets labeled, making it easy to protect the system from his successes—"Oh well, that's Wayne. He's good, but he's crazy."

The school culture can reinforce isolation as the accepted way to get along. Surveys of teachers show that seeking a colleague's help with classroom problems is associated with fear of adverse job evaluation, and thus viewed with suspicion. Conversely, taking leadership seems like joining with, or seeking favor from, the boss. Thus, while many schools are attempting some form of faculty collaboration such as mentoring or peer coaching, the effort must be approached thoughtfully or it will break down.

Be sensitive to organizational details. Mentoring offers a good case study of complexities and pitfalls. A recent gathering of high school department chairpersons discussed the following realities: 1) Time (again!): Unless mentor and protégé have matching schedules, it is difficult for the two to get together. One chairperson coped by placing the new teacher in a room next to the mentor, so brief informal exchanges could occur. Teachers report that much gets said between neighbors during passing periods. 2) Arbitrary pairings: Personalities, styles, and needs differ. Some chairpersons let protégés make their own choice of mentors, after large-group get-acquainted sessions. Some realized that designating someone as a mentor gave the appearance of favoritism, engendering jealousy among others in the department. One solution was to plan the mentoring program collaboratively with the whole department. 3) Evaluation: In some locations, mentors are required to conduct evaluations of their protégés. This undermines the entire program, since the new teachers are motivated to conceal, rather than share, the problems they encounter. Just as it requires thoughtful structure to make the classroom more interactive, so it does for a school faculty.

Effective collaboration depends on the whole school culture, not just an isolated program. Comparisons of schools where peer coaching was tried showed that it was most positively viewed in the buildings where a rich variety of regular exchange activities took place (Judith Little, 1988). Exchange can occur at a number of levels:

- one-on-one interchange for growth and improving classroom strategies
- wider communication and planning within departments or grade levels
- major one-time initiatives at the building or district level
- formal instructional leadership roles, taken by a few, or shared widely

Any of these can provide a starting place, but a key to success is using each to support the others.

Allow for differences. Once teachers become more active, talk isn't automatically productive. Committees can bog down and factions wrangle. The problem is how to keep innovation going *without* alienating the more traditional teachers and turning a building into a battleground.

One way to ameliorate this is to avoid absolute mandates for an entire school or district, and to ask instead that each teacher choose which of several improvements to work on. Successful reform in places like East Harlem involve multiple teacher groups, each organizing their own smaller "schools." A number of Theodore Sizer's "Essential Schools" have started by setting up a voluntary new course cluster, or an experimental school-within-a-school. When each group learns to appreciate the strengths of the other, change is more likely for all.

Build mutual respect. This is so essential to collaborative change that it simply must take priority over installing "correct" practices. A powerful tool for building cohesion among staff members is the gradual sharing of individual histories and past learning experiences. This opens communication and builds understanding so that teachers can live with their natural, human disagreements. Group dynamics theorists call this "maintenance" activity, and assert that every effective group needs plenty of it. Good administrators and staff development leaders incorporate such self-disclosure, sharing, and story-telling into just about any meeting or inservice session. In a session on lump-sum budgeting, for example, a good workshop leader began by asking participants to pair up and describe to each other the gains and trade-offs resulting from a recent personal purchase. The talk led to principles for analyzing the budget process. But the one-to-one exchange was vitally important to build trust, to open channels, and to begin a conversation first.

3. Administrative Support for New Efforts

Any group working on change can be undermined and burn out as it encounters resistance and contradictions. We've watched districts adopt new tests encouraging rote teaching of isolated skills, just as a staff development committee introduced a higher-order thinking-skills approach to the same subject. It's no surprise when teachers feel whipsawed and planners get discouraged. They need to know that the school administration is behind the new ideas—and yet also that programs won't be rammed down their throats. Districts must choose a few areas to work on and create a long-range development plan, instead of jumping from one inservice fad to another every year—yet the teachers need choices and a strong role in drawing up that plan.

What are some steps that principals and other administrators can take to support teachers as they change? We'll sketch out three areas, though we know they overlap a good bit: A) the school culture—the context in which a change effort will take place; B) the principal's own actions as a guide and a model; and C) supporting collaborative teacher groups to work on the effort. Within all of these however, what matters most are the implicit messages of commitment, openness, and trust rather than the formal structures that the principal sets up. What this really adds up to is building a healthy, adult working community in an organization not well-designed for it.

Nurture a positive school culture. Because schools are such complex places, says school researcher Michael Fullan (1985), effective leaders cannot depend on just a few strategies, and instead need a broader "feel for the process." School administrators, he says, should learn from Hewlett Packard Corporation's very successful policy of "management by wandering around."

Fullan speaks of the need for "intense interaction and communication." A principal who practices listening, who doesn't react defensively or jump to conclusions when events occur, who seeks as much feedback as possible, will be able to gather information about how a new activity is going. Student achievement scores or surveys of classroom applications will never yield such information. One needs to discover the particular obstacles or supports at work, and it's hard to prescribe how to do this because the best information-gathering is informal. Yet involvement must also be balanced with autonomy and respect for the sanctity of instructional time. As one teacher explained to a researcher:

> An administrator can walk in and interrupt what I am doing with any cockamamie thing . . . He butts into my classroom with all sorts of nit-picky stuff. The message is clear. What I am doing is not important. The kids can pick this up. (Pfeifer, 1986)

Teacher evaluation by principals can especially influence change in the classroom for good or ill. Making the teacher evaluation process dialogical rather than just an awkward ritual, asking teachers to set goals for their own development and to write responses to the principal's comments, supporting experiment in which a teacher's performance may not be perfect the first time something is tried—all set the stage for change to flourish. Otherwise it can seem safer for a teacher to quietly undermine a new program, rather than risk seriously trying it. Susan Ohanian, long-time teacher and free-lance writer, has described the more unproductive approach to supervision vividly:

> Once, while I presented for my supervisor a required lesson on *Julius Caesar*, a belligerent girl (whose attendance had improved dramatically since the appearance of self-chosen books) steadfastly read her novel. My department chairman leaned over and whispered to her, "Don't you think you should put that book away and pay attention to the teacher?" "Who the hell are you?" demanded the girl. "If she wants me to put it away, let her tell me." She went back to her book, and I continued my performance. Later, it was hard to convince my boss that the girl's devotion to that book was an excellent moment for me, much more valid than my gyrations . . . For 50 minutes twice a year, we all pretend that school is what everybody outside the classroom claims it should be. No student even asks to go to the bathroom. (Ohanian, 1985)

Be a guide and a model. Almost every national reform advocate calls for the principal to enunciate a vision of the school and of objectives embodied in any new effort, in order to help teachers set priorities. As long as he or she doesn't deny obstacles and realities, such rhetoric can help everyone maintain commitment. Henry Levin describes this role as "keeper of the dream." A principal's actions will be read very carefully as a school change initiative proceeds. The principal who protects the faculty from arbitrary district rules or bends a few to help a project along will prove her commitment.

The principal must model the attitudes the rest of the staff should adopt and learn new concepts along with everyone else. We know principals who regularly invite and answer letters from students throughout the school, to encourage written communication. They are also the ones who attend inservice workshops with their teachers and take the risk of writing, sharing, and joining in all the activities. And we know others who slip out of the meeting room as soon as the inservice session begins, or who sit off to the side conspicuously taking notes on participants' behavior, not the content of the session. The difference is not lost on the teachers.

A principal must be careful to avoid making contradictory demands, and, as much as possible, protect teachers from such demands from higher up. Otherwise teachers quickly become demoralized and avoid the new activity so as not to get caught in a bind. We observed one inner-city principal who wanted students to do more writing, but started marking grammar errors herself on papers collected from each classroom, and nagged teachers more and more about drilling kids to shore up the falling test scores from the previous year. After several months she was frustrated because teachers were assigning *less* writing, and were less committed than ever to trying new writing activities.

Support collaborative effort. Nothing breeds teacher cynicism faster than evidence that a committee task involves a pre-determined outcome. "Why should I take the time for this?" the teachers ask. In an authentic curriculum study, it's helpful, on the other hand, to provide constructive guidelines—clarifying the mission, choosing a reachable goal, requiring input from the rest of the staff, setting a reasonable timetable for a final report, and insuring that the results are put to use.

And then there are a myriad of unanticipated ways in which a good administrator must help. In one study of principals promoting an innovation, Hall and Hord (1984) report that nearly two thousand separate interventions were required of each of them during one school year. One of us sat in a principal's office recently and waited while she made phone calls around her building in immediate response to a teacher's report that the building engineer wouldn't unlock the room containing the laminating machine. It was frustrating for the visitor to wait as each stage of the drama played itself out, but the principal had her priorities right—and teachers were very committed to her and to the school.

We've seen a few promising school change projects come unglued because districts didn't make consistent changes in each of the interlocking elements that combine to create the school experience for kids. For example, if you want a true Whole Language literacy program, you *must* have lots of books in each classroom—period. If the budget for books isn't there, then whole language won't fully be there either, no matter what other ingredients may be in place.

So we've started using the following checklist in working with school districts and it seems to help. The point is simple: if you really want deep, lasting change to occur across classrooms, it has to be supported by parallel, congruent changes in each factor listed:

- curriculum
- instruction
- materials
- space
- scheduling
- grouping
- special education
- staff development
- faculty hiring
- evaluation/grading/report cards
- standardized testing—state assessment
- administrative leadership
- parent and community education
- board support
- budget

This may be a good place to also acknowledge some realities. It's fine to outline rational and revolutionary approaches to school improvement, but we are working in the real world, and we must start with what exists. Not every school system, administrator, or teacher is ready to face real issues or seek change. Therefore, some valuable efforts are initiated under the noses of unsupportive, autocratic—but fortunately often unwitting—people. It is important to help caring teachers do a more meaningful job *especially* when circumstances are difficult. More than once, grass-roots efforts have ultimately led to wider acceptance. We simply need to be honest about the scope of change likely under such conditions, and not burn out in the process.

4. Teachers' Attitudes—Professionalism and the Desire to Grow

Teachers' attitudes are crucial to whether in-depth curricular innovation succeeds or not. This is just one reason why change mandated from above is likely to bog down in the long run. In surveying many studies of school change, Michael Fullan concludes that narrowly defined innovations can be made to work with a top-down approach, but complex school-wide changes need deeper commitment. What are some practical ways to promote this commitment?

Provide incentives. Among teachers in the city of Chicago, continuing professional development was stunted until the Board of Education finally adopted pay incentives in line with those in suburban school districts. One might feel cynical about such motivation—but the fact is that Chicago teachers are now taking graduate courses and board-credit courses in record numbers. In a society where valued actions are materially rewarded, the lack of reward sends a negative signal. On the other hand, one particular district offered such unusually high pay for a summer program that some teachers showed up just for the money and sat in the back of the room reading the newspaper.

Look for the best in teachers. School systems, with their detailed curriculum guides, objectives, and standardized tests in each subject area, seem to expect very little initiative from teachers. Administrators or consultants who regard teachers as less than responsible can easily, unconsciously signal this, even when they're trying a more participatory approach—and so defensive responses continue. Truly changing the relationship means asking the teachers to set their own agenda at the beginning of a meeting or inservice session, asking for their analyses of problems in the school or in children's learning, and respecting the realities within their answers, even when we sometimes disagree with them.

When we visit schools we begin by asking teachers to talk about their successes and their problems, instead of starting right in to lecture them about the best new way to approach teaching. We usually see faces change from glazed blankness to surprise, to engagement and pleasure. When asked, they have plenty to say about what is working and what the obstacles are. Again and again we observe that when workshops and inservice activities respect teachers—by offering them ownership and control, immersing them in new perspectives on their own teaching and learning abilities, and providing opportunities to express themselves honestly—many respond with great energy. Often, the moment this begins, teachers start thinking and acting more for themselves. Self-fulfilling prophesy was never more in evidence than here.

5. Concrete Experience of New Possibilities

The workshop leaders are meeting in a branch library with seventy-five teachers to introduce a writing/reading inservice program. After introductions, the teachers are asked to jot on a 4 x 6 card their own goals and concerns about teaching writing and connecting it with the reading program. In pairs they discuss what they've written, and only after that do the leaders begin to hear people's thoughts and record them on a master list on the overhead.

With the list fresh in mind, the group embarks on a reading-writing activity. One leader reads aloud the book *Wednesday Surprise* by Eve Bunting. It's a moving story about a child and her grandmother and learning to read. The other leader then guides the group through several rounds of "dialogue journal" writing. In a dialogue journal, partners each jot down thoughts about a topic, and then trade notebooks, responding to the ideas and reactions of the other—a legitimized kind of note-passing. With this particular book, the teachers invariably write about their own experiences with literacy—and illiteracy—in their families. People are involved and moved as volunteers read some of these aloud. Grudgingly, the teachers conclude their sharing, and then go on to discuss implications of the activity for their initial concerns, and uses the approach with their own students.

Build inservice around experiential activity. Of course it's important to talk about beliefs and educational theories, for even when unconsciously held, these guide teachers' actions. But direct talk is not always the most effective way. If schools are immensely complex places with innumerable factors influencing change, so are individual classrooms. Because they know this, teachers need in-depth experiential enactments to help them visualize how a new approach works.

These activities are far more than just the "demonstrations" talked about in some training or coaching programs. We are not just training teachers to use a new tool. Rather, the best activities provide a mirror in which teachers see themselves in new ways. They draw on teachers' prior knowledge and abilities, instead of implying deficiency, and help them construct a new approach of their own, rather than just imitating an instructor. They help people renew and enjoy their own learning, something that teachers desperately need. They provide space for teachers to reconceptualize what learning and teaching can be. Only then are people well equipped—enriched, heartened, drawn into a supportive group—and ready to reflect on the activities, to bring to the surface implicitly challenged beliefs about instruction and children's learning, and to reconsider and reconstruct these beliefs and revise their practices accordingly.

It's not easy to bring this kind of learning into school districts. Judith Little points out that schools are not really structured to influence actual teaching. Not only do teachers work out of sight of one another, but the observations carried out by principals or department chairs are infrequent and the depth of their conceptual exploration is usually severely limited. But with focused effort, experiential inquiry can be extended throughout the cycle of staff development and classroom application. Schools can be more demanding consumers of inservice education, inquiring whether the consultants who advocate more active learning for children use such strategies with teachers. Then, because we know that inquiry and even guided practice do not lead all teachers to use a new approach, schools can schedule follow-up classroom visits by facilitators, to observe, co-teach lessons, and meet with teachers who ask for help. Team-teaching, peer coaching, inquiry groups that study a new approach together and then try it out, are all structures that bring teachers into one another's classrooms and help them engage new ideas in practice.

6. New Knowledge

Approach theory authentically. Some academics consider teachers anti-intellectual, unresponsive to theory. But teachers remember their first year teaching, when all that theory seemed to evaporate under the pressures of the moment, since there was virtually no apprenticeship system to help make the connections. We've observed in many settings as teachers do or do not embrace new ideas, and we've tried to understand the causes. We've seen whole districts where few teachers pursue ideas any further than the talk in immediate workshop sessions. They come, let us entertain them, and go back to their classrooms to do what they've always done. We can only say these are often places where the administrations send out extremely mixed signals—for example, paying teachers handsomely to attend a summer workshop, but then discouraging individuals from organizing teacher-led groups that could keep the new program developing.

But we've also watched as a workshop leader unobtrusively leaves stacks of articles on a table at the end of an inservice session and then initiates discussion with individuals as they enter the room the following week. At first a few teachers read the pieces; then others grow curious, and ultimately the class organizes small-group "literature circles" to compare ideas about the articles they choose to read.

There are places—like the Oak Park schools, described shortly—where administrators encourage interested teacher-groups to explore on their own, read about a new approach, meet informally to discuss it, and try it out, critiquing and adjusting both the ideas and their practice. In some schools, one can find a rack with new literature on education, set up by the principal in the teacher's lounge—even better when the principal leaves Post-It notes with short comments on some of the articles, if for no other reason than to show that someone is really reading the stuff. Some schools spend money to buy copies of a key book for everyone who participated in a recent workshop on the subject.

As with Lois Strickland, the process is contagious. At first a teacher tries one or two new strategies, perhaps inspired more by a workshop activity than by any revolution in her thinking. But then, when it shows promise, she wants to know more, to extend the practice, and to trouble-shoot the parts that aren't working as well. Just as with children, when teachers rediscover their need for new thinking, and see a likelihood of results, their hunger for learning bursts forth, even if long-suppressed. But the best way to see how all the Lois Stricklands can be encouraged in a staff development program is to see a strong one at work. The story of one such district-wide program is told on the following pages.

EXEMPLARY PROGRAM
A Ten-Year District-Wide Staff Development Effort
School District 97
Oak Park, Illinois

Oak Park Elementary District 97 provides schooling in grades K-8 for the children of a suburb just on the western boundary of Chicago. Oak Park has a long-standing tradition as a very progressive community, with a wide social and ethnic mix in its population. The town has worked hard to keep neighborhoods integrated and to keep the schools strong. This doesn't mean it's been easy or automatic.

Oak Park began work on teaching writing in 1981 when the Director of Reading and Language Arts, Mary Schneider, was inspired at a national conference and approached teachers in one building to gather research and try a few new strategies for teaching writing. After several short presentations by visitors and positive recommendations from six Oak Park teachers who attended a longer workshop nearby, Schneider convinced her administration to involve the Illinois Writing Project. A total of 50 teachers participated in two thirty-hour Writing Project inservice workshops in the spring of 1983, and then Schneider and two outstanding teachers, Irene Bergman and Chris Davis, joined in further training at a three-week Writing Project summer leadership institute.

State Board of Education funds paid for two more workshops in 1983 and '84, and the superintendent gave support by freeing participant teachers from other obligations. A copy of one of the best books on the subject, Donald Graves' *Writing: Teachers and Children at Work*, was purchased for each participating teacher. The district revised its language arts curriculum to emphasize process approaches to teaching writing.

And Mary began meeting with groups of teachers in each building to help them implement ideas learned in the workshops.

This was the beginning. Schneider and the two teachers who attended the leadership institute began to offer thirty-hour workshops each semester and during the summer, and over the next few years reached over half the three hundred-member faculty in the district. Then teachers began asking for follow-up sessions. Everyone knew that some teachers were using the new approaches more than others. Some had great success. Some marched kids through the writing process in an artificial, lock-step way. Others were trying hard, but not every strategy worked, and it wasn't easy to figure out on one's own what was going wrong.

Not only did teachers have many unanswered questions, but newer, more powerful strategies for teaching writing continued developing around the country, and the teachers wanted to know about them. Knowledge in such a field is not static. Nationally, reading and writing experts had gained understanding of how their two areas interlocked, and teachers wanted to learn about the "whole language" approaches that combined both.

By 1989 the three leaders realized the task was more than they could handle without burning out, so they organized a larger leadership team. Two other teachers, Georgiann Schulte and Cathy Schroer, had been experimenting with heterogeneous grouping of students, using a "workshop"-style structure for students to pursue reading and writing. They had been meeting regularly with a group of teachers, and then offered a fifteen-hour inservice program on this topic. Another teacher, Mary Berg, led a group developing thematic literature units. Ellie Aldridge-Bell had attended a more recent IWP summer leadership institute. And so the leadership team coalesced around these committed and innovative professionals.

One goal of the team became further development of their own and others' leadership skills. Additional interested teachers were encouraged to join in order to acquire such skills. Newer members served as interns and partners with more experienced inservice leaders. The team has now become a more formal part of the district teacher development program, and has renamed itself the Whole Language Leadership Committee. Inservice courses are offered on "The Classroom Workshop Structure," "Mini-lessons and Writing: Is There a Teacher in This Room?", "Writing Across the Curriculum" for junior high teachers, "Whole Language Teaching," and "Teachers' Own Writing." A separate district committee is grappling with the language arts textbook question, and another will soon begin studying the thorny issue of standardized tests, which many agree undermine the efforts to change. And now, teacher-leadership groups are beginning to coalesce in other subject areas such as math, science, and multi-cultural education to meet together and co-ordinate their efforts. Thus, the process continues, and the goals and tasks widen. As the teachers continue to grow, they seek still more development, rather than concluding that they've now "done" their improving. Change is gradual in Oak Park, and there's much more to do. But the commitment is deep.

Works Cited

Brandt, Ron. 1988. On Changing Secondary Schools: A Conversation with Ted Sizer. *Educational Leadership* (February).

Comer, James P. 1980. *School Power*. New York, Free Press.

Fullan, Michael. 1985. Change Processes and Strategies at the Local Level. *Elementary School Journal* (January).

Goodlad, John L. 1988. Understanding Schools Is Basic to Improving Them. *National Forum of Applied Educational Research Journal*.

Hall, Gene and Shirley Hord. 1984. Analyzing What Change Facilitators Do. *Knowledge: Creation, Diffusion, Utilization*.

————. 1987. *Change in Schools: Facilitating the Process*. Albany, NY: State University of New York Press.

Haynes, Norris M., James P. Comer, and Muriel Hamilton-Lee. 1988. The School Development Program: A Model for School Improvement. *Journal of Negro Education*.

Kidder, Tracy. 1989. *Among School Children*. Boston, MA: Houghton Mifflin Co.

Levin, Henry M. 1988. *Accelerated Schools for At-Risk Students*. New Brunswick: Center for Policy Research in Education.

————. 1990. Accelerated Schools After Three Years. *Educational Leadership* (April).

Lieberman, Ann. 1988, Expanding the Leadership Team. *Educational Leadership* (February).

Lieberman, Ann and Lynne Miller. 1990. Restructuring Schools: What Matters and What Works. *Phi Delta Kappan* (June).

Little, Judith Warren. Assessing the Prospects for Teacher Leadership. *Building a Professional Culture in Schools*. Edited by Ann Lieberman. New York: Teachers College Press.

Lortie, Dan. 1972. *Schoolteacher*. Chicago, IL: University of Chicago Press.

Ohanian, Susan. 1985. Huffing and Puffing and Blowing Schools Excellent. *Phi Delta Kappan* (January).

Pfeifer, R. Scott. 1986. *Enabling Teacher Effectiveness*. Washington, D.C.: American Educational Research Association.

Sizer, Theodore. 1985. *Horace's Compromise: the Dilemma of the American High School*. Boston, MA: Houghton Mifflin Co.

9

But What About Evaluation, Test Scores, Tracking, Special Students, Classroom Management, Parents, and Other Concerns?

What about evaluation and grading?

In Chapter 7 and in the earlier subject-area chapters, we've outlined some promising practices in what is now being called "authentic assessment." Today, teachers are no longer satisfied to assess students' growth solely on the basis of classroom quizzes and standardized achievement tests, which tend to treat the curriculum as a pyramid of atomized subskills, and which often miss what kids can really do with coordinated, higher-order activities like writing, researching, experimenting, or problem solving. Instead, innovative teachers are increasingly using kidwatching, observational notes, interviews, questionnaires, checklists, student artifacts and work samples, performance assessment, student self-evaluation, evaluation conferences, portfolios, and other tools to get a better understanding of kids' learning and more clearly explain their progress.

Recently, there has been a burst of helpful literature on new forms of evaluation, providing several books worth of guidance on ways to better gauge, guide, and report students' learning. We won't attempt here to reiterate the ideas so carefully crafted by Jean Kerr Stenmark in *Mathematics Assessment* (1991), Bill Harp in *Assessment and Evaluation in Whole Language Classrooms* (1991), Pat Belanoff and Marcia Dickson in *Portfolios: Process and Product* (1991), Robert Tierney in *Portfolio Assessment in the Reading-Writing Classroom* (1991), Angela Jaggar and Trika Smith-Burke in *Observing the Language Learner* (1985), Ken and Yetta Goodman and Wendy Hood in *The Whole Language Evaluation Book* (1989). Special issues of major professional journals have also covered promising practices in assessment—including the February 1992 issue of *Social Education*, the April 1989 issue of *Educational Leadership*, and the May 1989 issue of *Phi Delta Kappan*. We might also direct the interested reader to Chapter 16 of our own previous book, *A Community of Writers* (1988), entitled "The English Teacher's Red Pen: History of an Obsession."

Still, we want to say a few words here about the general problem of evaluation in education and its relation to the movement we've called Best Practice. Very plainly, we think teachers and schools evaluate students badly, unfairly, and far too much. As we argued in *Community of Writers*, American schoolchildren, teachers, parents, taxpayers, politicians and policy-makers are downright obsessed with grades and tests. Everyone involved spends far more time worrying about test scores themselves than thinking up ways to increase student learning, which might actually raise achievement scores. Instead, we tinker with our measuring devices, planning and conducting more and more evaluations, tests, and exams. We are a country full of measurement-obsessed people who seem to believe that you can raise the temperature by improving your thermometer.

What's so bad about the way we evaluate kids in school? To begin with, the socio-economic function of evaluation in American education has always been problematic and unsavory. Grading and testing have historically been harnessed to the screening, sorting, and classifying of children into categories of "merit" or "intelligence." These certified categories of students are then allocated certain current or future rewards, such as school prizes, invitations to honors classes, admission to good colleges, or entry to high-paying careers. As scholars like Michael Katz (1968), Joel Spring (1972), Stephen Jay Gould (1981), and Alan Chase (1977) have convincingly shown over the past twenty-five years, this vaunted American meritocracy is largely a sham. School tests and grades are part of a system that merely camouflages the replication of the existing the social hierarchy: kids from wealthy, culturally mainstream homes are certified by schools as "deserving" rewards, while students from poor, culturally different homes are proven by tests and grades to "need" a vocational education, or to be "unable to benefit" from a college preparatory program.

Though this historical interpretation is uncomfortable to many teachers, its reality is undeniable. The school grading system has been abused, co-opted, and enlisted in the service of some shamefully undemocratic arrangements in our culture. Even today, after the wide distribution of work by social historians and the many exposés of standardized test bias, our two most famous educational exams—the Scholastic Aptitude Test and the American College Test—brazenly continue to show a near-perfect correlation between family income and score levels, and still deliver a huge score penalty for being African-American or Hispanic. Understanding this distasteful history, Best Practice teachers must avoid, through every means available to them, complicity in such undemocratic and retrograde uses of educational evaluation.

But even if we admit that educational evaluation has often been mis-used by the society at large, don't we use it more responsibly within the institution of school? Sadly, most teachers are still wedded to evaluation procedures that are ineffective, time-consuming, and hurtful to students. One example from the field of writing is particularly illustrative. Every-one is familiar with the deep-rooted school tradition called "intensive correction," where the teacher marks every error in every paper that every student ever writes. Indeed, in American schools this practice is generally considered to be *the* basic, standard treatment for responding to student writing. But George Hillocks' (1986) meta-analysis of research showed that such intensive correction is *completely useless*. Marking all the errors in a student paper is no more effective, in terms of future growth or improvement, than marking none of them. The only difference is the huge expenditure of teacher time and the student demoralization which accompany this practice.

This kind of inefficient and discouraging evaluation is all too preva-lent across the curriculum. Under pressure to "justify" grades with copi-ous scores and marks in their record books, teachers expend enormous energy feeding the grading machine—finding ways to quantify, measure, score, compute, and record assorted aspects of kids' behaviors. This futile expenditure of time should remind us that the main legitimate purpose of evaluation in education is to guide instruction. Anything we do to gather and interpret information about kids' learning should provide accurate, helpful input for nurturing children's further growth. If we are generating data to feed a fake meritocracy, or simply out of habit and tradition, we aren't doing valid educational evaluation.

Back in their pre-service Educational Psychology courses, every teacher learned the distinction between summative and formative evalu-ation. Formative evaluation is the basic, everyday kind of assessment which teachers continually do to understand students' growth and help them learn further; summative evaluation doesn't aim to nurture future learning, but merely quantifies what has been learned up to a given point, translating it into a score or symbol that allows students to be ranked against each other. Summative evaluation isn't actually educational; it is just a way of reporting periodically to outsiders about what has been stud-ied or learned.

One of the side effects of our over-emphasis on summative evaluation and standardized testing is that we simply evaluate kids' work too much. We have a norm of grading every piece of work that students ever attempt in any school subject, duly placing a carefully computed grade in the record book after each attempt. We don't even laugh at the absurdity of high school course grading systems with point totals ballooning into the thou-sands, pseudo-scientific schemes that leave the teacher who invented them pounding a calculator for days just to generate "accurate" grades at the end of each marking period. Indeed, in many classrooms the compulsion to evaluate every piece of student work actually becomes an instructional bottleneck, limiting the amount of student practice to a level that the teacher has time to grade. The sad irony here, of course, is that practice—unmonitored practice—is the main way in which humans learn almost every valuable activity in life, from piano-playing to roof-shingling. But in school, kids aren't allowed to practice anything without being evaluated (we can't let their errors take root!), and so we adjust, counterproductively, by having kids just read less, write less, and think less.

We grade and test and score kids far more than is needed to effectively guide instruction. In classrooms where teachers are constantly watching, talking, and working with kids, elaborate grading systems are unnecessary, redundant, and sometimes contradictory. As far as the demand for official grades and records is concerned, teachers can produce a perfectly adequate documentation of students' growth through the occasional sampling of their work, periodic observations, once-in-a-while examination of their products. Especially when records are backed up by a portfolio of students' actual work—the raw material upon which any grade ought to be based—there should be no problem in justifying a given grade. When teachers make this change, substituting descriptive evaluation for grading, they are essentially making a trade: They are swapping time previously spent on scoring, computing, recording, averaging, and justifying grades, and exchanging it for time to collect, save, discuss, and reflect upon kids' real work.

But for teachers to change evaluation procedures can be one of the trickiest elements of moving toward Best Practice. We have been concerned to see many well-meaning Whole Language teachers and aspiring Best Practice districts reinventing evaluation systems that are numbingly complex, that pit kids against each other, that devour teachers' time and goodwill, that cater to the public's hunger for official ranking of children, that promise little formative feedback, and that ultimately threaten to undermine progressive innovation. As we've said, the evaluation obsession runs deep in all of us, and there is always a terrible tendency to bring it back in some new form.

Teachers are very susceptible to the evaluation obsession themselves. When we do a workshop with teachers, we always begin by asking what concerns or topics they would like to discuss during the course. Evaluation is usually the first topic to be mentioned, and it *always* ends up being listed as the top priority of every group. Indeed, we've worked with more than one group of teachers who, given a completely free choice, would spend every single minute of any workshop or course on evaluation alone. To be fair, part of this obsession simply reflects the pressure that teachers feel from the public, taxpayers, the media, state assessments, and so forth. But it also reveals that teachers are, finally, just another group of Americans—and they have acquired the evaluation fixation just as deeply, and in much the same way, as any other citizens.

But let's return to the bright side. As teachers and schools move toward Best Practice, there is a clear mandate for new forms of assessment, evaluation, grading, and reporting student progress. Across subject fields, Best Practice in evaluation means:

- the purpose of most assessment is formative, not summative
- most evaluation is descriptive or narrative, not scored and numerical
- students are involved in record-keeping and in judging their own work
- teachers triangulate their assessments, looking at each child from several angles, by drawing on observation, conversation, artifacts, performances, etc.
- evaluation activities are part of instruction (such as in teacher-student conferences), rather than separate from it
- teachers spend a moderate amount of their time on evaluation and assessment, not allowing it to rule their professional lives or consume their instruction
- where possible, competitive grading systems are abolished or deemphasized
- parent education programs help community members to understand the value of new approaches—why, for example, a portfolio of work samples actually provides far better information about student growth than an "83" or a "B-."

But what about standardized test scores during the transition to new forms of assessment?

As the Whole Language/Integrated Curriculum/Best Practice movement grows, everyone wants to know if test scores will go up. Of course, after all we said earlier about evaluation, it's obvious that we think the current measures are exceedingly poor and that the redesign of educational testing is an urgent priority. But in the meantime, until new and better tests are in place, the question remains: Will results on the existing, customary measures show progress or decline as teachers implement Best Practice ideas? Mostly, the answer to this is encouraging. For years, collaborative education researchers have published studies confirming significant achievement gains in a wide range of content areas when classrooms were redesigned to include ample cooperative activity—one of the fundamental components of the Best Practice paradigm (Johnson & Johnson, 1991). Similarly, there is a twenty-year-old body of research on literature-based reading programs which shows standardized achievement score gains for students in Whole Language-style programs, not just in regular education but among students with ESL, special education, or disadvantaged backgrounds. (Tunnell and Jacobs, 1989).

However, we must be patient in waiting for further validation from educational research. It is still quite early in the development of this reform era, and much more research is still to come. Some of the most interesting and inspiring research is coming from teacher-researchers, who are simultaneously bringing Best Practice to their students and carefully tracking its impact. One of our favorite examples of this data comes from Carol Carlson, a junior high teacher in a Chicago suburb who monitored her team's implementation of a workshop-style classroom, as the kids started the program in seventh grade and continued through eighth. Below are Carol's descriptions of the kids and the program, just as she reported it, including standardized test scores for her students over the phase-in of the workshop.

"The Starblazers"

105 middle school students

Heterogeneously grouped

Lower-middle income community

20% Hispanic

Mainstreamed LD students included

Writing program = writing workshop, 45 minutes daily

Reading program = mixed workshop and guided, 45 minutes daily

Grades = once per term on portfolios, via conference + 10% for "daily Oral Language" exercises

CALIFORNIA ACHIEVEMENT TEST RESULTS

	Language Mechanics	Language Expression	Total Language
1990 Sixth	10.2	8.3	8.8
1991 Seventh	10.2	9.4	9.8
1992 Eighth	12.9	12.9	12.9

What we first notice in looking at this data is its "Lake Wobegon effect," the phenomenon that on most American standardized tests, all kids turn out to be "above average," even students from ordinary middle-class schools like Mannheim Junior High. But looking at these grade level scores relatively, they show exactly the kinds of changes one might expect when teachers move toward new, student-centered classroom structures. In 1991, the first year of implementation, expression rises as kids' fluency grows from increased writing practice time, choosing their own topics, regularly enjoying an audience, and so forth. Then, in the second year, as kids continue to write daily, constantly revising, editing, and publishing their work and consistently meeting with their teachers in conferences, the mechanics score rises along with another sizeable jump in expression.

As another check on her findings, Carol looked back at the last year she herself taught eighth graders through the old, teacher-centered model and came up with these figures:

	Language Mechanics	Language Expression	Total Language
1990B	10.7	9.9	10.3

All these findings gave Carol and her colleagues the boost of confidence they needed to stay with the workshop and move on to the next level of innovation. Though it wasn't needed in Carol's district, the research could also have been used to persuade administrators, parents, or board members that teachers' instructional choices were valid and valuable. Carol's research serves as a good reminder to teachers: if you want evidence that Best Practice can work for your kids, you needn't wait for university researchers or government agencies to provide the data you seek—you can do great, powerful research yourself.

What about tracking and ability grouping?

One of the signal contributions of recent educational research has been the explicit rejection of tracking and the affirmation of heterogeneous grouping. One of the most shameful and unnecessary practices in American schools has been the routine division of children into different classrooms or instructional groups on the basis of "ability." Indeed, one of the earliest common experiences of most American schoolchildren (which many remember clearly and painfully as adults) is being assigned to either the low, middle, or high reading group—sometimes disguised with cutesy and, to the children, entirely transparent, euphemistic names like "Bluebirds," "Robins," and "Owls." Thanks to researchers like Jeannie Oakes (1985) and Anne Wheelock (1992), we now have conclusive evidence that such ability grouping is academically *harmful* to kids labeled low and middle—their measured achievement is depressed when they are segregated by levels. The evidence of tracking's benefits for "high" kids is slight, ambiguous, and still under hot debate among achievement researchers. This set of findings is certainly no ringing mandate for the widespread grouping practices that exist in most schools. And then there are the social effects of ability grouping: interpersonally, tracking is destructive for *everyone*, and undermines the American values of democracy, diversity, and pluralism.

Ability-grouping is a fact of life in most American schools, and it will take some time to dismantle it. Most elementary teachers have been trained to teach reading in those three leveled groups. Even though we now understand that this arrangement will shortchange most children in the room, teachers will continue to use it until two things happen: 1) they have an alternative structure that they feel comfortable using; 2) they receive administrative support and encouragement to make the change.

The good news is that the key ingredients of Best Practice classrooms —the eight structures outlined in our Chapter 7—offer specific models of how heterogeneous grouping can work. Classrooms that are run as workshops, using learning logs, cooperative groups, conferences, and other such activities, are *inherently individualized*. Every student doesn't need to be at the same level for the class to work together, for various temporary teams to be formed, for the teacher to teach one-on-one. In a writing workshop, for example, kids pick their own topics for writing, work at their own level in developing their drafts, conference with the teacher, join in heterogeneous peer writing groups to respond and help with writing in progress, and so forth. This is a rich, collaborative, active design for learning—but there is absolutely no need to track such a class and no benefit in doing so. Indeed, such communities of writers usually find that they prefer a wide range of values, experiences, responses, styles, and attitudes among their classroom audience. Teachers like the workshop classroom because all the students' writing is different—instead of grading one hundred and twenty-five identical essays on "The Color Symbolism in *The Scarlet Letter*" (assignments which ultimately leave the teacher who made them bored and angry on Sunday afternoons), they receive a rich array of self-selected, varied writings for which they can be genuine, open readers.

When teachers say they prefer tracked classes, or claim that mixed ability groups are harder to teach, they are being sincere. But they are also usually envisioning classes run in one, traditional way: teacher-directed, presentational, whole-class, lecture-test instruction. Indeed, the durability of ability grouping in schools has always stemmed from teachers' devotion to this single model of teaching. In this familiar kind of classroom, the teacher is the center: she or he tells, presents, explains, and gives assignments. When they are not listening to the teacher and taking notes, students work quietly and individually at their desks, writing answers to questions about what the teacher has presented. The teacher is a pitcher of knowledge; students are vessels being filled up. For students, the day is filled mostly with transforming what they have heard into short written repetitions: blanks filled in, bubbles darkened, and rarely, sentences or paragraphs composed.

In this narrow classroom model, there *is* a premium placed on silence, obedience, and "listening fast," and it feels convenient for teachers to sort kids into groups by squirminess or IQ or whatever factor will make them more amenable to this style of teaching. But once teachers become aware of the much wider repertoire of available classroom structures, ones that work to teach even heavy "content" subjects like math and science to heterogeneous groups, their feeling that tracking is "necessary" fades away.

What about special education students?

Our response to the tracking question above also expresses most of our thoughts about children with special learning needs or handicaps: their traditional segregation from the mainstream has not resulted mainly from their differentness but from the inability of educators to offer classrooms where they could learn along with other children. Again, the key classroom structures outlined in Chapter 7—the ones that lead to a decentralized, student-centered, inherently individualized classroom—invite the mainstreaming of kids with all sorts of difficulties and challenges. This becomes even more practical as special education teachers are increasingly delivering their assistance in the regular classroom, rather than pulling children out of that community.

As with tracking, once we discard the fantasy that everyone in a classroom ought to have the exact same IQ score or exhibit the exact same behaviors or study the exact same content, then a whole new range of appealing, exciting alternatives presents itself. We can follow the advice of educators like Lynn Rhodes and Curt Dudley-Marling (1988) and Susan Stires (1991), who have shared in recent books a variety of strategies for making mainstreaming work in regular Whole Language/Best Practice classrooms—and, where kids' problems genuinely impede such mainstreaming, developing self-contained programs that draw on principles of holistic, integrated learning. These experts have shown us that holistic approaches are not, as some teachers fear, inappropriate for special education students—on the contrary, they are the answer. For so many such children, the problem is not to accumulate subskills, as the old, dying model of special education had it, but rather to "join the club." As our colleague and reading teacher Marilyn Bizar says about struggling readers, the initial key is to "get the big picture," to get the gestalt of reading. The same goes for the feel of authorship, the sense of the scientific process, the approach of the problem solver. Above all, special kids need to connect with each school subject in a holistic way (as regular education kids usually did earlier in life, without much help), to see and feel themselves as thinkers, readers, writers, investigators, scientists, mathematicians, readers, and citizens.

What about parents?

Not all contemporary parents immediately support the ideas described in this book. Either individually or in groups, they may object to collaborative learning, untracked classes, journal-keeping, independent reading programs, or other structures that are part of the Best Practice paradigm. Sometimes parents may even organize to demand more of something they prefer—such as phonics or math drills—or less of something they think they oppose, such as "Whole Language."

Why does this happen? To begin with, most American parents were schooled under a quite different educational paradigm, and since these grownups naturally feel that they turned out pretty well, they want the same kind of education for their own children. But these parents aren't accurately remembering what school was really like for them, how it felt, or what really worked. Nor are they factoring in the enormous learning they've done outside of school and since school; ironically, people tend to give schools credit for everything they know and can do as forty-year-olds. As a result, these modern parents may quite passionately request for their children what they think worked for them—leveled reading groups, Friday spelling tests, red ink spread over writing assignments, or even a few teacherly whacks on the behind.

This phenomenon has another dimension, and James Moffett has described it at length in his book *Coming on Center* (1988). Moffett reminds us that parents in this culture are always deeply ambivalent about passing on the reigns of control and the tools of power to the next generation. While we grownups always want the next generation to succeed, we also usually feel that our youngsters are not quite ready, that they need to be protected, that **we** really should run things a bit longer. Moffett says this ambivalence is reflected in American parents' fixation on skills-oriented schooling—activities like diagramming sentences, studying spelling lists, filling out phonics worksheets, memorizing state capitals, computing sheets of decontextualized problems. If schools can keep kids busy with such atomized, essentially meaningless drills, then their true empowerment is delayed. They are "protected" from big, dangerous ideas—from reading whole, real books or writing their own, potentially serious ideas. The current wave of book censorship is obviously part of this picture; across America, even acknowledged classics are being banned from classrooms and libraries by "concerned" parents. It seems that the only approaches to schooling American parents ever passionately advocate are those that take meaning out of the center of the curriculum —and the only kinds of schooling they oppose in any organized fashion are those which allow kids to hear, discuss, and grapple with major ideas and values of our culture.

In spite of the complexity of this problem, we have nevertheless found that enlisting parent support for Best Practice teaching is actually one of the easier elements of the school change process. In schools and districts that have developed comprehensive parent education and involvement programs, parents quickly "buy in" to the new methods and curricula, becoming boosters of the program. How can teachers and principals promote this buy-in? Our experience has shown that there are two distinct levels of parental thinking about education. The first, more superficial level is composed of unexamined personal memories mixed with media generalities and educational one-liners. It's from this level of thinking that parents speak up for more skill-and-drill, higher test scores, more ability grouping, and so forth. But at a deeper level, most parents also have some more sophisticated and progressive ideas about education. Surfacing this deeper level of thinking requires re-connecting parents to their own real experience as students. If parent education programs take the time to help adults carefully recover the details, events, feelings of their own schooling, those grown ups typically come to some very different conclusions about what really worked for them as learners —and what they really want for their own children.

We've conducted parent workshops to explore this deeper understanding in various content areas, but for illustration here we'll focus on writing. To begin with, we invite parents from a building or district to a voluntary evening meeting, usually titled "How to Help Your Child Become Better at Writing (Math, Science, Reading, etc.)." Now, if the leader were to begin this meeting by asking parents what they think the writing curriculum ought to contain, people would quickly offer a list of superficial received wisdom and undistilled nostalgia that would probably include just about everything that's *not* Best Practice. So, instead we start by helping audience members to think back over their lifetime as writers. We do a slow, careful topic search, just like a good writing teacher might in a classroom with kids, taking people step by step back through their writing history, starting with how they used writing earlier this week, and then moving back gradually through their adult life, their jobs, their personal writing and correspondence, then moving down through the levels of formal education, and all the way back to the role of writing in their childhood homes.

Our goal is to help people rediscover some key moments or turning points in their development as writers. Though few adults think of themselves as "real" writers, everyone has had memorable experiences with writing, some positive and some negative, and this exercise helps dig up fresh, detailed memories of those moments. So we take a full ten or fifteen minutes pitching these prompts at people, inviting them to make notes as we go: What was the best paper you ever wrote in college? What was the biggest reaction a piece of your writing ever got? Can you remember some of your high school English teachers? What was the most important letter you ever wrote? Where did you do your writing when you had a school assignment? What was the role of writing in your mother's life? Your father's?

Next, we ask everyone to identify one experience that stood out from the rest—either good or bad—an event or moment that was particularly memorable or significant. We hand out 5 x 7 index cards and ask people to quickly write "the story of this experience." We stress that this is a one-shot rough draft, and even joke a bit about how it is not for a grade. After giving people ten minutes to write, we ask them to share with their neighbor, wherever they are sitting. They can read the card aloud, summarize it, or even talk about why they don't want to read it—just share something comfortable. Next we invite volunteers to read their stories to the whole group. Invariably, people start offering their experiences, slowly at first, but with increasing eagerness. Typically, people tell happy stories about writing that was praised or encouraged, about having some kind of real audience, about writing on topics of their own choosing, about writing collaboratively with someone, about writing experiences that were tied in with strong personal relationships. Usually, very few of these happy writing stories happened in school. Alternately, people will volunteer painful, negative experiences with writing, most of which *did* happen in school: They'll tell about endless grammar drills, teachers who drenched papers in red ink or belittled student writers, dry and rigid term paper assignments, about feeling that writing was painful and they were bad writers.

About this time, we introduce a summary of Best Practice research findings—for writing, we use a handout of fifteen items based on George Hillocks' meta-analysis—and say something like: "We thought you were just an ordinary group of parents—we didn't know that you have all been studying the research on writing instruction!" And we go through the research summary point by point, tying the research findings to the stories the parents have just been telling: praise is more important than criticism in helping writers grow; isolated, rote grammar instruction does not improve writing; writers should choose their own topics; collaboration improves the quality of texts; and the rest. What the research does is validate parents' own personal experience.

At this point, we can explain the Best Practice/Whole Language approach to parents in an especially powerful way: "Remember all those ineffective, hurtful things that happened to you in the name of learning to write? We don't *ever* want those things to happen to your children in this school. And the good, growthful things that happened for you, once in a while along the way? We want those things to happen to your child *every single day*."

We've done this workshop with more than twenty groups ranging in size from a half dozen to two hundred and fifty. Each and every time it shows that parents have Best Practice in their hearts, in their guts; they've learned from their own real lives what works and what doesn't in helping children grow. Sometimes, that deep, true knowledge gets distorted by the haze of time and replaced by the superficial educational platitudes spewed through our culture. But happily, that deep understanding can be recovered quickly, and can lead to a true commitment to supporting better ways of teaching and learning.

After this beginning, teachers and parents can build a Best Practice partnership that's strong and enduring. Of course there are many ingredients to such successful collaboration. To begin with, teachers need to keep parents informed of the nature of the program and the progress of their kids, using frequent notes or newsletters, go-to-school nights, going over kids' portfolios during parent conferences, making sure that enough work samples go home so that parents always have a sense of what's up. Parents are also a real part of the instructional program in Best Practice classrooms. In the early grades, this might mean setting up regular systems by which parents read aloud with kids each night, or serve as audiences for kids' writing, or do "kitchen science" research together. As they become part of the instructional team in such activities, parents also become important evaluators and record-keepers, all the way from sending daily reading reports back to the classroom to adding their own observations on the official quarterly report card.

Parents also need genuine invitations to participate in the classroom. In elementary grades, Moms and Dads can serve as one-time featured readers, bringing in a favorite children's book to read aloud, or as continuing volunteer editors who help kids prepare their writing for classroom publication. As students get older, parent participation may need to step back a notch, but there are plenty of helpful roles at a distance. For example, we know many schools which have a parent-run publishing center, a spot where groups of volunteer parents regularly meet to print and bind anthologies, books, and magazines written by students. This way, parents can even assist in the work of their teenage kids, without anyone having to actually be seen together!

How does Best Practice connect with movements like Whole Language, Language Across the Curriculum, and Integrated Curriculum?

All of the issues raised in this chapter revolve around the fact that curriculum change doesn't occur in a vacuum. When a teacher decides to approach biology or American history in a new way, he must also think

about a whole range of related pieces in the complex culture called school
—from grading to standardized test pressures, to tracking, to parents,
and onward. Now, in this book we've described Best Practice strategies
for each of the major school subjects separately, because we wanted to
show how they're all converging on the same underlying progressive philosophy. However, some important, growing educational movements in
this country are striving to embody the principles we've outlined in a
more fully integrated way that transforms many of the aspects of school
all together.

Before we discuss each of these movements briefly, we want to say a
word about integration itself. The curriculum theorist and middle school
leader James Beane defines two important dimensions of genuine educational integration:

> First, integration implies wholeness and unity rather than separation
> and fragmentation. Second, real curriculum integration occurs when
> young people confront personally meaningful questions and engage in
> experiences related to those questions—experiences they can integrate
> into their own system of meanings. When we seek to integrate the cur-
> riculum, we need to inquire into the questions and meanings that young
> people create rather than contrive connections across academically con-
> structed subject boundaries.

We would add a complementary idea: that boundary-breeching thematic
or interdisciplinary units are not automatically integrative, especially if
teachers construct and conduct them without genuinely sharing responsibility with students.

Whole Language

Whole Language is a strong, grass-roots movement of mostly elementary
teachers that is adding adherents daily. All around the country, teachers
gather in local TAWL (Teachers Applying Whole Language) groups,
attend conferences, and study the books of Ken Goodman, Regie Routman, Nancie Atwell, and others. Their fundamental theoretical orientation is psycholinguistic: that is, Whole Language teachers want to make
the classroom a scaffolded language-learning environment that parallels
the natural, efficient learning of home and community. In practice,
Whole Language teachers follow virtually all the principles of the progressive model outlined in this book. Mature Whole Language classrooms are child-centered, sociable, cognitive places where students are
deployed in choice-rich reading and writing workshops, conferences with
peers and adults, and thematic group investigations. Without question,
Whole Language is the largest, strongest, and most coherent manifestation of the neo-progressive movement in American schools. Though it is

now large enough to have its own set of internal frictions and factions, Whole Language has mostly retained its bottom-up politics and its steadfast philosophical orientation. The movement is also well supplied with books which we won't rewrite here, but will enthusiastically list among the suggested readings at the end of this chapter.

These Whole Language pioneers have had some special advantages where change is concerned. Because most elementary teachers still have a single group of children for the whole day and are responsible for all subjects, they enjoy some latitude and time to experiment. Putting administrative constraints aside (which is not always easy), an elementary teacher who wants to change, to seek integration, to move toward Whole Language, is free to do so within the six-hour day that she and her children spend together. For teachers in these self-contained classrooms, breaking down subject barriers and integrating instruction doesn't require a faculty vote or a working team of colleagues; often, it's simply an individual, professional decision.

Once schooling becomes departmentalized, typically beginning around fifth or sixth grade, experimentation gets trickier. The cellular organization, bell schedule, and specialized faculty become major barriers to innovation, and especially to multi-subject integration. Still, individual secondary teachers can move toward integration in their own forty-five-minute blocks by making the class more whole, more active, more collaborative, more experiential—as some of their colleagues from the lower grades might say, "more whole language." If a progressive math teacher cannot enlist English, science, and other colleagues to create a wider program, then she can at least implement many of the elements of Best Practice on her own limited turf, as many of the teachers introduced in this book have done.

Critical Literacy

Another steadily growing integrative trend, this one rooted mostly in secondary schools, is Critical Literacy (sometimes called "Writing and Reading Across the Curriculum"), a movement which brings the strategies of writing-to-learn and critical reading to the so-called content areas. Typically, what this means is showing science, math, shop, physical education, history, and other teachers some of the key experiential, cognitive, collaborative strategies that have been developed mostly in literacy education, and adapting them to the new subject matter. For example, students and teachers in any classroom can learn to harness the power of such writing strategies as clustering, free writing, learning logs, peer editing, and such reading strategies as predicting, reading aloud, literature circles, and semantic mapping. While spreading these activities through a school does not abolish the customary departments, it does have some positive effects.

First of all, the staff development effort itself, the inservice program in which teachers learn these ideas, typically provides an important faculty conversation about the nature of learning, teaching, and evaluation. For students in the classroom these new activities may help their teachers break the presentational habit and create a more active, cognitive, and collaborative classroom. Critical literacy, at its best, opens the door for teachers to a wider conception of thinking and learning processes in their own subjects, and invites cooperation among faculty.

Interdisciplinary Programs.

Beyond change within individual secondary classrooms, there is a diffuse and modest national trend toward interdisciplinary, thematic programs, in which groups of teachers and students identify large chunks of subject matter within or beyond the traditional curriculum, develop a new class and schedule, and go to work. The most venerable and familiar version of this is American Studies, which co-author Harvey Daniels taught twenty years ago. In American Studies, one social studies teacher and one English teacher are assigned two groups of students and two periods a day to intertwine American history and literature.

Today, some educators, many of them working in middle schools, are showing the way to embody truly progressive principles in such interdisciplinary programs. At Marquette Middle School in Madison, Wisconsin, teachers and students recently designed and undertook a study which became virtually the school's entire curriculum. As reported by Beane (1991), the program began when students brainstormed questions about themselves and their world, identifying categories of curiosity within their list, and eventually deciding on the main theme: Living in the Future. Next, students began listing activities that could help them answer the questions they had raised, and then they organized themselves into investigating teams. Beane tells what eventually resulted:

> One [project] involved designing a model for the city of Madison for the year 2020 and required integrating the work of committees on the environment, transportation, government, education, and health. Another activity called for investigating family health histories to determine personal risk factors in the future. A third brought an artist into the school to sketch pictures of how the kids might look in 30 years and to discuss the physical effects of aging. A fourth involved creating, distributing, tabulating, and analyzing a survey sent to several middle schools to find out what their peers predicted for the future. Still another activity found students investigating the accuracy of predictions made for this century 100 years ago.

These energizing investigations required students to use a wide variety of thinking skills: researching, reading, writing, debating, tabulating, calculating, graphing, charting, experimenting, interviewing, presenting, drawing, and so on. Key underlying features of the program included a strong student voice in planning, the constructivist assumption that students can make their own meanings, the jigsawing of a huge knowledge base, the blending of affect and cognition as students pursued personally relevant topics, and the fact that the program was not a segment of the day or a temporary treat—it was the whole curriculum. Perhaps most emblematic, "Living in the Future" will never be repeated at Marquette Middle School—not unless the next group of students who start the process authentically generates the exact same list of questions about themselves and their world, and freely makes the same choices.

While such interdisciplinary programs can be genuinely progressive, they don't always work that way. For example, in Los Angeles there is a nationally noted interdisciplinary high school program called "Humanitas" which illustrates both the benefits and the difficulties of such ambitious innovations in secondary schools. "Humanitas" is basically a thematic three-period high school course in English, social studies, and art. Three teachers are given paid summer planning time to develop courses around themes such as "The Protestant Ethic and the Spirit of Capitalism" or "Women, Race, and Social Protest." Students meet in these three classes daily, and teachers have an hour of common planning time. According to a recent laudatory article by the project's official outside evaluator (in Aschbacher, 1991), Humanitas has many positive effects on students: they score higher on standardized tests, they write better essays, and they have a higher rate of school retention. These are significant and valuable outcomes, and the quality of time kids spend in this daily block is evidently more involving and challenging than the rest of their school day.

However, the Humanitas program has shortcomings which compromise the full embodiment of progressive practice. Teachers plan the courses by themselves, in the summer. While they undoubtedly take student interests into account, there is no official provision for any student involvement, goal-setting, or decision-making—or, for that matter, is there any mention of student collaboration within any strand of the course. Project research shows that Humanitas pupils spend more time in substantive discussions than students in regular classes—six minutes more per day, to be exact. This is a disturbingly modest achievement for any program claiming progressive ambitions. The official project report mentions that "some" Humanitas faculty team-teach upon occasion, but apparently the standard deployment of Humanitas students is still groups of thirty kids who cycle for one period each among the three teachers.

One of the highlighted aspects of the teachers' summer work is that they "develop essay questions early in the unit-planning process to clarify their objectives in teaching about the theme to identify the significant issues to discuss, and to guide their selection of materials and lesson plans." This strict pre-planning of evaluation instruments would seem to effectively constrict digressions during the course, and to exert great pressure against reorienting the program in response to students, or giving time to interests or questions discovered along the way. The one sample essay question featured in the evaluator's report begins: "The cosmology of a traditional culture permeates every aspect of that culture. This is illustrated in the following three cultural groups: the Eskimos, the Southwest Indians, and the Meso-Americans. Specifically, discuss the spirit world that each group believed in, and explain how it influenced their culture and values. . . . " If every student must write on predetermined questions like this one, then Humanitas is not an integrated program as we and James Beane define it. Based upon the program's self-description, we conclude that it lacks the cognitive challenge, authenticity, and student responsibility to be classed as a genuinely progressive program. Instead, Humanitas is a refined, polished, elegant delivery system for traditional teacher-centered, transmission-oriented instruction.

We have no wish to malign this generally admirable program, or to overly exalt the Marquette project. We simply aim to illustrate the inherent difficulties of large-scale multidisciplinary programs. If teachers merely throw together the ingredients of existing courses and then present this material to students in the same old way, then no meaningful form of curriculum integration—or Best Practice—has been achieved. Students might well be better off following the bell schedule from one room to another if the teachers in those forty-five-minute segments are practicing progressive principles within their cells.

How can traditionally trained teachers manage the new, student-centered classroom?

If we want to decentralize the classroom, to transfer more responsibility and choice to students, to have configurations other than thirty kids listening to one teacher, then there are only a few basic alternatives: after all, there aren't an infinite number of ways to reshuffle a teacher and thirty children. Students can work alone, in pairs, in teams, or in groups. Kids need to be able to initiate, carry out, record, report on, and evaluate their work and the work of peers. Each of these alternate structures *does* ask teachers to redeploy the basic ingredients of schooling—kids, time, space, materials, themselves—in new and different combinations that neither they nor the children are accustomed to. Teachers need the management expertise to make these new alternatives work.

But many teachers lack, or feel they lack, the management skills to operate these varied structures. For example, when they hear about the research that links strong growth in students' writing to regular one-to-one teacher conferences, many teachers worry: "I'd love to do conferences with one kid at a time, but if I do, the other twenty-nine will go crazy." Teachers need ways to organize their classrooms so that structures like conferencing work, because these are the only powerful and proven alternatives we have. But these new configurations require a functional, orderly, trusting, productive, self-regulating classroom community—what some people call discipline. If kids can't work independently and in various smaller groups, then we're thrown right back to the teacher-controlling-the-whole-class model.

As classroom teachers ourselves, we are well aware of the luck of the draw and the year-to-year roulette of "good" and "bad" classes of students. Yet we believe that groups are mainly made, not inherited. There are specific, reliable ways for teachers to establish a productive classroom climate, and thus open the way to many promising innovations. According to the literature on group dynamics and development, a field of study oddly neglected by educators, there are six ingredients that teachers must, and can, shape to create that initial climate (Schmuck and Schmuck, 1988):

- positive expectations
- mutually developed norms
- shared leadership
- diffuse friendship patterns
- open channels of communication
- mechanisms for resolving conflicts

Wise teachers nurture these six factors, especially during the early life of a class, to create a widely overlapping network of positive interdependence. They consciously distribute acquaintance, power, responsibility among everyone, opening up every possible channel of communication, verbal, nonverbal, written, and artistic. Once this richly interdependent community has been created, when the time comes to institute complex structures like reading workshop or hands-on science projects, students are able to adjust and make the transition.

Unfortunately, some competing models of classroom management are currently being touted around the country, approaches that are entirely incompatible with Best Practice teaching. One we've observed in many schools is something called "Assertive Discipline," an approach founded on an adversarial relationship between teacher and students, upon control rather than community. Under this system, the school year starts out not with building of friendship and distribution of responsibility, but with the teacher reciting a menu of possible infractions and an elaborate system of contingencies and punishments. The underlying message to children is: "You are not trustworthy." Obviously, the possibilities for genuine cooperative learning in such classrooms is compromised: since they've been trained to function only under direct teacher oversight, either the kids won't work independently or they'll do it superficially, just enough to avoid sanctions.

While the Assertive Discipline system sometimes does create quiet, orderly classrooms, it works by suppressing students, not by empowering them or transferring responsibility to them. Once the system is loosened or kids pass on to the next teacher, control and suppression must start again, because kids have internalized nothing about monitoring themselves. Much like ability-grouping, Assertive Discipline is a system devised to legitimize the archaic and authoritarian model of the teacher-centered classroom. In such classrooms, the inevitable (and unsolvable) problem is to get children to be silent and motionless while an adult talks at them. But teachers who use Best Practice structures don't *need* Assertive Discipline—their classrooms already have order, discipline, and productivity which arise out of children's engagement in work, not their fear of humiliation and punishment.

Isn't Best Practice just another educational fad? And is any of this stuff really new? Sounds like open classroom to me, and that was a failure!

What we are calling the Best Practice movement of the 1990s certainly has a very familiar ring to those of us school veterans who lived through the late sixties and early seventies. Yet we find it puzzling that this earlier period of progressive reform is now scoffed at by most educators. In fact, we think the ideas of the late 60s and early 70s were important if imperfect precursors to today's developments, and it's worth understanding what went wrong back then as well as what useful foundations were laid. Maybe we should look at one specific and controversial innovation from this era, to help us re-value our heritage.

In the "open classroom" movement of the 1970s we got a memorable demonstration of how an innovation can fail, especially when the barriers to change aren't dealt with. Schools plunged into the open classroom experiment, tearing down walls, offering teachers a one-day inservice at the end of the summer in which some administrator or outside consultant essentially announced: "OK, next week we want you to throw away the one model of teaching and classroom organization that you were trained for and are experienced in, and instead we expect you to run your classroom in ten other ways you've never tried and we've never trained you for and quite frankly we haven't thought about either or tried ourselves.

Have a nice year." The great open education movement inevitably collapsed because teachers did not have in their professional repertoire the structures and strategies to run a variety of student-directed, independent, and small-group activities. Kids went bananas and many teachers who were working in huge rooms with hundreds of kids started sneaking in cardboard boxes, shelves, and other large objects with which they could gradually and surreptitiously rebuild a classroom-like space inside the trackless waste of the "pod."

But today, if you go into Joanne Trahanas' eighth grade language arts class in Glenview, Illinois, you'll see something that looks very much like an open classroom. You'll see thirteen-year-olds—an age group not usually noted for self-discipline—working industriously and without overt supervision on their writing skills every day. They come into Joanne's room, get out their writing folders, and get ready to work. There's a quick round of the class during which each kid announces what he or she is planning to work on that day, and then everyone, including the teacher, goes to work. Some draft new pieces, others go back and edit ongoing drafts. A few quietly seek out a partner for a quick conference. After a while, Joanne starts to see kids one at a time on a schedule she keeps, and as she confers with each student about his or her writing, she jots a phrase or two in the book where she tracks progress. A couple of times a week, the group gathers for ten minutes of reading aloud and discussion of their writing strategies and progress.

This is an open classroom, an open classroom that works. It works because Joanne has set up the structure, the norms, the schedule, the procedures, and the materials in such a way that kids quickly grow into responsible use of this special time and space. What's even more impressive to us is that Joanne has *six* writing workshops each day, with six different sets of kids. She has made the structure work not just with one group of children that she can train for six hours every day, but with one hundred twenty-five kids who pass briefly through her room for three hours a week. Joanne's workshop reminds us that there are important links between contemporary Best Practice ideas and past innovations, and demonstrates that we've learned a lot about how to make things really stick this time around.

Is anything ever going to change? Doesn't the educational pendulum just swing back and forth from progressivism to conservatism?

One tendency we have pretty successfully avoided in this book is quoting ourselves. But on the subject of school change and the pendulum metaphor, we are unlikely to improve on what we wrote in 1988 in *A Community of Writers*:

Those of us in teaching often use the image of a swinging pendulum to describe changing trends in education; indeed, the pendulum metaphor seems to be one of our favorite ways of talking about the history of our field. How impartial and content-free this image is, tempting us to believe that the fluctuations in educational practice merely result from pointless, random, eternal variation. However, shifting educational trends hardly reflect some impartial pendulum swings; instead this is more like the battlefront in a war, a line that moves back and forth with assaults and retreats. The practice of education reflects a historical struggle of one set of ideas against another, continually being fought out in close relation to the social-political-economic issues outside of schools. . . .

The cyclic vacillations between authoritarian and progressive education in this culture are not random pendulum swings, but advances and retreats along a battlefront—the playing out, over a huge span of time, of a war for the soul of schooling in this society. In the end, the student-centered, developmental approach will win out over the authoritarian model because it parallels the direction in which civilization itself progresses. If we look broadly enough, we can see evidence that this direction is already clearly marked: in matters of classroom management, teachers no longer whip their students in school or crown them with dunce caps; in enrollments, we now welcome females in equal numbers to all levels of education, though just a century ago they were effectively barred from anything above a grade-school education; in the curriculum, we no longer insist on endless copying of great authors' texts for penmanship practice or have kids stand and recite for elocution; and sentence diagramming, though far from dead, is quite evidently dying out of the schools even as we watch. As each of these unproductive practices is dropped, and as more effective, growth-producing methods prove themselves, we see gradual progress toward a better understanding of how human beings actually learn and grow. . . .

Of course there will always be regressions and short-term backslides. Change in schools never follows a straight, steady path, but is more like three-steps-forward-and-two-and-a-half-steps-back. Perhaps tomorrow a movement will spring up to restore the teaching of sentence diagramming to its "rightful, central place in the English curriculum," and such a trend might even catch on for a few years. Indeed, it is just this sort of event which misleads us, as individuals living in a particular brief lifetime, into believing that there's always a pendulum swinging back and forth between two eternal, fixed points, insuring that nothing ever really changes. But each time the progressive set of ideas comes back, it gains strength and coherence from the new research and practice that connects with it, and each time it appears it exerts more influence on the schools before it is once again suppressed. . . .

So we must not forget the half-step gained in every cycle. The larger, overall direction is heading the right way. The slow, long trend always prevails. And each cycle of regression, though probably inevitable, can be shortened if classroom teachers feel the confidence to push back at any pendulums that swing their way. . . .

Best Practice, Whole Language, Interdisciplinary Studies, if taught in their true, genuine forms—reflect a set of deep educational ideas, ideas that are partisan, that are contrary to other ideas, and that contend with opposing models and paradigms. To refer to this continuing struggle as the vacillation of vacuous fads or the swinging of a pendulum cheapens the efforts of people who are working, often against much resistance, to put these ideas into practice and to show how they work.

Works Cited

Aschbacher, Pamela. 1991. Humanitas: A Thematic Curriculum. *Educational Leadership* (October).

Beane, James. 1991. Middle School: The Natural Home of Integrated Curriculum. *Educational Leadership* (October).

Chase, Alan. 1977. *The Legacy of Malthus*. New York: Alfred A. Knopf.

Gould, Steven Jay. 1981. *The Mismeasure of Man*. New York: Norton.

Hillocks, George. 1986. *Research on Written Composition*. Urbana, IL: National Council of Teachers of English.

Johnson, David W., Roger T. Johnson, Edythe Holubec, and Patricia Roy. 1991. *Cooperation in the Classroom*. Edina, MN: Interaction Book Company.

Katz, Michael B. 1968. *The Irony of Early School Reform: Educational Innovation in Mid-Nineteenth Century Massachusetts*. Cambridge, MA: Harvard University Press.

Moffett, James. 1988. *Coming on Center: Essays in English Education*. Portsmouth, NH: Boynton/Cook.

Oakes, Jeannie. 1985. *Keeping Track: How Schools Structure Inequality*. New Haven: Yale University Press.

Rhodes, Lynn K. and Curt Dudley-Marling. 1988. *Readers and Writers with a Difference*. Portsmouth, NH: Heinemann Educational Books.

Schmuck, Richard and Patricia Schmuck. 1988. *Group Processes in the Classroom*. Dubuque, IA: William C. Brown.

Slavin, Robert, Sharon Schlomo, Karen Spencer, Clark Webb, and Robert Schmuck. 1985. *Learning to Cooperate, Cooperating to Learn*. New York: Plenum Press.

Spring, Joel. 1972. *Education and the Rise of the Corporate State*. Boston, MA: Beacon Press.

Stires, Susan. 1991. *With Promise: Redefining Reading and Writing Needs for Special Students.*. Portsmouth, NH: Heinemann Educational Books.

Tunnell, Michael and James Jacobs. 1989. Using "Real" Books: Research Findings on Literature Based Reading Instruction. *Reading Teacher* (March).

Wheelock, Anne. 1992. *Crossing the Tracks*. New York: The New Press.

Zemelman, Steven and Harvey Daniels. 1988. *A Community of Writers: Teaching Writing in the Junior and Senior High School.*. Portsmouth, NH: Heinemann Educational Books.

Suggested Readings on Whole Language, Critical Literacy, Reading and Writing Across the Curriculum, and Authentic Assessment

Atwell, Nancie. 1987. *In The Middle: Writing, Reading, and Learning with Adolescents*. Portsmouth, NH: Boynton/Cook.

Bayer, Anne Shea. 1990. *Collaborative-Apprenticeship Learning*. Mountain View, CA: Mayfield Publishers.

Belanoff, Pat and Marcia Dickson. 1991. *Portfolios: Process and Product*. Portsmouth, NH: Boynton/Cook.

Bird, Lois Bridges, ed. 1989. *Becoming A Whole Language School*. New York: Richard C. Owen.

Crafton, Linda. 1991. *Whole Language: Getting Started, Moving Forward*. New York: Richard C. Owen.

Countryman, Joan. 1992. *Writing to Learn Mathematics*. Portsmouth, NH: Heinemann Educational Books.

Edelsky, Carole, Bess Altwerger, and Barbara Flores. 1990. *Whole Language: What's the Difference?*. Portsmouth, NH: Heinemann Educational Books.

Fulwiler, Toby. 1987. *The Journal Book*. Portsmouth, NH: Heinemann Educational Books.

Fulwiler, Toby and Art Young. 1982. *Language Connections: Writing and Reading Across the Curriculum*. Urbana, IL: National Council of Teachers of English.

Gere, Ann. 1986. *Roots in the Sawdust*. Urbana, IL: National Council of Teachers of English.

Goodman, Kenneth. 1988. *What's Whole in Whole Language?* Portsmouth, NH: Heinemann Educational Books.

Goodman, Kenneth, E. Brooks Smith, Robert Meredith, and Yetta Goodman. 1987. *Language and Thinking in School*. New York: Richard C. Owen.

Goodman, Kenneth, Yetta Goodman, and Wendy Hood. 1989. *The Whole Language Evaluation Book*. Portsmouth, NH: Heinemann Educational Books.

Graves, Donald, and Bonnie Sunstein. 1992. *Portfolio Portraits*. Portsmouth, NH: Heinemann Educational Books.

Hansen, Jane. 1987. *When Writers Read*. Portsmouth, NH: Heinemann Educational Books.

Harp, Bill. 1991. *Assessment and Evaluation in Whole Language Classrooms*. Norwood, MA: Christopher Gordon.

Harste, Jerome, Kathy Short, with Carolyn Burke. 1988. *Creating Classrooms for Authors*. Portsmouth, NH: Heinemann Educational Books.

Heald-Taylor, Gail. 1989. *The Administrator's Guide to Whole Language*. New York: Richard C. Owen.

Integrating the Curriculum. 1991. *Educational Leadership (October)*.

Jaggar, Angela and Trika Smith-Burke. 1985. *Observing the Language Learner*. Newark, DE: International Reading Association.

Manning, Gary and Maryann Manning, eds. 1989. *Whole Language: Beliefs and Practices K-8*. Washington, D.C.: National Education Association.

Mayher, John. 1990. *Uncommon Sense: Theoretical Practice in Lanaguage and Education*. Portsmouth, NH: Boynton/Cook.

Nickell, Pat, ed. 1992. Student Assessment in Social Studies. *Social Education* (February).

Parker, Robert and Vera Goodkin. 1987. *The Consequences of Writing*. Portsmouth, NH: Boynton/Cook.

Peterson, Ralph and Maryann Eeds. 1990. *Grand Conversations: Liaterature Groups in Action*. Ontario, Canada: Scholastic.

Rief, Linda. 1992. *Seeking Diversity: Language Arts with Adolescents.*. Portsmouth, NH: Heinemann Educational Books.

Routman, Regie. 1988. *Transitions: From Literature to Literacy*. Portsmouth, NH: Heinemann Educational Books.

————. 1991. *Invitations: Changing as Teachers and Learners K–12*. Portsmouth, NH: Heinemann Educational Books.

Shanahan, Timothy. 1990. *Reading and Writing Together*. Norwood, MA: Christopher Gordon.

Stenmark, Jean Kerr. 1991. *Mathematics Assessment*. Reston, VA: National Council of Teachers of Mathematics.

Stires, Susan, ed. 1991. *With Promise: Redefining Reading and Writing Needs for Special Students*. Portsmouth, NH: Heinemann Educational Books.

Theme Issue on Assessment. 1989. *Educational Leadership* (April).

Theme Issue on Assessment. 1989. *Phi Delta Kappan* (May).

Tierney, Robert, ed. 1991. *Portfolio Assessment in the Reading-Writing Classroom*. Norwood, MA: Christopher Gordon.

Weaver, Constance. 1990. *Understanding Whole Language*. Portsmouth, NH: Heinemann Educational Books.

Weaver, Constance and Linda Henke, eds. *Supporting Whole Language*. Portsmouth, NH: Heinemann Educational Books.

10

Yes, But . . . Can It Work in City Schools?

Throughout this book, we've described everyday teachers who teach beautifully and who are improving. We've pictured everyday kids who can learn and grow. We've visited a number of poor, inner-city, all minority schools that are working. Yet most people conclude that, by and large, urban schools across the country are *not* working, that so-called "at risk" kids *aren't* learning as well as they might, and that too many city teachers *haven't* discovered the secrets of Best Practice. If you study national achievement scores, or, better yet, visit some urban schools, you realize that the disparity is genuinely catastrophic. In a very real sense, America has two school systems: perhaps three-quarters of our kids attend decent public and private schools in towns and suburbs, while the other fourth attend big-city schools that are often weighed down with grievous problems. Only by averaging these two separate and different systems can you derive the picture—the false and misleading picture—that America's main educational problem is mediocrity.

But we've also argued throughout this book—and research strongly confirms—that all kids can and do learn well under even some pretty trying circumstances. So if the children aren't really dumb, and if learning is so natural to human beings, if the teachers and their schools are not really hopeless, then what goes wrong? What makes learning and teaching so much harder in the inner city? If we are ever to achieve school reform beyond the successes of a few charismatic individual teachers and principals, we had better be clear about what is standing in the way. In this chapter we'll review the factors we believe to be most damaging, and we'll try to separate some of the myths from the realities of urban education. We want to show that the state-of-the-art instructional practices described in this book are just as applicable in inner city schools as they are in prosperous suburban ones.

210

Poverty

No one questions the deadening effects of poverty, and we've witnessed its devastations all too often. A most unfortunate effect on schools is instability. One example: Woodson South School has an excellent daily attendance record, over ninety percent—however, children enter and leave Woodson's attendance area at a rate of forty percent per year. Thus, even if Woodson develops the most outstanding of programs, forty percent of the children who benefit from them will be gone before the year is over. A similar number will arrive in the middle of the year, forcing teachers to try to catch up each new pupil on what he or she has missed.

This saps energy from the teachers, slows down the progress of the class, and requires the constant readjustment of the group dynamics each time a child comes or goes. As we've explained repeatedly throughout this book, the key structures of Best Practice teaching require a cohesive, interactive, interdependent classroom community where students assume high levels of responsibility for their own and classmates' learning. In schools where the classroom community is constantly reshuffled, teachers are, at best, driven back to the early stages of group-building, and, at worst, constantly preoccupied with discipline.

Outside of school, instability in families and violence in neighborhoods also pressures children mightily. In our observation, the younger kids—in grades one to four or five—nevertheless remain quite open to schooling, though some are withdrawn, overly needy of attention because of troubles at home or in the neighborhood, or untrained in self-discipline and social cooperation. It's the older children who are increasingly drawn away from school by the magnetism and self-destructiveness of the streets, especially when they compare this with repeated experiences of failure in school.

Yet the culture of poverty has also been overly blamed and deeply misunderstood. The common belief among middle class people and many city teachers is that poor children speak a defective language and have little exposure to learning outside school because their parents are either too overworked, lazy, or illiterate to help them. Repeatedly, sociology and linguistics researchers—and even court cases—have shown how wrong this is. For example, Black English ("Black English Vernacular" to sociolinguists) differs from school dialect in relatively minor ways (even if those stand out sharply to the middle class ear), and involves just as rich and complex, if different, uses of thought and expression as any other version of English. Similarly, children of Hispanic background may be limited in English, but may also be well on their way to literacy in Spanish, giving them much to build on.

Further, ethnographic study of children's activity in poor homes shows that many are quite involved in literacy activities through play, drawing, and even television, which, contrary to the standard platitudes, is actually full of print (Taylor and Dorsey-Gaines, 1988). These "at-risk" children often engage more print at home than during the school day itself. And detailed research on children's literacy development during their early years reveals that at age three, children have acquired all the basic concepts for reading (such as the stability of meaning, representation of reality through symbols, linear directionality of print) and that *there are no observable differences of such acquisition at this stage between any groups, rich or poor, urban or rural, black or white* (Harste, 1984).

Perhaps the most helpful explanation of this puzzle is provided by the anthropologist Shirley Brice Heath, who found, by comparing different working-class communities, that some had family customs for language use which were in harmony with the usual patterns of student-teacher communication, while other groups did not (Heath, 1983). In other words, pre-school-age children in some cultural groups get lots of practice using school-type talk, answering questions about toys and books, or giving factual information. In other groups, the kids simply acquire a different communication style. If these kids don't pick up the new talk quickly in school, or get specific help learning it, they fall behind and stay behind. Thus, the repeated experience with failure that drives children to reject school later on.

Class Issues

School teachers are just about one hundred percent middle class people, while many of the children they work with in the inner city are poor, and considerable friction and misunderstanding occur as a result. This is not a matter of race, though race issues can certainly be present. Black, White, Hispanic teachers, all are middle class by income, and many come from families that struggled hard to get there. The motives of most of these teachers working with poorer children are positive—they want earnestly to help the next generation escape from poverty, just as they or their parents did.

But it's not so simple, because class in urban America isn't just a matter of how much money you have. Class involves the way you talk, the games you play, the music you listen to, your family's attitude toward single parenthood, your beliefs about education. Sociologists help us understand that there's not just one *right* approach to these things (i.e., *my* approach); social groups simply do differ about them. However, the cultural gap between teachers and their students—which would already be present anyway because the younger generation always needs to distinguish itself—can grow to unfortunate proportions.

Teachers (*and* students) can make dysfunctional assumptions or take damaging actions as a result. One research project showed how some urban teachers grossly underestimated parents' willingness to intervene and help their kids or support the teacher's policies. In a sample study, the teacher failed to contact parents whose children were having trouble, and when contact was finally made very late in the year, the teacher was surprised at the cooperation and resulting improvement that took place (Allen and Mason, 1989). Of course, *every* community has parents who don't help when children are having trouble with school. But the *assumption* that they won't, or the failure to communicate clearly or sympathetically with the parents can mean unfortunate lost opportunities.

More heartbreaking is the amount of anger and hostility we sometimes see in urban schools. The kids can seem wild, and the teachers feel the need to yell at them frequently and to label them harshly to their faces, just to maintain basic control. In workshops, the teachers assert quite openly that these kids lack discipline and manners in their homes and therefore respond only to such tactics. Of course, we've seen suburban teachers take this stance too—though not as frequently or as strongly. What makes this phenomenon puzzling is that in the many effective urban classrooms we've observed in the poorest areas, discipline isn't a problem at all. The kids are industrious and polite, the teachers calm and positive.

It appears that an unfortunate cycle of conflict perpetuates itself in the more negative classrooms. Based on past experiences and a sense of social differences, the teachers expect the worst of the kids and don't believe these kids have the internal resources to control themselves. The children come to believe this themselves since, after all, the adults dealing with them tell them so in words and actions. The children's anger and self-dislike are then acted out, providing apparent confirmation of the teachers' negative beliefs.

Serious urban teachers and writers have argued that only a skills-worksheets-discipline approach will succeed with minority disadvantaged children. Lisa Delpit, writing in the *Harvard Educational Review* (1985) is one of the most outspoken of these critics. She claims that when she offered White and Black children the same "open classroom" type activities, the White kids prospered, while the Black kids went nowhere. We weren't present to see just how she prepared the children or maintained order. But we've observed so many inner-city classrooms (some of which are described in this book) where kids of *all* colors and backgrounds thrived on self-directed and collaborative tasks, that we know the problem must be a deeper, more subtle one.

There's both danger and irony in this sad cycle. If schools decide that "these kids" are already accustomed to authoritarian discipline at home, and that they will "only" respond to rigid controls, then the schools merely reproduce stereotypical and dysfunctional elements of a poverty culture right in the classroom. Instead, it's arguable that these kids especially should experience a middle-class culture in school, being part of classroom communities that enact self-control, responsibility, self-monitoring, sharing, cooperation, and some deferral of gratification. If city kids never see these values enacted, never internalize them, how can they ever escape poverty and function in mainstream society?

Other factors can cause problems with learning, but it all gets ascribed instead to the children's social background. For example, as we observed one teacher trying unsuccessfully to help her third graders with punctuation, she turned to us in frustration, saying, "These kids just don't *want* to learn!" When we asked one child to read a sample aloud, she read in monotones, like a robot. It was clear that she had learned to decode words but not to read for meaning—a problem typical of the school's skills-oriented reading program, not a problem of attitude. She had never been trained to listen to sentences rather than just individual words, and so she couldn't find where to add punctuation. However, when we asked for volunteers from among the children who *couldn't* understand, she raised her hand again and again, bravely risking embarrassment because she wanted so badly to learn!

Thus, in spite of the best of intentions, many teachers and children become embroiled in what seem like endless skirmishes of a class war, a war that eats up all too much energy. In still another way, then, too many urban kids experience school as a succession of failures, and while they tolerate this for a few early years, they ultimately tune themselves out of what is for them an unproductive setting.

Yet—when we work with teachers who have struggled in this saddening whirlpool, it nearly always turns out that they are desperate to escape it. They are delighted to discover that meaningful classroom activities yield the side effect of improving children's behavior. And such activities almost always have this effect because they communicate respect for children's voices and allow the children to realize they are smarter than they thought. Under the battle-scarred surface of almost every angry teacher there still lives the idealist, the believer in kids' ability to grow and learn. The class war does not have to cycle on forever.

Resources

It's standard politics these days to assert that just throwing money at a problem like education won't solve it. And it's certainly true that a considerable amount of money has been wasted over the years on programs which didn't work. On the other hand, without the funds, how will we ever retrain the twenty thousand teachers in a city like Chicago, most of whom need to learn new methods of teaching writing, reading, math, science, and social studies? Jonathan Kozol (1991) has reminded us, in

Savage Inequalities, that city kids, teachers, and schools simply don't get their fair share of the money available for education in this society.

It's instructive to compare the situation in a large city with that of a comfortable (but not rich) suburb like Oak Park, which we described just a few pages ago. By offering several thirty-hour inservice workshops per year on teaching writing, Oak Park helped over half of its staff during a five-year period. Now, morale and success in this area of the curriculum are high, and an expanded team of in-district teacher-leaders is offering advanced workshops on special topics and techniques.

Oak Park employs three hundred teachers. What would it take to deliver the same services for a staff of twenty thousand? Our own recent two-year program in Chicago trained two hundred and fifty, nearly the equivalent of that entire suburban staff, and yet in a large city it's such a tiny drop in the bucket that it can't possibly build momentum for system-wide change we've seen in smaller districts. The estimated cost for retraining just one fourth of the Chicago staff in one subject area, such as reading or math (i.e., five thousand teachers, a number which, though limited, would create a significant impact and very likely influence even the non-participants), would total about $400,000 per year for five years. Ask anyone at the Chicago Board of Education how difficult it would be to find an extra $2,000,000 right now! Yet this number is based on very conservative calculations for materials, administrative costs, and pay for the time of workshop leaders and teachers.

"Why didn't the teachers get this training in college, so they wouldn't need it now?" one might ask. It's a good question, of course, but because the Best Practice processes of teaching described in this book were far less understood twenty years ago, very few teachers received the help needed then. It will be years before a significant proportion of the staffs turn over—even though teacher pre-service training is gradually being brought up to date. This deficit affects small, rich suburbs just as much as it does big cities. But our example shows how much harder it is to make up for the lack in the larger setting where proportionately fewer resources are available to do the job.

Size

We've already said a lot about size by talking about resources. But there's another aspect of size that was just briefly mentioned: momentum. In any large organization or community, change depends on more than just a *few* individuals. There's plenty of pressure for all to behave alike, and even if variety is tolerated, the very different ones are isolated or labeled so their example will pose no threat: "Oh, Ms. Wilde? Yes, she sure uses some unusual methods, and they work great for **her**. But you have to be a little crazy to be able to do it that way!" Teachers aren't the only ones who operate this way. It's hard to find a group of human beings who don't.

This means that for new ideas to take hold beyond an enthusiastic few, a critical mass of adherents must be established. A "movement" needs enough people to encourage and support one another, to exert some social pressure on the others, and to demonstrate that the new approaches work not just for the far-out risk-takers, but for any ordinary professional who wants to try them. However, too many big-city programs involve training for one or two "experts" per building, or one or two "lighthouse" schools. These programs usually don't spread because it's easy for the "example" folks to be kept isolated, labeled, and ultimately discouraged and burned out. The process is rarely malicious or anti-anything. It's just the way people seem to operate in large systems. Ask any manager trying to initiate change in a large corporation.

Bureaucracy

Americans love to sneer at it. We have more than our share of it. To a certain extent, we need it—after all, should classroom teachers be ordering toilet paper and writing the checks to pay for repairing school buses? But bureaucracy almost inevitably creates obstacles to change, and larger urban school systems simply have more of it to deal with. In big-city bureaucracies, programs need to be approved at more levels. People can pass the buck more easily. Politics and policies come to serve the needs of the system more than the needs of teachers and children.

Here's one typical way the politics of a large bureaucracy can undermine change. As the program is being launched, an administrator worries that people in one building or area will be offended if services are offered elsewhere, but not for them. Yet, there isn't enough money to do the job right in every location. So the administrator decides to give a little bit to *each* location, but not enough to run the program fully in any one place. The program limps along in its many sites, isolated planners and change agents get discouraged, the program finally fails.

The city of Chicago is presently experimenting with a system of local school governance that may address this problem. While there are plenty of ways for the local control approach to stumble, too, it does offer real hope. Individual schools are able to arrange for special programs and improvements on their own, and they *are* doing so. Whether other political forces will impede this process or undo it before it has a chance to succeed remains a major question.

Misguided Curriculum

People outside the educational world assume that teaching is teaching; a teacher either has got what it takes or not. Ordinary citizens can hardly be expected to be aware of the revolutions that have occurred over the past twenty years in our understanding of what and how to teach. But the fact is that we really do know more now about how learning works, and this isn't a matter of fads or philosophical pendulum swings. From detailed psycholinguistic studies, we know that all language learning—speaking, reading, writing—is active and holistic. Children don't learn rules first and then apply them, or sounds first and then words. From the very beginning, young children engage in full, actual communication: requests, complaints, expressions of love, surprise, hurt, questions, answers.

And so we've found that to teach school subjects, creating real purposes and options for real communication works. Assigning rote, audience-less topics like "What I did last summer" doesn't. Helping kids employ the processes of pre-writing and revision that actual writers use works. Following arbitrary textbook outlining doesn't. Similarly with reading, practicing whole-group reading with "predictable" stories (i.e., with patterns and refrains children can repeat) works. Teachers reading good children's literature aloud works. Practicing separate sound-decoding skills doesn't, because it leaves many children reproducing sounds but never learning to look for meaning in the sentences. Teachers are shifting to these more effective Best Practice approaches to reading and writing in tremendous numbers. But larger, older school districts are sometimes the last to change.

The isolated-skills approach to learning is not the "traditional" approach. It was, in fact, an innovation that started in the 1920s. Many nineteenth century educators actually came closer to Best Practice strategies, though we now understand the rationale and effective application of them far more completely. However, a massive bureaucratic support system, including reams of competency testing, grew up around the isolated-skills method. A tremendous amount of energy and resources was expended on all the basal readers, workbooks, scope-and-sequence curriculum plans, that were used to guide teachers' every classroom action. These systems were especially embraced by large-city schools looking for ways to assure uniform, if minimum, performance by huge teaching staffs.

One thing that strikes an observer in urban schools is just how much class time is taken with testing and preparation for testing. And, of course, the children who have trouble with reading and writing have particular trouble with the tests *because they can't read the directions*! It's a vicious circle, because more time on effective reading methods would especially help those kids who do poorly on the tests—the very tests that are supposed to assure that the teachers are doing their jobs.

The result? We've certainly not become a nation of avid readers, as any newspaper circulation manager will tell you, nor are we fluent writers or eager mathematicians or active citizens. Kids in well-off schools have still learned to read tolerably well, partly because children will generally learn what society and families expect of them, barring major disruptions in their lives. The toll on learning exacted on poorer urban children has been far more visible, however, because those children and their schools have been vulnerable in the other ways we've described. That is, the kids who have needed the most effective support have suffered the most when they didn't get it.

Resistance to Change

Another perspective on the slowness of change in urban schools is that change is actually slow *everywhere*, because that's just what human beings do—resist change. Think of some new technology you are now comfortable with and recall your feelings just before you tried it, and as you moved into learning it. For Steve, a good example was cash machines. The first time he tried one, it ate his card. He went to the main office of the bank feeling like an utter fool, and a condescending "account representative" walked him through the process a few times. Who wants to go through that? Co-author Harvey Daniels doesn't: he's never even attempted a cash machine.

Even for some of the most enjoyable activities, many of us find a dozen reasons to put them off if they're new—until finally some supportive but urgent friend, or perhaps a growing inner need of our own, or the pressure of necessity (like no cash on a Sunday afternoon) brings us to take the plunge. At the opposite pole, psychologists tell us that a person who is unhappy or dissatisfied clings to unrewarding situations and behaviors—at least in part because they are predictable, familiar, part of the definition of self and world the person has depended on for a long time.

Therefore, many of us who work to help teachers and schools change their approaches to teaching have learned to be patient, to respect the educators we work with, and to listen supportively. We've found that the most effective path to change is not through arguing and accusing, but through simply immersing people in activities that are new, enjoyable, and filled with implications about their work, and then giving them a chance to talk with each other about the experience and what it means. This sort of change process takes time, but it's deep and lasting.

EXEMPLARY PROGRAM

Building-Level Change
Washington Irving School
Chicago, Illinois

What has excited us most during the past several years of close work with city teachers and kids is that once a good thing takes hold in a classroom or a workshop—an effective strategy for using math manipulatives, or getting writing edited, or making self-selected reading work—teachers and kids alike embrace it with great energy and real results. Principals manage to find resources, teachers flock to workshops on teaching hands-on science, whole language, math, and complain when we haven't scheduled more. Kids dig in, work hard, produce, and have a good time. Improving teaching and learning doesn't seem nearly as difficult as we thought. Just as the many negatives can combine to weigh a school down and discourage its teachers, so a strategic selection of positives can add up, synergistically.

We can best illustrate this with a final story about how one school has changed. School reform experts and researchers have asserted for years that the most potent locus for educational change is not individual classrooms or teachers, whole districts or states, but the individual school building. Here, after all, we have one complete but manageable educational community, with all of the elements and ingredients necessary to sustain itself and to grow. And while the three of us know many heroic (sometimes crafty) teachers who manage to excel and innovate in unsupportive buildings, our predominant experience in city and suburban schools generally bears out the axiom: change works best at the level of whole buildings, as long as they aren't too large (two to three hundred kids is optimal).

In the fall of 1991, the PBS television affiliate in Chicago aired a one-hour documentary about Washington Irving School, a half-Black, half-Hispanic elementary building on Chicago's West Side. The Washington Irving building was new, replacing a crumbling structure that was torn down to make way for a medical research park. Still, Irving continued struggling under the burden of Chicago's weighty bureaucracy and the educational disconnection of its poverty-stricken attendance area. With a new building, however, came a new principal, Madeleine Maraldi, the driving force in Irving's development. Maraldi challenged the teachers to do more, rather than just blame the kids for their own low achievement. She obtained grants, organized new labs for writing, reading, math, and science, scheduled inservice workshops (on writing first because it was the teachers' chosen priority), regularly circulated articles on new teaching methods, and signaled that she would support experimental teaching efforts, even if they didn't yield immediate results.

We were happy to watch the documentary on Washington Irving for several reasons. First, after years of media reports relentlessly exposing the failures and foibles of public education in Chicago, this program spent sixty minutes showing how one school improved itself. Second, we were happy because the show focused on curriculum renewal as the engine of reform. The program showed a whole school community—teachers, parents, kids, principal, and a few outside helpers—thinking seriously, regularly, and sometimes passionately, about what gets taught and how. Finally, we enjoyed the program because all three of us, in different roles, had worked with Irving School for two years, assisting in their approach to curriculum reform, teacher empowerment, and parent involvement.

The professional development work at Irving began with a thirty-hour after-school teachers' workshop on teaching writing, offered to volunteers and taught by two talented teacher-leaders from another Chicago school. Then, when other teachers got interested, a second section of the same workshop was offered, enrolling a mix of Irving and outside teachers, as well as a few principals who had heard about things percolating at Irving. Next, the teachers asked for further support with writing, and so the workshop leaders, Tom and Kathy Daniels, agreed to hold an after-school writing program at Irving, half the time writing with kids and half the time talking about instruction with teachers. Meanwhile, the faculty started asking for ideas about math, and so the project brought in its thirty-hour math workshop, which uses the same processes as the writing workshop: personal exploration, direct experience, professional discussion of research, trying and debriefing classroom experiments (as well as eating lots of after-school snacks). Another group of outside teacher-leaders facilitated the math course, helping Irving teachers incorporate the new strategies into their own teaching. Through all these teacher development activities were stranded parent involvement efforts and many supportive interventions by the principal. When the PBS camera crew eventually came along, what they were able to document was the fertile, exciting start of what needs to be a five- or six- year cycle of school-based, teacher-led, curriculum-driven change.

An important finding of school-change research is that the principal plays an absolutely key role. This is especially true in city schools like Irving where the stultifying bureaucracy can crush teachers, and where years of teaching in degraded conditions leave a great need for morale boosting. Madeleine Maraldi is extraordinarily skilled at both deflecting bureaucracy and uplifting teachers. But more important than these skills, she knows curriculum, understands the research on best educational practice, and trusts teachers and kids. She sees her main role as that of facilitator, not as a boss or an expert, though she *is* both. It's deeply symbolic that at our workshops, though Madeleine participated as a regular member of the group, she always found time to check the level in the coffee pot, adjust the temperature in the room, or roll the photocopying machine from the office into the meeting room. With each of these actions, she signaled to teachers the importance of the work they were doing in studying curriculum and planning changes in instruction.

Staff development at Irving began with some very important cues from Madeleine. (In a less archaic school system, some of these ideas might have come from a teacher committee—but in Chicago, hierarchies still prevail). The first nudge came from Madeleine's decision that the school's improvement would come best through teacher renewal in key content areas. She might instead have invested in one of the now-popular "effective schools" projects that focuses on generic issues like discipline, critical thinking, or cooperative learning. Instead, Madeleine committed herself to an inservice program rooted in subject fields. While arguments can certainly be made for the content-free, across-the-curriculum approach, it has been our experience that most of the useful strategies promoted in generic courses eventually come up in our curriculum-based workshops. For example, teachers in a writing workshop must learn how to train and organize children for the collaborative structure called peer editing, just as in our math workshop teachers must know how to prepare and supervise kids in problem-solving teams.

Tom and Kathy Daniels, the teacher-consultants who led the first wave of inservice programs along with Emily Garland, Pam Sourelis, and Dee Wozniak, describe below how the workshops unfolded. In their words, we think, are eloquently woven the themes already well established in this book about how anyone, adult or child, learns best.

When we first approached the Washington Irving School we had no idea how special this experience was going to be. We thought we were just going to begin another 30-hour writing-across-the-curriculum workshop for some fellow teachers. We had been conducting similar workshops in a wide variety of Chicago schools for about five years. As we drove through this near West Side neighborhood, we noticed a large abandoned and vandalized factory, lots of old, smallish houses, empty lots, and evidence of some new housing construction. We were totally unprepared for the school building itself, which was brand new and graffiti-free.

As we walked through the clean, cheery halls, full of familiar prints beautifully presented, and lots of student work arranged with pride, it affirmed our hunch that something good was already going on here. Even the name of the school, taken from the old American storyteller, seemed to fit with the writing workshop we were about to start. In fact, the group of teachers we met that night would soon name themselves after one of Washington Irving's legends: we called our Wednesday night writing workshop "The Sleepy Hollow Gang."

We plugged in the coffee and set out the snacks, and participants began to arrive for the first session. Although there were a few teachers from nearby Brown and Jefferson schools, the majority were from Irving itself. We noticed several men and even a couple of young teachers, rare commodities in our prior workshops. The smiling Irving principal, Madeleine Maraldi, took her place with the other participants.

We always start our sessions by inviting pairs of teachers to interview each other, to seek out unusual stories and experiences, and then to write a paragraph introducing—or re-introducing—their colleagues to the group. The Irving teachers took their time listening carefully to each other, and struggled with their paragraphs to get the words just right. From the beginning, everyone wanted to read his or her paper aloud. People told about their experiences and attitudes toward writing, teaching, and life. The principal wrote every assignment, read hers aloud, and shared her personal struggles fearlessly. The eagerness to share and listen built a strong sense of community.

We began each weekly meeting by sharing and troubleshooting experiences with particular writing strategies: brainstorming, clustering, journals, guided imagery, and the rest. There are always a few reluctant "show me" personalities in any workshop, but when our group's skeptics announced their doubts to the group, there was lots of practical and encouraging advice from those with similar problems. Several teachers began to emerge as cheerleaders, and by the time we got to the middle of the third session, almost everybody felt we were riding a tidal wave moving toward conversion of the whole group.

Watching the Group Grow

Some veteran teachers came into the first session pessimistic and discouraged about the state of their teaching and the attitude of their students. They had been trying hard for a long time, and seemed likely candidates for "burn-out." But by the third session, they were trying out variations of the classroom strategies we discussed. Enthusiasm crept into their descriptions and experiences. At first, the younger teachers were rather quiet. As more and more teachers shared their personal and classroom struggles, and reported trying new strategies with their students, these younger teachers began to experiment and share their results. Veteran teachers reached out to the new teachers, and the new teachers brought their enthusiasm and idealism. Everyone seemed eager to contribute something to the group. People started to bring in their favorite classroom literature; each week we began with an oral reading from at least one beloved book, and so we built a considerable list of favorite titles for a classroom library.

It had also become obvious that having the principal there every session, writing every time, carefully listening to every teacher, was an enormous advantage for the teachers and students of Washington Irving. She supported a strong writing program. She modeled by writing to students and having them write to her. She recognized the powerful connection between reading and writing, and supported classroom libraries and a Whole Language approach. Toward the end of the workshop, she purchased a number of professional books on teaching and literacy for her teachers, and over the summer both she and they read voraciously.

By September, 1990, each classroom had a set of portfolios for student writing, the basals were set aside in favor of real books, and a literature lab had been established. In addition, a follow-up writing workshop was planned, this time including both kids and teachers, as part of an after-school program. Twelve teachers and thirty-five students would meet twice a week to work on writing, using the computer labs. Before the program started, we held a few planning sessions with the teachers to brainstorm possibilities and work out details. Half were familiar faces from the workshop but there were newcomers without the writing process background, including a few doubters who didn't think kids would come after school to do more school stuff.

The teachers decided to work in pairs and a sort of buddy system developed between the workshop "graduates" and the nonworkshoppers. Teachers who had never team-taught before worked together, sharing ideas and encouraging each other. By the time the kids' after-school writing program got underway, it was just a couple of weeks before Halloween, a natural time for spooky stories filled with terror and screaming. Older kids made up raps, put them to music, and performed them on videotape. Others wrote and illustrated their stories, made books and banners, and performed their tales of horror and thrills. They composed their pieces both individually and collectively, using the word processors. Most of them acted, sang, danced, mugged, and rapped their words for the video camera. At the end of each session, teachers got together with us to share, ask for suggestions, read works in progress, and encourage each other to continue.

Involving Parents

Our culminating activity was the "Washington Irving Family Album Night," which took place in December. We carefully selected this name, feeling that our initial label, "Family Writing Night" might scare away parents for whom writing is a challenge. Over a hundred parents, students, and relatives showed up for a simple meal, a night of reading and writing, and rich fellowship. Families had been encouraged to bring photographs that held special memories, and Madeleine had purchased a photo album for each family to take home as a souvenir. After a dinner of hot dogs, chips, and punch, and a short welcoming speech in English and Spanish, students in the after-school writing program stood up and introduced their families. The introductions were carefully videotaped one-by-one. Then all of the students and teachers got up and performed a rap that they had written about Irving School.

Next, we wanted to create a generation-spanning, cafeteria-wide writing workshop, so we set the mood by reading aloud a wonderful children's book about memory called *Wilfred Gordon McDonald Partridge* by Mem Fox. We introduced the idea of everyone's writing a personal memoir: children writing a memory of their parents, and parents of their children. We passed paper to everyone, young and old. Instructions were given in English and Spanish, and writing was invited in either language. To our delight, everyone started writing. Occasionally kids or parents would stop writing to read to each other, to check a fact, or to get help finding the right word or the right spelling. Kids who were too young or too tired to write found a corner we had set up with books and pillows and read to themselves or to each other. As everyone wrote, we took Polaroid pictures of each family. Someone helped glue their pictures on the memoirs, and we photocopied everything on the machine that Madeleine had wheeled into the lunchroom. Families kept their original memoirs, and the school kept copies, which were later published in a special album. As families lined up at the copy machine, Joe Perlstein, one the teachers, played the videotape of the family introductions and the kids' Halloween stories on the big screen television. Families who previously seemed ready to leave stayed to watch themselves and their children on TV. As they left, many asked if Family Album Night would become an annual event, as they enjoyed themselves so much. As we cleaned up that night, we were exhausted and elated.

Staff development at Irving continued in a number of other forms. A thirty-hour inservice workshop on teaching math was conducted by Arthur Hyde and teachers Eva Belisle-Chatte, Kathy Schaller, and Donna Nowatski. A third inservice series on writing was attended not only by Irving staff, but also by teachers and principals from other nearby schools. The Daniels' provided help designing curriculum plans to institutionalize the Irving teachers' long-term change. And the teachers requested a further workshop series on helping students to revise their writing.

Maraldi and her teachers, meanwhile, introduced more and more initiatives to complement the inservice training and regular classroom activity. Collaborative working groups replaced ability-grouping in reading instruction. A school-wide reading program has students discussing their books with any adult in the school in order to have their reading "verified" for report-card tallies. In the reading lab, seventh-eighth-grade teacher Joe Perlstein gives out buttons to new members of the "thousand club," when they've completed a thousand pages of reading. A grant funds monthly trips to a bookstore, where children pick out books for their own classroom libraries. The children don't own the books, but inside each is a stamp that reads:

THIS BOOK WAS SELECTED

FOR THE IRVING SCHOOL LIBRARY

BY _____

ON _____

The children eagerly start reading "their" books on the bus ride back and then add them to the permanent classroom collection with their names as selector forever inscribed inside. At holiday time, another grant allows each child to choose a book they can keep and take home—for many, the first book they have ever owned. Classes regularly visit the local library. Two computer labs facilitate kids' copious writing and revising work. Twice-weekly visits to the math and science labs help classroom teachers and kids strengthen their use of hands-on learning. And a radically redesigned report card for fourth through eighth grades provides for teacher check-off of significant reading behaviors, student self-evaluation, and parents' evaluation of their children's progress.

Perhaps no one of these strategies alone would have kick-started improvement in the school. But taken together they've begun to make a tremendous difference. Parents are involved and active. Kids are coming to school with enthusiasm, plunging into activities in the math lab and science lab, reading and writing with pride and fascination. The children sometimes surprise themselves. As one eighth-grade girl put it:

> When I came to Irving, I told my friends, "I ain't readin' no books, I ain't readin' no books." And then I saw this book by Judy Blume. It was called *Superfudge*, and I read it and it was *good*. And then I read another one. And I found myself reading *another* one of her books. I got to the point where I had read almost all her books. I've got about two more to read.

Even scores on standardized tests, which don't really measure the true import of the changes, are up dramatically; between 1989 and 1990, for example, state reading assessment scores rose twenty-five percent in eighth grade and eighteen percent in third grade.

A camera crew videotaped one teacher inservice session at Irving as part of the documentary on Chicago school reform, and the surprised grins on the faces of the camera crew offered an unexpected validation for our work. As these strangers eavesdropped on the workshop, listened to the teachers writing, sharing, and debating, they were drawn into their spirit. The crew exclaimed about the passion and professionalism of the teachers they had taped. All the teachers who were interviewed in the documentary spoke honestly and eloquently about the anxieties, pleasures, and rewards of change in their own classrooms. Second-grade teacher Norma Barron-High admitted feeling pressured by the principal's enthusiasm and the sheer volume of ideas:

> I sometimes feel like I'm still in school at the university level, because she [Maraldi] gives us so much material that I feel a little bit overwhelmed by everything in there. . . . It's not familiar territory. It means letting go of what I've been trained to use. . . . One thing that relaxes me a little bit about this is that she has stated over and over that she is evaluating us and the program according to whether or not our children are reading more and writing more. They may not be writing perfect English papers, but they are *definitely* writing more.

Pat Mark, the computer lab teacher who has taught at Irving for thirty years, explained:

> When people asked me "What do you do for a living?" I would never say, "Teacher." . . . I wasn't proud to be named a Chicago teacher. But now I boast about it. . . . If we would walk into a suburban school we would not see the kind of work that's coming out of Irving School today. . . . I'm rejuvenated. I can't wait to get here in the morning. And when I go home, I hurry up with dinner because I'm [always] down at the computer trying to think of what I should do tomorrow.

And as Joe Perlstein, the energetic, prematurely gray-haired twenty-year veteran says at the end of the documentary:

> It's very difficult to change. It takes a lot out of a person. However, you don't mind if there's a payback, if you feel that the children are growing, that they appreciate what is going on. If you see a light at the end of the tunnel, then you say to yourself, "Don't stop now. Keep pushing, keep pressing." Because it will all be worth it in the end.

Works Cited

Allen, Jo Beth, and Jana Mason. 1989. *Risk Makers, Risk Takers, Risk Breakers: Reducing the Risks for Young Literacy Learners*. Portsmouth, NH: Heinemann Educational Books.

Delpit, Lisa. 1985. "Skills and Other Dilemmas of a Progressive Black Educator," *Harvard Educational Review*, Nov.

Harste, Jerome, Virginia A. Woodward, and Carolyn L. Burke. 1984. *Language Stories and Literacy Lessons*. Portsmouth, NH: Heinemann Educational Books.

Shirley Brice Heath, *Ways with Words: Language, Life, and Work in Communities and Classrooms*. New York, Cambridge U P.

Kozol, Jonathan. 1991. *Savage Inequalities: Children in America's Schools*. New York: Crown Publishers.

Taylor, Denny and Catherine Dorsey-Gaines. 1988. *Growing Up Literate: Learning from Inner-City Families*. Portsmouth, NH: Heinemann Educational Books.

Index

For more than fifteen years, Zemelman, Daniels, and Hyde have worked on school renewal projects in Chicago and around the country. Their most recent collaboration, the Best Practice network, has brought models of state-of-the-art instruction to thousands of teachers, across the curriculum and up through the grades.

STEVE ZEMELMAN is professor of Humanities at Roosevelt University in Chicago, where he teaches writing to adult and inner-city students and works with teachers at all grade levels. He is founder and co-director of the Illinois Writing Project, one of the most active and innovative staff development organizations in the country. His other books include *A Writing Project* (Heinemann 1985) and *A Community of Writers* (Heinemann 1988), both co-authored with Harvey Daniels.

HARVEY DANIELS is a professor of Interdisciplinary Studies at National-Louis University, where his students are veteran teachers earning graduate degrees in nontraditional, school-based programs. He also directs Walloon Institute, a national summer seminar for teacher and parent leaders. Daniels is the author of five other books on education, the most recent of which is *Not Only English* (National Council of Teachers of English, 1990).

ARTHUR HYDE teaches Mathematics Education at National-Louis University and conducts staff development on mathematics, problem solving, and curriculum integration. His previous books include *Mathwise* (Heinemann 1991), *Thinking in Context: Teaching Cognitive Processes Across the Elementary School Curriculum* (Longman 1989), and *Effective Staff Development for School Change* (Ablex 1992).

Also available from Heinemann. . .

Teach Me!
Produced by **WTTW, Chicago**

1991-92 Chicago Emmy Award Recipient, Outstanding Achievement for a
Documentary of Current Significance

Teach Me! follows a Chicago public school as it works with authors
Zemelman, Daniels, and Hyde in moving toward Best Practice instruction.
With a student population that is 86% poverty-level and 96% Hispanic and
Black, and with test scores in the bottom quartile of the nation, Washington
Irving School is typical of Chicago and other urban school systems in America.
What's different is that Irving is tossing aside excuses and asking teachers to
re-examine how they teach. It hasn't been easy.

Viewers will be introduced to veteran teachers from first through eighth grade,
many with twenty to thirty years in the system. This is the story of their
exhilaration and exhaustion, their rising enthusiasm tempered with self doubt,
as they slowly let go of familiar, but ineffective, methods and embrace techniques that involve and excite children about learning.

It is also the story of the kind of environment, support, and leadership required
to take teachers successfully through this kind of transformation and the
reaction of students and parents to the change.

As cities throughout the country struggle with failing students and teacher
shortages, this program clearly presents what the research reveals about best
educational practice and how to bring it into the classrooms of our present
cadre of teachers.

Time: 58 minutes
Format: 1/2" VHS

Contact your local supplier or call Heinemann direct.

Heinemann
361 Hanover Street
Portsmouth, NH 03801-3912
1-800-541-2086